The birthplace of the nation-state and modern nationalism at the end of the eighteenth century, Europe was supposed to be their graveyard at the end of the twentieth. Yet, far from moving *beyond* the nation-state, *fin-de-siècle* Europe has been moving *back to* the nation-state, most spectacularly with the disintegration of the Soviet Union, Yugoslavia, and Czechoslovakia into a score of nationally defined successor states. This massive reorganization of political space along national lines has engendered distinctive, dynamically interlocking, and in some cases explosive forms of nationalism: the autonomist nationalisms of national minorities, the "nationalizing" nationalisms of the new states in which they live, and the transborder nationalisms of the "external national homelands" to which they belong by shared ethnicity though not by citizenship. Drawing on Pierre Bourdieu and the "new institutionalist" sociology, and comparing contemporary nationalisms with those of interwar Europe, Rogers Brubaker provides a theoretically sophisticated and historically rich account of one of the most important problems facing the "New Europe."

Nationalism reframed

Nationalism reframed

Nationhood and the national question in the New Europe

Rogers Brubaker

CAMBRIDGE
UNIVERSITY PRESS

Published by the Press Syndicate of the University of Cambridge
The Pitt Building, Trumpington Street, Cambridge CB2 1RP
40 West 20th Street, New York, NY 10011-4211, USA
10 Stamford Road, Oakleigh, Melbourne 3166, Australia

First published 1996

Printed in Great Britain at the University Press, Cambridge

A catalogue record for this book is available from the British Library

Library of Congress cataloguing in publication data

Brubaker, Rogers.
Nationalism reframed: nationhood and the national question in the
New Europe / Rogers Brubaker.
p.   cm.
Includes bibliographical references.
ISBN 0 521 57224 X – ISBN 0 521 57649 0 (pbk.)
1. Nationalism – Europe, Eastern. 2. Nationalism – Former Soviet
Republics. 3. Nationalism – Europe. 4. Europe, Eastern – Politics
and government – 1989– . 5. Former Soviet republics – Politics and
government. 6. Europe – Politics and government – Twentieth
century. I. Title.
DJK51.B78 1996
320.5'4'0947 – dc20   96–10873 CIP

ISBN 0 521 57224 X hardback
ISBN 0 521 57649 0 paperback

WD

For Zsuzsa

Contents

Acknowledgments

It was my good fortune to be able to present earlier versions of several chapters to a variety of audiences in Europe and America, and I benefited a great deal from the critical comments I received in those settings. I am grateful, in addition, to the many colleagues, students, and friends here and abroad who commented on earlier versions of one or more chapters. Although I cannot name them all, I would like to thank Jeffrey Alexander, Perry Anderson, Dominique Arel, Jeremy Azrael, Omer Bartov, Rainer Bauböck, Mark Beissinger, Ivan Berend, Zsuzsa Berend, Ian Bremmer, Craig Calhoun, Geoff Eley, Bruce Grant, Stephen Graubard, John Hall, Nikki Keddie, Larry King, Pål Kolstø, Victoria Koroteyeva, David Laitin, David Lake, John Meyer, Gusztav Molnár, Alexander Motyl, László Neményi, T. K. Oommen, Sigrid Rausing, Philip Roeder, Shigeki Sato, Philippe Schmitter, Jack Snyder, David Stark, Monique Djokic Stark, Alfred Stepan, Dariusz Stola, Ronald Suny, Ivan Szelenyi, Rafael Vago, Veljko Vujacic, and Loïc Wacquant. Thanks also to Scott Bruckner, Stephan De Spiegeleire, Carla Thorson, Andrea Lannoux, Jon Fox, and Amanda Binder for their research assistance, and to Alina Tso for help with the final preparation of the manuscript.

For generous institutional support, I thank the MacArthur Foundation, the National Science Foundation, the German Marshall Fund of the United States, the Howard Foundation, the Collegium Budapest, the Center for Advanced Study in the Behavioral Sciences, the Center for German and European Studies of the University of California, and the Committee on Research of the Academic Senate, UCLA. Chapter 3 developed in the context of a collaborative Research Planning Group on National Minorities, Nationalizing States, and External National Homelands in the New Europe and was considerably enriched by the group's discussions in Los Angeles and Bellagio; support for the group from the Council for European Studies, the Project on Ethnic Relations, the Rockefeller Foundation, and the Social Science Research Council is gratefully acknowledged.

Earlier versions of several chapters have been previously published. Chapter 1, "Rethinking Nationhood: Nation as Institutionalized Form, Practical Category, Contingent Event," originally appeared in *Contention* 4, no. 1 (1994), 3–14. A version of Chapter 2 was published as "Nationhood and the National Question in the Soviet Union and Post-Soviet Eurasia: An Institutionalist Account" in *Theory and Society* 23, no. 1 (1994), 47–78, ©1994 Kluwer Academic Publishers. A version of Chapter 3, "National Minorities, Nationalizing States, and External National Homelands in the New Europe," was originally published in *Daedalus*, Journal of the American Academy of Arts and Sciences, in the issue entitled "What Future for the State?" (124, no. 2 [1995], 107–32). The initial version of Chapter 4, "Nationalizing States in the Old 'New Europe' – and the New," was written for and will appear in *Understanding Nationalism: Ethnic Minorities and Nation-Building in the Post-Communist States*, ed. Ian Bremmer. A version of this chapter has appeared in *Ethnic and Racial Studies* 19, no. 2 (1996), 411–37, published by Routledge. Chapter 6, "Aftermaths of Empire and the Unmixing of Peoples," was initially commissioned by RAND for a Conference on Migration From and Within the Former USSR, The Hague, March 4–5, 1993, and has appeared as a RAND report, no. DRU-563-FF, November 1993. A subsequent version appeared in *Ethnic and Racial Studies* 18, no. 2 (1995), 189–218, published by Routledge.

Introduction

I

Europe was the birthplace of the nation-state and modern nationalism at the end of the eighteenth century, and it was supposed to be their graveyard at the end of the twentieth. If we take 1792, when war and nationhood were first expressly linked and mutually energized on the battlefield of Valmy,[1] as symbolizing their birth, we might take 1992 as symbolizing their anticipated death, or at least a decisive moment in their expected transcendence. Chosen by Jacques Delors as the target date for the completion of the ambitious program of the Single European Act, "1992" came to stand for the abolition of national frontiers within Europe; for the free movement of persons as well as goods and capital; for the emergence of a European citizenship; and – with the signing of the Treaty of Maastricht in 1991 – for the prospect of a common European currency, defense, and foreign policy. Just as Europe took the lead in inventing (and propagating) nationhood and nationalism, so now it would take the lead in transcending them; and "1992" served as a resonant symbol of that anticipated transcendence.

Deeper and more general forces, too, were seen as undermining the nation-state and rendering nationalism obsolete. Nationalism, discredited by the "Thirty Years War" of the first half of the century, seemed to have been dissolved in Western Europe by the subsequent thirty years of prosperity – "les trentes glorieuses," as they are called in France. Moreover, the organization of political space along national

---

[1] On September 20, 1792, at Valmy, in northeastern France, the ragtag French army, under fire from the much better trained and better equipped Prussian infantry, held its ground to the revolutionary battle-cry of "Vive la Nation." This led Goethe, who was present at the battle, to declare – notwithstanding the immediate military insignificance of the battle – that "this date and place mark a new epoch in world history." See François Furet and Denis Richet, *La Révolution française* (Paris: Hachette, 1965), p. 185; Albert Soboul, "De l'Ancien Régime à l'Empire: problème national et réalités sociales," *L'Information historique* (1960), 58.

lines seemed increasingly ill-matched to social, economic, and cultural realities.[2] The nation-state was seen as simultaneously too small and too large: too small to serve as an effective unit of coordination in an increasingly internationalized world, too large and remote to be a plausible and legitimate unit of identification. Global financial integration, dense global networks of trade and migration, a global communications infrastructure purveying an incipient global mass culture, the global reach of transnational corporations, the border-spanning jurisdictions of a host of other transnational organizations, and the inherently transnational nature of terrorism, drug trafficking, nuclear weaponry, and ecological problems all reinforced the conviction that the world was moving beyond the nation-state. The drive toward institutionalized supranationality symbolized by "1992" may have been unparalleled outside Europe. But since underlying forces were seen as working in the same direction elsewhere, an incipiently post-national Europe was seen as showing the rest of the world "the image of its own future."

The future displayed recently by Europe to the world, however, looks distressingly like the past. The first half of the 1990s has seen not the anticipated eclipse but the spectacular revival and rebirth of the nation-state and the national idea in Europe. "1992" was rudely preempted by 1991, when war, once again entwined with powerfully mobilizing myths of nationhood, broke out in Europe. Other developments, too, have conspired to chasten the heralds of supranationality and to place the scheduled transcendence of nationalism and the nation-state on hold. Not only was "Europhoria" shattered by the unforeseen resistance to the Maastricht treaty, by the currency crisis of 1992–93, and by the ignominious failure of a common European response to the Yugoslav crisis. Not only has immigration sparked a major revival of nationalist rhetoric in most European countries. Not only has German unification in the heart of the continent – unification predicated on a conception of state-transcending nationhood – engendered concern about a revival of German nationalism. Most important, the spectacular reconfiguration of political space along national lines in Central and Eastern Europe and Eurasia has suggested that far from moving *beyond* the nation-state, history – European history at least – was moving *back to* the nation-state. The "short twentieth century"[3] seemed to be ending much as it had begun, with Europe entering not a post-national but a *post-multinational*

---

[2] See for example David Beetham, "The Future of the Nation-State," in Gregor McLennan *et al.*, eds., *The Idea of the Modern State* (Milton Keynes, UK and Philadelphia: Open University Press, 1984).

[3] Eric Hobsbawm, *The Age of Extremes: The Short Twentieth Century, 1914–1991* (London: Michael Joseph, 1994).

era through the wholesale nationalization of previously multinational political space.

Yet currently faddish sweeping pronouncements about the resurgence and ubiquity of nationalism, like earlier sweeping declarations of its demise and obsolescence, obscure more than they reveal. Rather than engage in an unproductive debate about nationalism and the nation-state in general, this book grapples with the "actually existing nationalisms" of a particular – and particularly volatile – region. The region can be roughly defined as the vast and variegated swath of Central and Eastern Europe and Eurasia that (along with parts of the Middle East and North Africa) was occupied in the nineteenth century by the Habsburg, Ottoman, and Romanov Empires. Their loosely integrated, polyethnic, polyreligious, and polylinguistic realms sprawled eastward and south-ward from the zone of more compact, consolidated, integrated states of Northern and Western Europe. As the category "nation" diffused east-ward in the second half of the nineteenth century as a salient "principle of vision and division" of the social world, to use Pierre Bourdieu's phrase, these imperial realms were increasingly perceived, experienced, and criticized as specifically *multinational* rather than simply polyethnic, polyreligious, and polylinguistic, and the "principle of nationality" – the conception of states as the states of and for particular nations – became the prime lever for reimagining and reorganizing political space.

Beginning with the gradual erosion of Ottoman rule in the Balkans in the nineteenth century, but occurring mainly in a concentrated burst of state-creation in the aftermath of World War I, the great multinational land empires were reorganized along ostensibly national lines. This massive reorganization of political space, to be sure, remained incomplete: the Soviet Union was reconstituted, largely within the frame of the Romanov territories, as an expressly multinational state; and Yugoslavia and Czechoslovakia, although constituted as national states, that is, as states of and for putative triune "South Slav" and diune Czechoslovak nations respectively, came increasingly to be understood and experienced as multi- and binational, respectively. Today, however, with the breakup of the Soviet Union, Yugoslavia, and Czechoslovakia, the last of the region's avowedly multinational states have disappeared. Everywhere, political authority has been reconfigured along putatively national lines.

Yet nationalism remains central to politics in and among the newly created nation-states, just as it remained central to politics in and among the newly created (or enlarged) nation-states that issued from the post-World War I settlement. Far from "solving" the region's national question, the most recent nationalizing reconfiguration of political space, like its early twentieth-century analog, has only reframed the national question, recast it in a new form.[4] It is this reframing of nationalism that I explore in this book.

II

Nationalism has been both cause and effect of the great reorganizations of political space that framed the "short twentieth century" in Central and Eastern Europe. But the forms of nationalism that have *resulted* from the nationalization of political space are different from – and less familiar than – those that helped *engender* it. The nationalist movements that preceded and (in conjunction with a variety of other factors) produced the redrawing of political boundaries have been intensively studied. By contrast, the nationalisms that (again in conjunction with a variety of other factors) were produced by this redrawing of political boundaries have received much less attention. This book addresses the distinctive forms and dynamics of these latter nationalisms, those that have emerged in the wake of the nationalization of political space.

These nationalisms are interlocking and interactive, bound together in a single relational nexus. This can be characterized on first approximation as a triad linking national minorities, the newly nationalizing states in which they live, and the external national "homelands" to which they belong, or can be construed as belonging, by ethnocultural affinity though not by legal citizenship.

This triadic nexus involves three distinct and mutually antagonistic nationalisms. The first are the "nationalizing" nationalisms of newly

---

4 Like the nationalization of political space, the other elements of the "triple transition" in the region – marketization and democratization – have also failed to attenuate nationalist tensions. Focusing on Romania, for example, but considering other countries in post-Communist Eastern Europe as well, Katherine Verdery has shown how privatization, electoral democracy, and other elements of "transition" have aggravated rather than alleviated nationalist conflicts. See her essay "Nationalism and National Sentiment in Post-Socialist Romania," *Slavic Review* 52 (Summer 1993), 184ff. On the connections between marketization, democratization, and nationalism, see also Jack Snyder, "Nationalism and the Crisis of the Post-Soviet State," *Survival* 35, no. 1 (1993), 14ff. On the "triple transition" – the simultaneous transformations of state identities, political regimes, and economic systems – see Claus Offe, "Capitalism by Democratic Design – Democratic Theory Facing the Triple Transition in East Central Europe," *Social Research* 58, no. 4 (1991) and "Das Dilemma der Gleichzeitigkeit: Demokratisierung, Marktwirtschaft und Territorialpolitik in Osteuropa," in Offe, *Der Tunnel am Ende des Lichts: Erkundungen der politischen Transformation im neuen Osten* (Frankfurt: Campus Verlag, 1994). For a sustained analysis of democratization and nationalism, see Juan J. Linz and Alfred Stepan, *Problems of Democratic Transition and Consolidation: Southern Europe, South America, and Post-Communist Europe* (Baltimore and London: Johns Hopkins University Press, 1996), especially chapters 2, 19, and 20.

independent (or newly reconfigured) states. Nationalizing nationalisms involve claims made in the name of a "core nation" or nationality, defined in ethnocultural terms, and sharply distinguished from the citizenry as a whole. The core nation is understood as the legitimate "owner" of the state, which is conceived as the state *of* and *for* the core nation. Despite having "its own" state, however, the core nation is conceived as being in a weak cultural, economic, or demographic position within the state. This weak position – seen as a legacy of discrimination against the nation before it attained independence – is held to justify the "remedial" or "compensatory" project of using state power to promote the specific (and previously inadequately served) interests of the core nation.

Directly challenging these "nationalizing" nationalisms are the transborder nationalisms of what I call "external national homelands." Homeland nationalisms assert states' right – indeed their obligation – to monitor the condition, promote the welfare, support the activities and institutions, assert the rights, and protect the interests of "their" ethnonational kin in other states. Such claims are typically made when the ethnonational kin in question are seen as threatened by the nationalizing (and thereby, from the point of view of the ethnonational kin, de-nationalizing) policies and practices of the state in which they live. Homeland nationalisms thus arise in direct opposition to and in dynamic interaction with nationalizing nationalisms. Against nationalizing states' characteristic assertion that the status of minorities is a strictly internal matter, "homeland" states claim that their rights and responsibilities *vis-à-vis* ethnonational kin transcend the boundaries of territory and citizenship. "Homeland," in this sense, is a political, not an ethnographic category. A state becomes an external national "homeland" when cultural or political elites construe certain residents and citizens of other states as co-nationals, as fellow members of a single transborder nation, and when they assert that this shared nationhood makes the state responsible, in some sense, not only for its own citizens but also for ethnic co-nationals who live in other states and possess other citizenships.

Caught between two mutually antagonistic nationalisms – those of the nationalizing states in which they live and those of the external national homelands to which they belong by ethnonational affinity though not by legal citizenship – are the national minorities. They have their own nationalism: they too make claims on the grounds of their nationality. Indeed it is such claims that make them a national minority. "National minority," like "external national homeland" or "nationalizing state," designates a political stance, not an ethnodemographic fact. Minority nationalist stances characteristically involve a self-understanding in specifically "national" rather than merely "ethnic" terms, a demand for state recognition of their distinct ethnocultural nationality, and the assertion of certain collective, nationality-based cultural or political rights. Although national minority and homeland nationalisms both define themselves in opposition to the "nationalizing" nationalisms of the state in which the minorities live, they are not necessarily harmoniously aligned. Divergence is especially likely when homeland nationalisms are strategically adopted by the homeland state as a means of advancing other, non-nationalist political goals; in this case ethnic co-nationals abroad may be precipitously abandoned when, for example, geopolitical goals require this.

The triadic relational interplay between national minorities, nationalizing states, and external national homelands has not been confined to Europe. One of the most important instances, for example, has involved the overseas Chinese, the nationalizing southeast Asian states in which they live, and China as external national homeland.[5] Within Europe, moreover, the triadic nexus existed before the great twentieth-century reconfigurations of political space: thus in the final "dualist" phase of the Habsburg Empire, when Hungary was (in the domestic sphere) virtually an independent state, there was a tense triadic relation between Hungarian Serbs as national minority, Hungary as nationalizing state, and the Kingdom of Serbia as external national homeland.

The locus classicus of the triadic nexus, however, was interwar East Central Europe. The post-World War I settlements, though ostensibly based on the principle of national self-determination, in fact assigned tens of millions of people to nation-states other than "their own" at the same time that they focused unprecedented attention on the national or putatively national quality of both persons and territories. Most fatefully, millions of Germans were left as minorities in the region's new or reconstituted (and strongly nationalizing) states, especially Poland and Czechoslovakia. They belonged by citizenship to these new states but by ethnic nationality to an initially prostrate but obviously still powerful external national homeland. Similarly, more than three million Hungarians suddenly became national minorities in Romania, Czechoslovakia, and Yugoslavia, linked by shared ethnicity to their openly irredentist "homeland"; while substantial Bulgarian and Macedonian minorities, assigned to Yugoslavia, Greece, and Romania,

---

[5] For an overview, see Milton Esman, "The Chinese Diaspora in Southeast Asia," in Gabriel Sheffer, ed., *Modern Diasporas in International Politics* (London and Sydney: Croom Helm, 1986).

were linked by shared (or in the case of Macedonians, putatively shared) ethnic nationality to equally irredentist Bulgaria. Some 6 or 7 million Ukrainians and Belarusians in the eastern borderlands of nationalizing Poland were linked to larger co-ethnic populations in the Soviet Union who possessed their own nominally sovereign (and in the 1920s, culturally quite autonomous) "national states" in the Soviet federal scheme.

The post-Communist reorganization of political space has had similar consequences. Again, tens of millions of people became residents and citizens of new states conceived as "belonging to" an ethnic nationality other than their own. Most dramatically, some 25 million ethnic Russians have been transformed, by a drastic shrinkage of political space, from privileged national group, culturally and politically at home throughout the Soviet Union, into minorities of precarious status, disputed membership, and uncertain identity in a host of incipient non-Russian nation-states. But many other groups in the region – including large numbers of Hungarians, Albanians, Serbs, Turks, and Armenians – found themselves similarly "mismatched," attached by formal citizenship to one state (in most cases a new – and nationalizing – state) yet by ethnonational affinity to another.

III

This is a book of essays, not a monograph. The essays are linked by a common concern with the recasting of nationalist politics in post-Communist Europe and Eurasia, but they approach this subject from a number of distinct angles. The book is in two parts. My theoretical argument is developed in most sustained fashion in the first part. The opening chapter argues that the upsurge in nationalism should not lead us to reify nations. Nationalism can and should be understood without invoking "nations" as substantial entities. Instead of focusing on nations as real groups, we should focus on nationhood and nationness, on "nation" as practical category, institutionalized form, and contingent event. "Nation" is a category of practice, not (in the first instance) a category of analysis. To understand nationalism, we have to understand the practical uses of the category "nation," the ways it can come to structure perception, to inform thought and experience, to organize discourse and political action.

Chapter 2 takes up this challenge in relation to the Soviet Union and its successor states. Drawing on "new institutionalist" sociology, it analyzes the unique Soviet system of institutionalized multinationality and its unintended political consequences. The Soviet regime repressed nationalism, of course. But this does not mean (as is often assumed) that it repressed nationhood and nationality. Quite the contrary: in fact the regime went to remarkable lengths, long before glasnost and perestroika, to institutionalize both territorial nationhood and ethnocultural nationality as basic cognitive and social categories. Once political space began to expand under Gorbachev, these categories quickly came to structure political perception, inform political rhetoric, and organize political action. They made claims to national autonomy, sovereignty, and secession conceivable, plausible, and ultimately compelling. And they continue to orient political understanding and political action in Soviet successor states today.

Chapter 3 develops a dynamic and relational approach to nationalism in post-Communist Europe and the former Soviet Union, focusing on the potentially explosive interplay, sketched above, between national minorities, the newly nationalizing states in which they live, and the external national "homelands" to which they belong by ethnocultural affinity though not by legal citizenship. National minority, nationalizing state, and external national homeland are bound together in a single relational nexus, linked by continuous mutual monitoring and interaction. Moreover, the three "elements" in the triadic relation are themselves not fixed entities but fields of differentiated and competing positions, arenas of struggle among competing stances. The triadic relation between these three "elements" is therefore a relation between relational fields, as it were; this is part of what makes it unstable and potentially explosive. This chapter illustrates the dynamics of the triadic relational nexus with a sustained discussion of the breakup of Yugoslavia.

The three essays comprising Part II develop historical and comparative perspectives on the national question in the "New Europe." They take as their point of departure a basic structural analogy between the interwar period and the present. Then, as now, a set of new states, conceived as nation-states, arose from the rubble of multinational empires. Then too the boundaries between states and nations did not coincide. Then too states with ethnic kin living as minorities in neighboring states presented themselves as the "homelands" of those minorities and sought to "protect" (and often to incorporate) them. Then too an elaborate international machinery was set up to monitor and protect the rights of national minorities. In the interwar period, national tensions contributed significantly to the outbreak of war. Without making prognoses, the historically informed chapters in Part II bring the past to bear on the present, focusing on key aspects of the national question today that have striking parallels in the interwar period.

The literature on nationalism has focused on state-seeking nationalisms, neglecting the "nationalizing" nationalisms of existing states. Chapter 4 reverses the emphasis, addressing what I call "nationalizing states." These are states that are conceived by their dominant elites as nation-states, as the states of and for particular ethnocultural nations, yet as "incomplete" or "unrealized" nation-states, as insufficiently "national" in a variety of senses. To remedy this defect, and to compensate for perceived past discrimination, nationalizing elites urge and undertake action to promote the language, culture, demographic preponderance, economic flourishing, or political hegemony of the core ethnocultural nation. The new states of post-Communist Eurasia, like the new states of interwar Europe, can usefully be conceptualized as nationalizing states in this sense, although there is of course great variation among states (and even within states: over time, across regions, among political parties, between government agencies) in the intensity and modalities of nationalizing policies and practices. This chapter analyzes one particular nationalizing state – interwar Poland – in detail in order to work out an analytical vocabulary for the comparative analysis of contemporary nationalizing nationalisms.

Chapter 5 takes as its point of departure the striking – and unsettling – similarities between Weimar Germany and post-Soviet Russia. These include loss of territory; a "humiliating" loss of status and standing as a Great Power; the retention of preponderant economic and military power *vis-à-vis* a neighboring zone of incipient and extremely weak states; deep economic crisis; incipient, fragile, and only weakly legitimate democratic institutions; and concerted mobilization by the radically nationalist extreme right. This chapter focuses on one further similarity: on the presence of millions of aggrieved and vulnerable co-ethnics in neighboring nationalizing states, more precisely on the responses to their predicament in Weimar Germany and contemporary Russia. I conceptualize those responses as variants of a distinctive form of nationalism, oriented to noncitizen co-ethnics in other states. The chapter probes the homeland nationalism of Weimar Germany in order to gain analytical leverage and comparative perspective on the homeland nationalism that has become so salient in post-Soviet Russia.

The final chapter analyzes post-imperial migrations of ethnic unmixing in historical and comparative perspective. Political reconfiguration always has important consequences for migration. This is true both for the expansion and for the contraction of political space. The expansion of political space – for example through the creation of empire – regularly induces large-scale migrations. By creating a political roof over a large multiethnic population, empires often promote the mixing of peoples. Much of the world's ethnic heterogeneity – and many of its severest conflicts – can be traced to movements of peoples under imperial regimes. But if empires tend to promote the mixing of peoples through migration, the shrinkage of political space in their aftermaths tends to promote unmixing. This chapter examines the post-Soviet reflux of ethnic Russians to Russia in the light of the migrations of other once-dominant "new minorities" engendered by transitions from multinational empire to incipient nation-states: Balkan Muslims during and after the disintegration of the Ottoman Empire, Hungarians after the collapse of the Habsburg Empire, and Germans after the collapse of the Habsburg Empire and the German Kaiserreich.

IV

This book is not about the resurgence of nationalism. Nationalism is not a "force" to be measured as resurgent or receding. It is a heterogeneous set of "nation"-oriented idioms, practices, and possibilities that are continuously available or "endemic" in modern cultural and political life.[6] "Nation" is so central, and protean, a category of modern political and cultural thought, discourse, and practice that it is hard indeed to imagine a world without nationalism. But precisely because nationalism is so protean and polymorphous, it makes little sense to ask how strong nationalism is, or whether it is receding or advancing.

My concern in this book is not with the resurgence but with the reframing of nationalism, not with how much nationalism there is but with what kind, not with the strength but with the characteristic structure and style of nationalist politics in post-Communist Europe and Eurasia. These old–new nationalisms, while strikingly similar in some respects to those of interwar Central and Eastern Europe, differ sharply from the state-seeking and nation-building nationalisms on which most theories of nationalism have been built. To attend seriously to the distinctive forms, dynamics, and consequences of these old–new nationalisms will be a key challenge for the study of nationalism in the next decade. This book is offered as a preliminary step toward meeting that challenge.

---

[6] I place "nation" in quotation marks to signal that I am talking about practices and discourses oriented to a *putative* nation, or invoking the *category* nation, and to refrain from treating the putative nation of nationalist practice and discourse as a real entity, a substantial collectivity. See Craig Calhoun, "Nationalism and Ethnicity," *Annual Review of Sociology* 19 (1993); Katherine Verdery, "Whither 'Nation' and 'Nationalism'?," *Daedalus* 122, no. 3 (Summer 1993); and Chapters 1-3 below.

Part I

Rethinking nationhood and nationalism

1   Rethinking nationhood: nation as institutionalized form, practical category, contingent event

Most discussions of nationhood are discussions of *nations*. Nations are understood as real entities, as communities, as substantial, enduring collectivities. *That* they exist is taken for granted, although *how* they exist – and how they came to exist – is much disputed.

A similar realism of the group long prevailed in many areas of sociology and kindred disciplines. Yet in the last decade or so, at least four developments in social theory have combined to undermine the treatment of groups as real, substantial entities. The first is the growing interest in network forms, the flourishing of network theory, and the increasing use of network as an overall orienting image or metaphor in social theory. Second, there is the challenge posed by theories of rational action, with their relentless methodological individualism, to realist understandings of groupness.[1] The third development is a shift from broadly structuralist to a variety of more "constructivist" theoretical stances; while the former envisioned groups as enduring components of social structure, the latter see groupness as constructed, contingent, and fluctuating. Finally, an emergent postmodernist theoretical sensibility emphasizes the fragmentary, the ephemeral, and the erosion of fixed forms and clear boundaries. These developments are disparate, even contradictory. But they have converged in problematizing groupness, and in undermining axioms of stable group being.

Yet this movement away from the realism of the group has been uneven. It has been striking, to take just one example, in the study of class, especially in the study of the working class – a term that is hard to use today without quotation marks or some other distancing device. Indeed *the* working class – understood as a real entity or substantial

---

[1] In this tradition, the collective action literature, from Mancur Olson's *The Logic of Collective Action: Public Goods and the Theory of Groups* (Cambridge, Mass.: Harvard University Press, 1971) through Michael Hechter's *Principles of Group Solidarity* (Berkeley: University of California Press, 1987), has been particularly important in challenging common-sense understandings of groupness and group-formation.

community – has largely dissolved as an object of analysis. It has been challenged both by theoretical statements and by detailed empirical research in social history, labor history, and the history of popular discourse and mobilization.[2] The study of class as a cultural and political idiom, as a mode of conflict, and as an underlying abstract dimension of economic structure remains vital; but it is no longer encumbered by an understanding of *classes* as real, enduring entities.

At the same time, an understanding of *nations* as real entities continues to inform the study of nationhood and nationalism. This realist, substantialist understanding of nations is shared by those who hold otherwise widely diverging views of nationhood and nationalism.

At one pole, it informs the view of nationalism held by nationalists themselves and by nationally minded scholars. On this view, nationalism presupposes the existence of nations, and expresses their strivings for autonomy and independence. Nations are conceived as collective individuals, capable of coherent, purposeful collective action. Nationalism is a drama in which nations are the key actors. One might think that this sociologically naïve view has no place in recent scholarship. But it has in fact flourished in recent years in interpretations of the national uprisings in the former Soviet Union.[3]

But the realist ontology of nations informs more sober and less celebratory scholarship as well. Consider just one indicator of this. Countless discussions of nationhood and nationalism begin with the question: what is a nation? This question is not as theoretically innocent as it seems: the very terms in which it is framed presuppose the existence of the entity that is to be defined. The question itself reflects the realist, substantialist belief that "a nation" is a real entity of some kind, though perhaps one that is elusive and difficult to define.

The treatment of nations as real entities and substantial collectivities is not confined to so-called primordialists, meaning those who emphasize the deep roots, ancient origins, and emotive power of national attach-

---

2 The great book of E. P. Thompson on *The Making of the English Working Class* (New York: Vintage, 1963) marked the beginning of this process. While stressing on the one hand that class is not a thing, that "'it' [i.e. class understood as a thing] does not exist," that class is rather "something . . . which happens," a "fluency," a "relationship" (pp. 9–11), Thompson nonetheless ends up treating the working class as a real entity, a community, an historical individual, characterizing his book as a "biography of the English working class from its adolescence until its early manhood," and summing up his findings as follows: "When every caution has been made, the outstanding fact of the period from 1790 to 1830 is the formation of the working class" (pp. 9–11, 194).

3 It mars even the work of so eminent a specialist on Soviet nationality affairs as Hélène Carrère d'Encausse. See *The End of the Soviet Empire: The Triumph of the Nations* (New York: Basic Books, 1993).

ments.[4] This view is also held by many "modernists" and "constructivists," who see nations as shaped by such forces as industrialization, uneven development, the growth of communication and transportation networks, and the powerfully integrative and homogenizing forces of the modern state. Nor is the substantialist approach confined to those who define nations "objectively," that is in terms of shared objective characteristics such as language, religion, etc.; it is equally characteristic of those who emphasize subjective factors such as shared myths, memories, or self-understandings.

Paradoxically, the realist and substantialist approach informs even accounts that seek to debunk and demystify nationalism by denying the real existence of nations. On this view, if the nation is an illusory or spurious community, an ideological smokescreen, then nationalism must be a case of false consciousness, of mistaken identity. This approach reduces the question of the reality or real efficacy of nationhood or nationness to the question of the reality of nations as concrete communities or collectivities, thereby foreclosing alternative and more theoretically promising ways of conceiving nationhood and nationness.

The problem with this substantialist treatment of nations as real entities is that it adopts *categories of practice* as *categories of analysis*. It takes a conception inherent in the *practice* of nationalism and in the workings of the modern state and state-system – namely the realist, reifying conception of nations as real communities – and it makes this conception central to the *theory* of nationalism. Reification is a social process, not only an intellectual practice. As such, it is central to the phenomenon of nationalism, as we have seen all too clearly in the last few years.[5] As

---

4 I stress that I am not simply criticizing primordialism – a long-dead horse that writers on ethnicity and nationalism continue to flog. No serious scholar today holds the view that is routinely attributed to primordialists in straw-man setups, namely that nations or ethnic groups are primordial, unchanging entities. Everyone agrees that nations are historically formed constructs, although there is disagreement about the relative weight of premodern traditions and modern transformations, of ancient memories and recent mobilizations, of "authentic" and "artificial" group feeling. What I am criticizing is not the straw man of primordialism, but the more pervasive substantialist, realist cast of mind that attributes real, enduring existence to nations as collectivities, however those collectivities are conceived.

5 As Pierre Bourdieu's work on the symbolic dimensions of group-making suggests, reification is central to the quasi-performative discourse of nationalist politicians which, at certain moments, can succeed in creating what it seems to presuppose – namely, the existence of nations as real, mobilized or mobilizable groups. Bourdieu has not written specifically on nationalism, but this theme is developed in his essay on regionalism, "L'identité et la représentation: éléments pour une réflexion critique sur l'idée de région," *Actes de la recherche en sciences sociales* 35 (November 1980), part of which is reprinted in Bourdieu, *Language and Symbolic Power* (Cambridge, Mass.: Harvard University Press, 1991), pp. 220–8; see also the conclusion to "Social Space and the Genesis of Classes" in that same collection (pp. 248–51).

analysts of nationalism, we should certainly try to *account* for this social process of reification – this process through which the political fiction of the nation becomes momentarily yet powerfully realized in practice. This may be one of the most important tasks of the theory of nationalism. But we should avoid unintentionally *reproducing* or *reinforcing* this reification of nations in practice with a reification of nations in theory.

To argue against the realist and substantialist way of thinking about nations is not to dispute the reality of nationhood.[6] It is rather to reconceptualize that reality. It is to decouple the study of nationhood and nationness from the study of nations as substantial entities, collectivities, or communities. It is to focus on nationness as a conceptual variable, to adopt J. P. Nettl's phrase,[7] not on nations as real collectivities. It is to treat nation not as substance but as institutionalized form; not as collectivity but as practical category; not as entity but as contingent event. Only in this way can we capture the reality of nationhood and the real power of nationalism without invoking in our theories the very "political fiction" of "the nation" whose potency in practice we wish to explain.[8]

We should not ask "what is a nation" but rather: how is nationhood as a political and cultural form institutionalized within and among states? How does nation work as practical category, as classificatory scheme, as cognitive frame? What makes the use of that category by or against states more or less resonant or effective? What makes the nation-evoking, nation-invoking efforts of political entrepreneurs more or less likely to succeed?[9]

---

6 Here I differ from those who, finding "nation" inadequate or hopelessly muddled as a designator of a putative real entity or collectivity, avoid engaging the phenomenon of nationhood or nationness altogether. This was the case notably for the influential work of Charles Tilly and his collaborators, *The Formation of National States in Western Europe* (Princeton: Princeton University Press, 1975). As Tilly wrote in the introductory essay to that volume, "'nation' remains one of the most puzzling and tendentious items in the political lexicon" (p. 6). Tilly shifted the focus of analysis from nation to state, marking a deliberate break with the older literature on nation-building. The adjective "national" appears throughout the book; yet it is strictly a term of scale and scope, meaning essentially "state-wide"; it has nothing to do with the phenomenon of nationhood or nationness.

7 See J. P. Nettl, "The State as a Conceptual Variable," *World Politics* 20 (1968).

8 On nation as political fiction, see Louis Pinto, "Une fiction politique: la nation," *Actes de la recherche en sciences sociales* 64 (1986), a Bourdieuian appreciation of the studies of nationalism carried out by the eminent Hungarian historian Jenö Szücs.

9 For suggestive recent discussions of nationalism that avoid treating "the nation" as a real entity, see Richard Handler, "Is 'Identity' a Useful Cross-Cultural Concept?," in John Gillis, ed., *Commemorations: The Politics of National Identity* (Princeton: Princeton University Press, 1994); Katherine Verdery, "Whither 'Nation' and 'Nationalism'?,"

This might seem an unpropitious moment for such an argument. The collapse of the Soviet Union, the national conflicts in the successor states, the ethnonational wars in Transcaucasia and the North Caucasus, the carnage in the former Yugoslavia: doesn't all this – it might be asked – vividly demonstrate the reality and power of nations? Doesn't it show that nations could survive as solidary groups, as foci of identity and loyalty and bases of collective action, despite the efforts of the Soviet and Yugoslav states to crush them?

In a context of rampant ethnonationalism, the temptation to adopt a nation-centered perspective is understandable. But the temptation should be resisted. Nationalism is not engendered by nations. It is produced – or better, it is induced – by *political fields* of particular kinds.[10] Its dynamics are governed by the properties of political fields, not by the properties of collectivities.[11]

Take for example the case of Soviet and post-Soviet nationalisms. To see these as the struggles of nations, of real, solidary groups who somehow survived despite Soviet attempts to crush them – to suggest that nations and nationalism flourish today *despite* the Soviet regime's ruthlessly antinational policies – is to get things exactly backwards. Nationhood and nationalism flourish today largely *because of* the regime's policies. Although antinational*ist*, those policies were anything but anti-*national*. Far from ruthlessly suppressing nationhood, the Soviet regime pervasively institutionalized it. The regime repressed *nationalism*, of course; but at the same time, as I argue in detail in Chapter 2, it went further than any other state before or since in institutionalizing territorial *nationhood* and ethnic *nationality* as fundamental social categories. In doing so it inadvertently created a political field supremely conducive to nationalism.

The regime did this in two ways. On the one hand, it carved up the Soviet state into more than fifty national territories, each expressly defined as the homeland of and for a particular ethnonational group. The top-level national territories – those that are today the independent

Daedalus 122, no. 3 (1993), and Craig Calhoun, "Nationalism and Ethnicity," *Annual Review of Sociology* 19 (1993).

10 Not only political fields but economic and cultural fields too can generate nationalism. See for example Katherine Verdery, "Nationalism and National Sentiment in Post-Socialist Romania," *Slavic Review* 52 (1993) for an argument about the nationalism-generating power of post-socialist economic restructuring.

11 I develop this line of analysis in detail in Chapter 3, using "field" in a sense broadly akin to that developed by Pierre Bourdieu. For a particularly clear exposition of the concept, see Pierre Bourdieu and Loïc Wacquant, *An Invitation to Reflexive Sociology* (Chicago: University of Chicago Press, 1992), pp. 94ff.

successor states – were defined as quasi-nation states, complete with their own territories, names, constitutions, legislatures, administrative staffs, cultural and scientific institutions, and so on.

On the other hand, the regime divided the citizenry into a set of exhaustive and mutually exclusive ethnic nationalities, over a hundred in all. Thus codified, ethnic nationality served not only as a *statistical category*, a fundamental unit of social accounting, but also, and more distinctively, as an *obligatory ascribed status*. It was assigned by the state at birth on the basis of descent. It was registered in personal identity documents. It was recorded in almost all bureaucratic encounters and official transactions. And it was used to control access to higher education and to certain desirable jobs, restricting the opportunities of some nationalities, especially Jews, and promoting others through preferential treatment policies for so-called "titular" nationalities in "their own" republics.

Long before Gorbachev, then, territorial nationhood and ethnic nationality were pervasively institutionalized social and cultural forms. These forms were by no means empty. They were scorned by Soviet-ologists – no doubt because the regime consistently and effectively repressed all signs of overt political nationalism, and sometimes even cultural nationalism. Yet the repression of nationalism went hand in hand with the establishment and consolidation of nationhood and nationality as fundamental cognitive and social forms. Under glasnost, these already pervasively institutionalized forms were readily politicized. They constituted elementary forms of political understanding, political rhetoric, political interest, and political identity. In the terms of Max Weber's "switchman" metaphor, they determined the tracks, the cognitive frame, along which action was pushed by the dynamic of material and ideal interests. In so doing, they contributed powerfully to the breakup of the Soviet Union and to the structuring of nationalist politics in its aftermath.

I have argued that we should think about nation not as substance but as institutionalized form, not as collectivity but as practical category, not as entity but as contingent event. Having talked about nationhood as institutionalized form, and as cognitive and sociopolitical category, I want to say a few words in conclusion about nationness as event. Here my remarks will be even more sketchy and programmatic. I want simply to point to a gap in the literature, and to suggest one potentially fruitful line of work.

In speaking of nationness as event, I signal a double contrast. The first is between nation as entity and nationness as a variable property of groups, of relationships, and of what Margaret Somers has recently called "relational settings."[12] The second contrast is between thinking of nationhood or nationness as something that *develops*, and thinking of it as something that *happens*. Here I want to focus on this second contrast, between developmentalist and eventful perspectives. I borrow the latter term from a recent paper by William Sewell, Jr.[13]

We have a large and mature developmentalist literature on nationhood and nationalism. This literature traces the long-term political, economic, and cultural changes that led, over centuries, to the gradual emergence of nations or, as I would prefer to put it, of nationness. The major works of the last decade on nationhood and nationalism – notably by Ernest Gellner, Benedict Anderson, Anthony Smith, and Eric Hobsbawm[14] – are all developmentalist in this sense.

By contrast, we lack theoretically sophisticated eventful analyses of nationness and nationalism. There are of course many studies of particular nationalisms geared to much shorter time spans than the decades or centuries characteristic of the developmentalist literature. But those conducted by sociologists and political scientists have tended to abstract from events in their search for generalized structural or cultural explanations, while historians, taking for granted the significance of contingent events, have not been inclined to theorize them.[15]

I know of no sustained analytical discussions of nationness as an event, as something that suddenly crystallizes rather than gradually develops, as a contingent, conjuncturally fluctuating, and precarious frame of vision and basis for individual and collective action, rather than as a relatively stable product of deep developmental trends in economy, polity, or culture. Yet a strong theoretical case can be made for an eventful

[12] Margaret R. Somers, "Narrativity, Narrative Identity, and Social Action: Rethinking English Working-Class Formation," *Social Science History* 16 (1992), 608ff. For an anthropological approach to the study of nationness as something produced and reproduced in everyday relationships, see John Borneman, *Belonging in the Two Berlins* (New York: Cambridge University Press, 1992); see also Verdery, "Whither 'Nation' and 'Nationalism'?," 41.

[13] William Sewell, Jr., "Three Temporalities: Toward an Eventful Sociology," forthcoming in Terrence J. McDonald, ed., *The Historic Turn in the Human Sciences* (Ann Arbor: University of Michigan Press).

[14] Ernest Gellner, *Nations and Nationalism* (Ithaca, NY: Cornell University Press, 1983); Benedict Anderson, *Imagined Communities: Reflections on the Origin and Spread of Nationalism* (London: Verso, revised edn, 1991); Anthony Smith, *The Ethnic Origins of Nations* (Oxford: Basil Blackwell, 1986); Eric Hobsbawm, *Nations and Nationalism since 1780* (Cambridge: Cambridge University Press, 1990).

[15] Sewell, "Three Temporalities"; cf. Marshall Sahlins, "The Return of the Event, Again: With Reflections on the Beginnings of the Great Fijian War of 1843 to 1855 between the Kingdoms of Bau and Rewa," in Aletta Biersack, ed., *Clio in Oceania: Toward a Historical Anthropology* (Washington and London: Smithsonian Institution Press, 1991), p. 38.

approach to nationness. As Craig Calhoun has recently argued, in a paper on the Chinese student protest movement of 1989, identity should be understood as a "changeable product of collective action," not as its stable underlying cause.[16] Much the same thing could be said about nationness.

A theoretically sophisticated eventful perspective on nationness and nationalism is today urgently needed. To make sense of the Soviet and Yugoslav collapse and their aftermaths, we need – among other things – to think theoretically about relatively sudden fluctuations in the "nationness" of groups and relational settings. We need to think theoretically about the process of being "overcome by nationhood," to use the poignant phrase of the Croatian writer Slavenka Drakulic. Drakulic was characterizing her own situation. Like many of her postwar generation, she was largely indifferent to nationality. Yet she came – against her will – to be defined by her nationality alone, imprisoned by an all-too-successfully reified category.[17] As predicaments go, in the former Yugoslavia, this one is not especially grave. But it illustrates in personal terms a more general and fateful occurrence – the relatively sudden and pervasive "nationalization" of public and even private life. This has involved the nationalization of narrative and interpretative frames, of perception and evaluation, of thinking and feeling. It has involved the silencing or marginalization of alternative, non-nationalist political languages. It has involved the nullification of complex identities by the terrible categorical simplicity of ascribed nationality. It has involved essentialist, demonizing characterizations of the national

16   Craig Calhoun, "The Problem of Identity in Collective Action," in Joan Huber, ed., *Macro-Micro Linkages in Sociology* (Newbury Park, Calif.: Sage, 1991), p. 59.
17   "Being Croat has become my destiny . . . I am defined by my nationality, and by it alone... Along with millions of other Croats, I was pinned to the wall of nationhood – not only by outside pressure from Serbia and the Federal Army but by national homogenization within Croatia itself. That is what the war is doing to us, reducing us to one dimension: the Nation. The trouble with this nationhood, however, is that whereas before, I was defined by my education, my job, my ideas, my character – and, yes, my nationality too – now I feel stripped of all that. I am nobody because I am not a person any more. I am one of 4.5 million Croats . . . I am not in a position to choose any longer. Nor, I think, is anyone else . . . something people cherished as a part of their cultural identity – an alternative to the all-embracing communism . . . – has become their political identity and turned into something like an ill-fitting shirt. You may feel the sleeves are too short, the collar too tight. You might not like the colour, and the cloth might itch. But there is no escape; there is nothing else to wear. One doesn't have to succumb voluntarily to this ideology of the nation – one is sucked into it. So right now, in the new state of Croatia, no one is allowed not to be a Croat" (Slavenka Drakulic, *The Balkan Express: Fragments from the Other Side of War* [New York: W. W. Norton, 1993], pp. 50–2).

"other," characterizations that transform Serbs into Chetniks, Croats into Ustashas, Muslims into Fundamentalists.

We know well from a variety of appalling testimony *that* this has happened; but we know too little about *how* it happened. This is where we need an eventful perspective. Following the lead of such thinkers as Marshall Sahlins, Andrew Abbott, and William Sewell, Jr., we must give serious theoretical attention to contingent events and to their transformative consequences.[18] Only in this way can we hope to understand the processual dynamics of nationalism. And it is the close study of such processual dynamics, I think, that will yield the most original and significant work on nationalism in the coming years, work that promises theoretical advances as well as a richer understanding of particular cases.[19]

I began with the question: how should we think about nationhood and nationness, and how are they implicated in nationalism? Reduced to a formula, my argument is that we should focus on nation as a category of practice, nationhood as an institutionalized cultural and political form, and nationness as a contingent event or happening, and refrain from using the analytically dubious notion of "nations" as substantial, enduring collectivities. A recent book by Julia Kristeva bears the English title *Nations without Nationalism*; but the analytical task at hand, I submit, is to think about nationalism without nations.

Ours is not, as is often asserted, even by as sophisticated a thinker as Anthony Smith, "a world of nations."[20] It is a world in which nationhood is pervasively institutionalized in the practice of states and the workings of the state system. It is a world in which nation is widely, if unevenly, available and resonant as a category of social vision and division. It is a world in which nationness may suddenly, and powerfully, "happen." But none of this implies a world of nations – of substantial, enduring collectivities.

---

[18] Sahlins, "The Return of the Event, Again"; Andrew Abbott, "From Causes to Events: Notes on Narrative Positivism," *Sociological Methods and Research* 20 (1992); Sewell, "Three Temporalities."

[19] Here the study of nationalism might fruitfully draw on the recent literature on revolution, with its attention to transformative events and processual dynamics. See for example the debate in *Contention* between Nikki Keddie, "Can Revolutions be Predicted? Can their Causes be Understood?" (1, no. 2 [1992]) and Jack Goldstone, "Predicting Revolutions: Why We Could (and Should) have Foreseen the Revolutions of 1989–1991 in the U.S.S.R. and Eastern Europe" (2, no. 2 [1993]). Although Keddie and Goldstone disagree about the predictability of revolution, they agree about the importance of transformative events, complex interactions, and rapid changes in ideas, stances, and behavior.

[20] Anthony Smith, *National Identity* (London: Penguin, 1991), p. 176

To understand the power of nationalism, we do not need to invoke nations. Nor should we, at the other extreme, dismiss nationhood altogether. We need, rather, to decouple categories of analysis from categories of practice, retaining as analytically indispensable the notions of nation as practical category, nationhood as institutionalized form, and nationness as event, but leaving "the nation" as enduring community to nationalists.

2   Nationhood and the national question in the Soviet Union and its successor states: an institutionalist account

The Soviet Union has collapsed, but the contradictory legacy of its unique accommodation to ethnonational heterogeneity lives on. That accommodation pivoted on *institutionalized multinationality*. The Soviet Union was a multinational state not only in *ethnodemographic* terms – not only in terms of the extraordinary ethnic heterogeneity of its population – but, more fundamentally, in *institutional* terms. The Soviet state not only passively tolerated but actively institutionalized the existence of multiple nations and nationalities as fundamental constituents of the state and its citizenry. It established nationhood and nationality as fundamental social categories sharply distinct from the overarching categories of statehood and citizenship. In so doing, it prepared the way for its own demise. For the institutional crystallizations of nationhood and nationality were by no means empty forms or legal fictions, although this was how they were viewed by most Sovietologists. Institutionalized definitions of nationhood, I argue in this chapter, not only played a major role in the disintegration of the Soviet state, but continue to shape and structure the national question in the incipient successor states.

The chapter is in two parts. The first part discusses the dual legacy inherited by the successor states from the Soviet encounter with the national question. It focuses on the two very different modes in which nationhood and nationality were institutionalized in the Soviet Union – territorial and political on the one hand, ethnocultural and personal on the other hand. The second part discusses the way in which this dual legacy shaped the breakup of the state and continues to structure nationalist politics in the successor states today.

The argument shares the broad analytic orientations of the "new institutionalism" in sociology. All social science institutionalisms, old and new, oppose decontextualized, atomistic accounts of action; all theorize about "how social choices are shaped, mediated, and channeled by institutional arrangements."[1] But by moving beyond a concern with the *institutional contexts of and constraints on interested action* to emphasize the *institutional constitution of both interests and actors*, the new institutionalism in sociology diverges from the older sociological institutionalism as well as from the new rational-choice institutionalisms of economics and political science.[2]

It is this emphasis on the constitutive rather than merely constraining role of institutions that informs the present analysis. The Soviet institutions of territorial nationhood and personal nationality comprised a pervasive system of social classification, an organizing "principle of vision and division" of the social world,[3] a standardized scheme of social accounting, an interpretative grid for public discussion, a set of boundary-markers, a legitimate form for public and private identities, and, when political space expanded under Gorbachev, a ready-made template for claims to sovereignty. Institutional definitions of nationhood did not so much constrain action as constitute basic categories of political understanding, central parameters of political rhetoric, specific types of political interest, and fundamental forms of political identity. As political space expanded, they made specific types of political action conceivable, plausible, even compelling, transforming the collapse of a regime into the disintegration of a state. And they continue to constitute elementary forms of political understanding and political action in the successor states.

Two caveats should be added here to forestall misunderstanding. First, as should be clear from the discussion in Chapter 1, my argument is about nationhood and nationality as institutionalized cultural and political forms, not about nations as concrete collectivities. To assert, and explore, the centrality of institutionalized definitions of nationhood to Soviet collapse and successor state politics is not to treat "nations" – taken as "real," solidary, internally homogeneous, externally sharply bounded social groups – as the chief protagonists of either. As I argued in Chapter 1, to take nationhood seriously does not require us to reify

[1] Paul J. DiMaggio and Walter L. Powell, "Introduction," in Powell and DiMaggio, eds., *The New Institutionalism in Organizational Analysis* (Chicago: University of Chicago Press, 1991), p. 2.
[2] *Ibid.*, pp. 2–15; John W. Meyer, "The World Polity and the Authority of the Nation-State," in George M. Thomas, John W. Meyer, Francisco O. Ramirez, and John Boli, *Institutional Structure: Constituting State, Society, and the Individual* (Newbury Park: Sage, 1987).
[3] Pierre Bourdieu, "Social Space and Symbolic Power," in Bourdieu, *In Other Words: Essays Towards a Reflexive Sociology* (Stanford: Stanford University Press, 1990), p. 134.

nations, to treat them as fixed and given, or even to presuppose that they exist.[4] Soviet and post-Soviet "national struggles" were and are not the struggles of nations, but the struggles of institutionally constituted national elites – that is elites institutionally defined *as national* – and aspiring counter-elites.[5] This chapter seeks to show how these struggles were and remain crucially framed, mediated, indeed constituted by institutionalized definitions of nationhood and nationality.

Second, my argument is about the enduring consequences of Soviet institutional definitions of nationhood, particularly those consequences that have survived the regime itself; it is not about the intentions that guided the architects of Soviet nationality policies. Those policies were intended to do two things: first, to harness, contain, channel, and control the potentially disruptive political expression of nationality by creating national-territorial administrative structures and by cultivating, co-opting, and (when they threatened to get out of line) repressing national elites;[6] and second, to drain nationality of its content even while legitimating it as a form, and thereby to promote the long-term withering away of nationality as a vital component of social life.[7] The annals of unintended consequences are rich indeed, but seldom have

---

4 For persuasive criticisms of static, essentialist, primordialist accounts of nationhood and nationality in the Soviet context, see Gail Lapidus, "Ethnonationalism and Political Stability: The Soviet Case," *World Politics* 36 (1984), 560; David Laitin, "The National Uprisings in the Soviet Union," *World Politics* 44 (1991), esp. 148–51; and John Comaroff, "Humanity, Ethnicity, Nationality: Conceptual and Comparative Perspectives on the U.S.S.R.," *Theory and Society* 20 (1991), esp. 670ff.

5 On the crucial role of institutionally constituted national elites, see Philip Roeder, "Soviet Federalism and Ethnic Mobilization," *World Politics* 43 (1991); Veljko Vujacic and Victor Zaslavsky, "The Causes of Disintegration in the USSR and Yugoslavia," *Telos* 88 (1991); Victor Zaslavsky, "Nationalism and Democratic Transition in Post-Communist Societies," *Daedalus* 121, no. 2 (1992); and Mark Beissinger, "Elites and Ethnic Identities in Soviet and Post-Soviet Politics," in Alexander J. Motyl, ed., *The Post-Soviet Nations: Perspectives on the Demise of the USSR* (New York: Columbia University Press, 1992).

6 See among others Richard Pipes, *The Formation of the Soviet Union*, revised edition (Cambridge, Mass.: Harvard University Press, 1964); Gregory J. Massell, "Modernization and National Policy in Soviet Central Asia: Problems and Prospects," in Paul Cocks *et al.*, eds., *The Dynamics of Soviet Politics* (Cambridge, Mass.: Harvard University Press, 1976), pp. 268–9; Lapidus, "Ethnonationalism and Political Stability," 578–9; G. E. Smith, "Ethnic Nationalism in the Soviet Union: Territory, Cleavage, and Control," *Environment and Planning C: Government and Policy* 3 (1985), 49–73; Allan Kagedan, "Territorial Units as Nationality Policy," in Henry R. Huttenbach, ed., *Soviet Nationality Policies* (London and New York: Mansell, 1990), pp. 163–76; Roeder, "Soviet Federalism and Ethnic Mobilization."

7 See for a particularly clear statement of this point Walker Connor, *The National Question in Marxist-Leninist Theory and Strategy* (Princeton: Princeton University Press, 1984), pp. 201ff.

intention and consequence diverged as spectacularly as they did in this case.[8]

The Soviet legacy

Institutionalized multinationality

The unprecedented and unparalleled nature of the Soviet system of institutionalized multinationality is worth underscoring. Most of the world's states are ethnically heterogeneous.[9] In some of these states, ethnicity is subjectively experienced and publicly articulated as *nationality*, ethnic heterogeneity as *national* heterogeneity. In such cases, at least some of the ethnic groups comprising the population (besides the dominant ethnic or national group) understand themselves, or are understood by others, as belonging to distinct nations, nationalities, or national groups.[10] This was true, for example, albeit to a limited extent, of the Romanov Empire in its last half-century.

It was not this subjective understanding of ethnicity as nationality that distinguished the Soviet case from its Romanov predecessor or from other polyethnic states. What was distinctive, rather, was the official, objectified codification[11] of ethnic heterogeneity as national hetero-geneity. More precisely, it is the *thoroughgoing state-sponsored codification*

---

[8] The first aim, to be sure, was realized to a considerable degree, although as Philip Roeder has persuasively argued, the center's ability to contain and control ethno-political mobilization had been gradually eroding for a quarter-century before Gorbachev took power. See Roeder, "Soviet Federalism and Ethnic Mobilization," 212ff.; for an earlier diagnosis along the same lines, see Grey Hodnett, "The Debate over Soviet Federalism," *Soviet Studies* 18, no. 4 (1967), 459–60. The second aim, however, was never realized on a large scale. Throughout the Soviet period, the net effect (although not the intention) of Soviet nationality policies was strongly to reinforce rather than to attenuate the salience and significance of nationality as a central organizing principle of social life.

[9] According to a calculation made by Walker Connor in 1972, only twelve of the world's (then) 132 states were "essentially homogeneous from an ethnic viewpoint." See Connor, "Nation-Building or Nation-Destroying?" *World Politics* 24 (1972), 320. For a more recent statement of the point, see Anthony Smith, "State-Making and Nation-Building," in John A. Hall, ed., *States in History* (Oxford: Basil Blackwell, 1986), p. 229.

[10] On the distinction between an ethnic group and a nation, see Anthony Smith, *The Ethnic Origins of Nations* (Oxford: Basil Blackwell, 1986), esp. pp. 21–31, 135–52; Benjamin Akzin, *States and Nations* (Garden City, NY: Doubleday, 1966), p. 51. I deliberately elide here the distinction between nation and nationality, crucial in some contexts (in the Hungarian half of the Habsburg Empire, for example, where it was used to justify major differences in political status and cultural standing) but not central to the Soviet nationality regime.

[11] On the social effects of codification generally, see Pierre Bourdieu, "Codification," in Bourdieu's *In Other Words*.

and institutionalization of nationhood and nationality exclusively on a sub-state rather than a state-wide level.[12]

In other cases where sub-state ethnicity is subjectively experienced as nationhood, the state may refuse to acknowledge, let alone positively institutionalize, this subjective definition, insisting that while the minority group in question may differ in language or religion, it nonetheless belongs fundamentally to the dominant nation (whether this is conceived as an ethnic nation or a state-nation embracing the entire citizenry). This was the case, for example, of the Hungarian half of the Habsburg Empire after 1867. Although Hungarian-speakers comprised only about half of the population, ruling elites insisted – against the increasingly vigorous protests of Romanians, Serbs, and (to a lesser extent) Slovaks – that Hungary contained a single nation, the Hungarian nation, with which all citizens, whatever their native language or ethnic origins, were expected to identify, and to which all were expected, eventually, to assimilate.[13]

In a second variant, the state may acknowledge the subjective claim to sub-state nationhood of a component ethnic group or groups yet at the same time seek to uphold and institutionalize a more encompassing state-wide sense of nationhood, a definition of the state-wide citizenry as a nation. Thus while French Canadians or Scots may be acknowledged as members of distinct sub-state nations, their respective states seek to sustain a wider sense of Canadian and British nationhood as well.

In a third variant, the state may accept, more or less grudgingly, the self-designation of a minority ethnic group as a national minority, without seeking, as in the second variant, to define that group as part of a more encompassing state-nation as well. But in this case the state is usually identified very closely with the dominant nation. It is conceived as a nation-state in the strong sense, that is as the state of and for a particular nation – and this despite the fact that its citizenry includes, besides members of that state-bearing, state-legitimating nation,

---

[12] This institutionalized multinationality sharply distinguished the Soviet state from its Romanov predecessor, to which it is too often casually assimilated as a modernized but essentially similar "prison of nations." The Romanov Empire was indeed for centuries a polyglot and polyreligious state; and it became by degrees a multinational state in the late nineteenth century as ethnolinguistic and ethnoreligious heterogeneity were increasingly interpreted as national heterogeneity. See Hugh Seton-Watson, *Nations and States* (Boulder, Colo.: Westview, 1977), pp. 143, 148, and *The Russian Empire 1801–1917* (Oxford: Oxford University Press, 1967), pp. 485ff. Its multinationality, however, while increasingly (although far from universally) *perceived* as a central political fact by some peripheral and central elites, was never *institutionalized*.

[13] Seton-Watson, *Nations and States*, p. 164; Oscar Jaszi, *The Dissolution of the Habsburg Monarchy* (Chicago: University of Chicago Press, 1929), pp. 304ff.

members of national minorities as well. This was the case, for example, of Germans in interwar Poland and of Hungarians in interwar Romania. They were recognized as national minorities (as were several other minorities in the "New Europe" that emerged from the settlement of the First World War); and they were accorded certain specific and limited cultural rights in that capacity by domestic law and international treaties.[14] But ruling elites of the states in which they lived defined those states as nation-states in the strong sense, as the states of and for the Polish and Romanian nations respectively.

The Soviet nationality regime was quite different. To begin with, the Soviet Union was not conceived or institutionalized as a nation-state. This was not the inevitable and automatic consequence of the *degree* of ethnic heterogeneity: many highly polyethnic states – including most postcolonial states of Asia and Africa – claim to be, or aspire to become, nation-states.[15] It resulted rather from the *form* in which ethnic hetero-geneity was institutionalized and the manner in which ethnic nationality was aligned with the organization of public life.

Soviet elites might have sought to organize the same territories and peoples as a nation-state – whether as a Soviet nation-state, founded on an emergent Soviet nation, or as a Russian nation-state. But they did neither. On the one hand, Soviet rulers never elaborated the idea of a *Soviet* nation. To be sure, they did seek to inculcate a state-wide Soviet identity, and in the 1960s and 1970s they developed the doctrine of the "Soviet People" (*sovetskii narod)* as a "new historical community." But this emergent entity was explicitly conceived as supra-national, not national.[16] The supra-national Soviet People was consistently distinguished from the individual sub-state Soviet nations. Nationhood remained the prerogative of sub-state ethnonational groups; it was never predicated of the state-wide citizenry.

On the other hand, the Soviet Union was never organized, in theory or in practice, as a *Russian* nation-state. Russians were indeed the dominant nationality, effectively controlling key party and state institutions; and

---

14   C. A. Macartney, *National States and National Minorities* (London: Oxford University Press, 1934).

15   See for instance Smith, "State-Making and Nation-Building," p. 232, and *State and Nation in the Third World* (New York: St. Martin's, 1983), p. 126; and Crawford Young, *The Politics of Cultural Pluralism* (Madison: University of Wisconsin Press, 1976), chapter 3.

16   Bohdan Nahaylo and Victor Swoboda, *Soviet Disunion: A History of the Nationalities Problem in the USSR* (New York: Free Press, 1990), p. 186. See also the detailed discussion in Yaroslav Bilinsky, "The Concept of the Soviet People and its Implications for Soviet Nationality Policy," *Annals of the Ukrainian Academy of Arts and Sciences in the United States* 14 (1978–80).

Russian was promoted by the state as its lingua franca.[17] But this did not make the state a Russian nation-state, any more than the dominance of Germans and the use of German as a lingua franca made the Austrian half of the Habsburg Empire a German nation-state. A whole series of features of the Soviet nationality regime – some of which are discussed in greater detail below – were radically incompatible with the organizational model of the nation-state. These included the Soviet system of ethno-territorial federalism; the elaborate codification of, and pervasive significance attached to, personal nationality; the cultivation of a large number of distinct national intelligentsias; the cultivation of distinct national cadres, allowed, for the most part, to live and work in "their own" national territories; the deliberate policy of nation-building, aimed at the consolidation of non-Russian nations, pursued in the 1920s and early 1930s; the cultivation and codification of a large number of national languages; and the development of an elaborate system of schooling, including higher education, in non-Russian languages.[18]

Thus the Soviet Union was neither conceived in theory nor organized in practice as a nation-state. Yet while it did not define the state or citizenry as a *whole* in national terms, it did define component *parts* of the state and the citizenry in national terms. Herein lies the distinctiveness of the Soviet nationality regime – in its unprecedented displacement of nationhood and nationality, as organizing principles of the social and political order, from the state-wide to the sub-state level. No other state has gone so far in sponsoring, codifying, institutionalizing, even (in some cases) inventing nationhood and nationality on the sub-state level, while at the same time doing nothing to institutionalize them on the level of the state as a whole.[19]

---

[17] For an analytically sophisticated account of Russian dominance of the Soviet state, see Alexander J. Motyl, *Will the Non-Russians Rebel?* (Ithaca and London: Cornell University Press, 1987), esp. pp. 41ff.

[18] On Soviet "nation-building," see now the brilliant article by Yuri Slezkine, "The USSR as a Communal Apartment, or How a Socialist State Promoted Ethnic Particularism," *Slavic Review* 53, no. 2 (1994); and Gerhard Simon, *Nationalism and Policy Toward the Nationalities in the Soviet Union* (Boulder, Colo.: Westview Press, 1991), chapter 2. For a concise and wide-ranging overview of Soviet language policy, see Jonathan Pool, "Soviet Language Planning: Goals, Results, Options," in Jeremy Azrael, ed., *Soviet Nationality Policies and Practices* (New York: Praeger, 1978).

[19] Yugoslavia comes closest, with its Soviet-inspired system of ethnoterritorial federalism; see Connor, *The National Question in Marxist-Leninist Theory and Strategy*, pp. 222–31, and Vujacic and Zaslavsky, "Causes of Disintegration." Yet the close ethnolinguistic kinship of the various South Slav peoples, comprising the very large majority of the Yugoslav population, made it possible to conceive of the citizenry as a whole as at least a potential or incipient Yugoslav (= South Slav) nation, and to institute the category "Yugoslav" as an official nationality (chosen as a self-designation by more than 5% of the population in the 1981 census).

Ethnoterritorial federalism and personal nationality

This institutionalization of nationhood and nationality had two independent aspects. One concerned the territorial organization of politics and administration; the other concerned the classification of persons. The Soviet system of ethnoterritorial federalism divided the territory of the state into a complex four-tiered set of national territories, endowed with varying degrees of autonomy and correspondingly more or less elaborate political and administrative institutions. At the top level of the ethnoterritorial hierarchy, which concerns us here, were the fifteen Union Republics, each bearing the name of a particular national group[20] (and corresponding to today's independent successor states). Constitutionally characterized as sovereign, the Union Republics enjoyed, on paper, a broad set of powers including the right to secede from the Union and to enter into relations with foreign states and the authority to coordinate and control production and administration on their territory.[21] In practice, of course, centralized party and ministerial control sharply, although variably, limited the sphere of effective republic autonomy. But the significance of the republics as institutional crystallizations of nationhood lay less in the constitutional fictions of sovereignty, statehood, and autonomy – symbolically potent and self-actualizing though they proved to be under Gorbachev – than in the durable institutional frame the republics provided for the long-term cultivation and consolidation of national administrative cadres and national intelligentsias (periodic purges notwithstanding) and for the long-term protection and cultivation of national languages and cultures (the promotion of Russian as a lingua franca notwithstanding).

Complementing – and crosscutting – this elaborate and distinctive system of ethnoterritorial federalism was an equally elaborate and distinctive system of personal nationality. While the former divided the territory of the state into a set of national jurisdictions, the latter divided

---

[20] Strictly speaking, as Pål Kolstø reminded me, the vast Russian Soviet Federated Socialist Republic (RSFSR), like the Russian Federation today, did not bear the name of a national group; it bore the territorial-political designation "Rossiiskii," not the ethnolinguistic designation "Russkii" – a distinction lost in English, which renders both as "Russian."

[21] Gregory Gleason, *Federalism and Nationalism: The Struggle for Republican Rights in the USSR* (Boulder, Colo.: Westview, 1990), pp. 82–3. Below the Union Republics – mainly in the vast Russian Republic but also in a few other Union Republics – were twenty Autonomous Republics and eighteen lower-level autonomous formations. For a discussion of the historical genesis, ethnic demography, and political significance of these autonomous formations, see Lee Schwartz, "Regional Population Redistribution and National Homelands in the USSR," in Huttenbach, ed., *Soviet Nationality Policies.*

the population of the state into an exhaustive and mutually exclusive set of national groups, over a hundred in all, twenty-two with more than a million members. Ethnic nationality (*natsional'nost'*) was not only a *statistical category*, a fundamental unit of social accounting, employed in censuses and other social surveys. It was, more distinctively, an obligatory and mainly ascriptive *legal category*, a key element of an individual's legal status. As such, it was registered in internal passports and other personal documents, transmitted by descent, and recorded in almost all bureaucratic encounters and official transactions.[22] In some contexts, notably admission to higher education and application for certain types of employment, legal nationality significantly shaped life chances, both negatively (especially for Jews)[23] and positively (for "titular" nationalities[24] in the non-Russian republics, who benefited from mainly tacit "affirmative action" or preferential treatment policies).

This dual – and unprecedentedly thoroughgoing – institutionalization of nationhood and nationality on the sub-state level was effected through state action. Yet it was not intended by state actors. It resulted rather from the unforeseen and unintended persistence over time of a set of

[22] When the system of internal passports was introduced in the early 1930s, nationality was initially registered by self-designation. But thereafter, nationality depended exclusively on parental nationality, not on residence, language, or subjective identity. There was no possibility of changing one's nationality, and no regard for individual choice, except for children of mixed-nationality marriages (and even their choice – made once and for all at age sixteen – was limited to the two parental nationalities). See Victor Zaslavsky and Yuri Luryi, "The Passport System in the USSR and Changes in Soviet Society," *Soviet Union* 6, Part 2 (1979), 147ff.; Rasma Karklins, *Ethnic Relations in the USSR: The Perspective from Below* (Boston: Allen & Unwin, 1986), pp. 23, 31–2, 42–3.

[23] Discrimination against Jews – treated as a nationality in the Soviet classificatory scheme – induced most children of mixed marriages involving Jews and non-Jews to choose the non-Jewish nationality for their passports, and probably to identify subjectively with the non-Jewish nationality as well (Zaslavsky and Luryi, "The Passport System in the USSR," 149). Since intermarriage rates for Jews were extremely high (see the data reported in the *Journal of Soviet Nationalities* 1, no. 2 [1990], 160ff.), this reclassification strategy contributed substantially to the apparently dramatic shrinkage of the Jewish population of the Soviet Union (from 2.2 million in 1959 to 1.4 million in 1989). More recently, of course, ethnonational reclassification has proceeded in the opposite direction, since the lifting of restrictions on emigration and the automatic immigration and citizenship rights extended by Israel to diaspora Jews have revalorized Jewish nationality, at least for would-be emigrants (see Brubaker, "Political Dimensions of Migration From and Among Soviet Successor States," in Myron Weiner, ed., *International Migration and Security* [Boulder, Colo.: Westview Press, 1993]). The more general analytical point is that even the rigidly ascriptive Soviet system of personal nationality did leave room at the margins – considerable room, for some groups – for the play of individual strategies.

[24] In standard Sovietological usage, the "titular" nationality of a particular ethnoterritorial unit is the nationality whose name the unit bears: thus Georgians were the titular nationality in the Georgian SSR, Kazakhs in the Kazakh SSR, and so on.

institutional arrangements cobbled together in *ad hoc* fashion as tactical responses to urgent situational imperatives.[25] Lenin, long opposed to ethnoterritorial federalism (or any other kind) on principle, embraced it as expedient in the aftermath of the Bolshevik seizure of power, believing it a necessary and effective means of reconstituting shattered state authority and cementing political loyalty in the ethnic borderlands, and expecting it to be a temporary transitional arrangement.[26] In the belief he was correct; in the expectation, mistaken.

Still less was it intended or foreseen that personal legal nationality would become an enduring ascribed status or an important determinant of life chances. Nationality as an official component of personal status was introduced in 1932 as one of a number of elements contained in the newly instituted system of internal passports. That system was central to the coercive control of the newly collectivized agrarian and increasingly industrialized urban labor force; more generally, it was central to the control and regulation of migration.[27] But it was the passport system as such, not the legal nationality that was encoded in it along with much other information, that was crucial for this purpose. Indeed the passport-based regulation and coercive control of labor supply and internal migration could have been effected just as easily without the encoding of nationality. The later uses of official nationality were unrelated to the original purposes for which internal passports were created.

It was thus through an irony of history, through the unintended consequences of a variety of *ad hoc* regime policies, that nationality became and remained a basic institutional building block of the avowedly internationalist, supra-nationalist, and anti-nationalist Soviet state, with the land partitioned into a set of bounded national territories, the polity comprised in part of a set of formally sovereign national republics, and the citizenry divided into a set of legally codified nationalities.

Territorial and ethnocultural models of nationhood

The dual scheme of ethnoterritorial federalism and personal nationality employed the same set of national categories. The same categories, that

[25] See Gleason, *Federalism and Nationalism*, p. 5.
[26] The most thorough account of the *ad hoc* development of ethnoterritorial federalism is Pipes, *The Formation of the Soviet Union*, which carries the story through 1923. See also E. H. Carr, *The Bolshevik Revolution* (London: Macmillan, 1950), vol. I, pp. 253ff.; Hélène Carrère d'Encausse, *Le grand défi: Bolcheviks et nations 1917–1930* (Paris: Flammarion, 1987), pp. 143ff.; and Gleason, *Federalism and Nationalism*, esp. chapter 2.
[27] Zaslavsky and Luryi, "The Passport System in the USSR."

is, were attached to territorial polities and to personal nationalities. There were, to be sure, far more of the latter, for the national classification of the citizenry included numerous small nationalities to whom no separate national territory was assigned.[28] But of the fifty-three national territories, almost all bore the names of one or more of the nationalities into which the Soviet citizenry had been divided. There was thus a correspondence, usually one-to-one, between particular national territorial jurisdictions and particular nationalities, for example between Ukraine as a national territory and Ukrainian as a personal nationality, between Estonia as a territory and Estonian as a nationality, and so on.

Yet while the national territorial jurisdictions *corresponded* to the nationalities for which they were named, the two were neither legally nor spatially nor even conceptually *congruent*. The jurisdiction of the national republics was territorially, not personally circumscribed. They had jurisdiction over certain matters occurring in their bounded territories, regardless of the nationality of the persons living in those territories. On the other hand, the nationality of persons did not depend on their place of residence. Personal nationality was an autonomous classification scheme, based on descent, not residence. It had no territorial component whatsoever. Moreover, vast and largely state-sponsored migrations, some ethnodemographically arbitrary administrative boundaries, and the sheer impossibility of constructing ethnodemographically "clean" frontiers in areas of historically mixed settlement[29] combined to engender a major mismatch between the frontiers of national territories and the spatial distribution of nationalities.[30] A substantial fraction of the

---

[28] Although twenty-two nationalities, according to the 1989 census, included over 1 million members, and thirty-three numbered between 100,000 and a million, another forty-seven individually enumerated nationalities (not counting twenty-six individually enumerated "peoples of the North") had fewer than 100,000 members, some only a few hundred. See Gosudarstvennyi komitet po statistike, *Natsional'nyi sostav naseleniia SSSR* (Moscow: Finansy i statistika, 1991), pp. 5–8.

[29] Julian Birch, "Border Disputes and Disputed Borders in the Soviet Federal System," *Nationalities Papers* 15, no. 1 (1987), 44.

[30] To a considerable extent, this spatial mismatch between the distribution of nationalities and the boundaries of "their" territories was induced or even directly imposed by the regime. Thus migrations of persons outside "their own" homeland were induced as a means of weakening homeland attachments and identities and promoting an emergent supra-national Soviet identity. And some territorial frontiers – notably in parts of Central Asia and Transcaucasia – were drawn in a manner that departed deliberately from the dictates of ethnic demography. This last point, however, should not be exaggerated: for the most part, national territorial borders reflected ethnic demography about as well as could be expected given mixed populations (Schwartz, "Regional Population Redistribution"). For a comparative discussion of the "redistribution and gerrymandering of ethnic groups" in multiethnic Communist states, see Walker Connor, *The National Question*, pp. 300ff.

population of most national territories belonged to "non-titular," i.e. conceptually "external" nationalities; conversely, a substantial fraction of the population of most national groups lived outside "their own" national territories.

The Soviet scheme of institutionalized multinationality was characterized not only by a legal incongruence and a spatial mismatch between its two components – national territories and personal nationalities – but also by a fundamental tension, at once conceptual and political, between two independent, even incompatible definitions of nationhood: one territorial and political, the other personal and ethnocultural. This tension is an old one, long familiar to students of comparative nationalism.[31] Usually, however, these opposed understandings of nationhood are associated with differing countries or regions. What is interesting, and distinctive, about the Soviet nationality regime was the simultaneous institutionalization of both conventionally opposed definitions of nationhood.

On one definition, the nation is a territorially bounded and self-governing collectivity, a collectivity pervasively shaped, indeed *constituted* by its territorial and political frame. Nationhood, on this view, is both conceptually and causally dependent on political territory. Not every territorial polity is a nation; but nationhood, at least its full realization, requires the form and frame of the territorial polity. Nationhood – at least fully realized nationhood – is an emergent property of certain territorial polities.

This understanding of nationhood captured well the historical experience of Western European state-nations, incubating and emerging within the protective and powerfully shaping territorial and institutional frame of large yet culturally relatively homogeneous territorial states. But in its stronger version – according to which political territory is essential not simply for the full realization, but for the mere existence of nationhood – it did not capture well the historical experience of Central and Eastern Europe. There political units were either much smaller than cultural units – as in the densely urban belt of statelets, principalities, city-states, and free cities along trans-Alpine medieval trade routes from the Mediterranean to the Rhine[32] – or much larger than cultural units, as

---

[31] See for example Hans Kohn, *The Idea of Nationalism* (New York: Collier Books, 1944), esp. pp. 329ff.; Theodor Schieder, "Typologie und Erscheinungsformen des Nationalstaats in Europa," in Schieder, *Nationalismus und Nationalstaat* (Göttingen: Vandenhoeck and Ruprecht, 1991); Jenö Szücs, *Nation und Geschichte* (Budapest: Corvina, 1974), pp. 21ff.; Smith, *The Ethnic Origins of Nations*.

[32] Stein Rokkan and Derek Urwin, *Economy, Territory, Identity: Politics of West European Peripheries* (London: Sage, 1983), pp. 26–7.

in the great multinational empires of the Ottomans, Habsburgs, and Romanovs. In the context of this radical discrepancy of scale between political authority and cultural commonality, a different conception of nationhood emerged. On this alternative view, the nation is neither conceptually nor causally dependent on political territory. The nation is an ethnocultural community, typically a community of language. It might span several political units (as in the case of pre-unification Germany or Italy), or it might be contained in a much larger political structure (as in the case of the "nonhistoric" ethnolinguistic nations – for example Slovaks and Slovenes – within the Habsburg Empire).[33]

The gap between the territorial-political and ethnocultural models of nationhood, to be sure, is not unbridgeable.[34] Under the standardizing, homogenizing influence of the modern, "citizen-mobilizing and citizen-influencing" state,[35] territorial polities may shape their citizenries into relatively homogeneous cultural communities. And from a very different starting point, state-spanning or intra-state ethnocultural nations may attain statehood, or at least territorial political autonomy within a wider state, and thus acquire a territorial and institutional frame.

In regions with highly intermixed ethnocultural communities, however, where political borders cannot be drawn to coincide with ethnocultural frontiers, the territorial-political and ethnocultural models of nationhood are not so easily reconciled. Widely dispersed ethnocultural nations, as well as those that overlap with other ethnocultural nations in inextricably intermixed frontier "shatter zones," cannot be neatly "territorialized," cannot easily acquire their own territorial states. And territorial polities that include substantial and self-conscious national minorities cannot, in the age of nationalism, be easily "nationalized," i.e. nationally homogenized. Thus in both the Austro-Hungarian and Russian Empires, ethnically mixed populations, increasingly resistant to assimilation, by the late nineteenth century, prevented a full convergence of the territorial-political and ethnocultural models of nationhood. A persisting tension between the two, and between corresponding proposals for national autonomy, is evident in the history of the national question in both empires.[36]

---

[33] On nonhistoric nations – those without an independent political history – in the Habsburg Empire, see Robert Kann, *The Multinational Empire: Nationalism and National Reform in the Habsburg Monarchy*, vol. I (New York: Columbia University Press, 1950), pp. 271ff.

[34] Smith, *The Ethnic Origins of Nations*, chapter 6.

[35] Eric Hobsbawm, *Nations and Nationalism since 1780* (Cambridge: Cambridge University Press, 1990), p. 83.

[36] Kann, *The Multinational Empire*, vol. II; Pipes, *The Formation of the Soviet Union*, chapter 1.

The duality of Soviet nationhood: tensions and contradictions

The Soviet nationality regime institutionalized both models of nation-hood – as well as the tension between them. Nations, we have seen, were defined simultaneously in territorial and political terms (as national republics) and in extra-territorial, cultural terms (as nationalities). Had the nationalities lived exclusively in "their own" national republics, the two definitions would have been congruent. But this was far from being the case when the system of ethnoterritorial federalism was established, and even less so after the massive state-sponsored and state-imposed migrations associated with industrialization, collectivization, and war.[37] At the time of the 1989 census, more than 73 million Soviet citizens, a quarter of the total Soviet population, lived outside "their own" national territory (or belonged to small nationalities without a national territory of their own). To give just a few examples: 17 percent of all Russians – 25 million in all – lived outside the Russian republic. Another 12 million lived in non-Russian national territories inside the Russian republic. One-third of all Armenians lived outside Armenia, while nearly three-fourths of all Tatars – nearly 5 million in all – lived outside the Tatar Autonomous Republic.[38]

The tensions arising from this dual and non-congruent institutional-ization of nationhood were attenuated by the strict limits the Soviet regime placed on nationalism. Nations were to be seen but not heard; culture (and, one might add, politics and administration as well) was to be "national in form but socialist in content."[39] The more purely formal the national categories – the smaller, that is, their substantive social significance – the less the lack of congruence between the territorial frame and the personal substrate of nationhood would matter. In the extreme case, it would not matter at all whether, and to what degree, Soviet citizens lived in "their own" national republics or elsewhere, for the republics would be national in name only; what was nominally "their own" national republic would in fact be no more "their own" than any other.

---

[37] On migrations induced or compelled by the state, see E. Glyn Lewis, "Migration and Language in the U.S.S.R.," in Joshua Fishman, ed., *Advances in the Sociology of Language*, vol. II (The Hague: Mouton, 1972); Simon, *Nationalism*, chapters 5, 7.

[38] Robert A. Lewis, "The Migration of Russians Outside Their Homeland," *Nationalities Papers* 20, no. 2 (1992), 36; Gosudarstvennyi komitet po statistike, *Natsional'nyi sostav naseleniia SSSR*.

[39] For an extended discussion of this formula, introduced by Stalin to characterize proletarian culture, but aptly summarizing the core idea informing Soviet nationality policy as a whole, see Connor, *The National Question*, pp. 202ff.

For many, perhaps most Sovietologists, this hypothetical limiting case came close to describing Soviet reality. Dominant currents within Sovietology either ignored nationality altogether or dismissed it as an ideological façade bearing little or no relation to "real" social and political structures. Yet as more perspicuous analysts recognized, even well before the Gorbachev era, nationality was not a purely formal construct, an ideological fig leaf, existing only on paper. It *was* of course a formal construct, an institutional form; but as such it powerfully shaped Soviet society. The repression of political nationalism was compatible with the pervasive institutionalization of nationhood and nationality as fundamental social categories. Nationalists' complaints – and Stalin's murderous policies – notwithstanding, the regime had no systematic policy of "nation-destroying."[40] It might have abolished national republics and ethnoterritorial federalism;[41] it might have abolished the legal category of personal nationality;[42] it might have ruthlessly Russified the Soviet educational system; it might have forcibly uprooted peripheral elites, and prevented them from making careers in "their own" republics.[43] It did none of the above. The repression of nationalism

---

[40] The expression is Walker Connor's; see his "Nation-Building or Nation-Destroying," *World Politics* 24 (1972). Under Stalin the regime did, of course, act with extraordinary brutality toward certain national groups, notably those accused of collaborating with the Germans in the Second World War, who were stripped of their national institutions, erased from history books, and deported in their entirety, with great loss of life, to remote regions of the state. Stalin also ordered the wholesale deportations of the elites of the newly reincorporated Western territories. But despite his murderous repression of particular national groups, he did not attack the social or legal foundations of institutionalized multinationality as such. On wartime deportations, see Simon, *Nationalism*, chapter 7; Aleksandr M. Nekrich, *The Punished Peoples* (New York: W. W. Norton, 1978); Robert Conquest, *The Nation Killers: The Soviet Deportation of Nationalities* (New York: Macmillan, 1970).

[41] For a discussion of the Soviet debate of the 1950s and 1960s concerning whether the federal forms and national republics had outlived their usefulness, see Hodnett, "The Debate over Soviet Federalism"; and Gleason, *Federalism and Nationalism*, chapter 4.

[42] Some consideration was given in the 1970s to abolishing the legal status of nationality, but it came to nothing. See Lapidus, "Ethnonationalism and Political Stability," 567–8; Zaslavsky and Luryi, "The Passport System in the USSR," 149–50; Karklins, *Ethnic Relations in the USSR*, p. 32.

[43] John Armstrong notes that "peculiar features of the official system facilitate retention of ethnic ties by permitting . . . upwardly mobile persons to obtain higher education and pursue subsequent careers in their home republics. Only those intent on highly specialized activities (from ballet to nuclear physics) or on very high level Party careers must prepare to merge in the all-Soviet (Russified) career pool . . . It is frankly puzzling why, decades ago, the Soviet regime did not take radical measures to integrate career patterns [rather than allowing the upwardly mobile to pursue careers in their own languages and in their own republics]. Even Stalin's totalitarianism eschewed the most extreme precedents for creating a supraethnic elite," notably the Ottoman Janissary system, which "entailed forcible removal, in early adolescence, of boys in Christian

went hand in hand with the consolidation of nationhood and nationality.[44]

The tensions arising from the dual institutionalization of nationality, and from the non-congruence between national territories and ethno-cultural nations, were indeed attenuated by the repression of nationalism. The problem of irredentism, for example, which might have been nourished by the mismatch between territorial and ethnocultural frontiers, did not arise; for popular demands for such ethnonationally rectificatory border changes were excluded from the universe of legitimate political discourse.[45] But tensions associated with the dual definition of nationhood, although attenuated, were not eliminated.

The institution of national republics, for example, defined as the states of and for particular nations, legitimated the preferential treatment of members of the "titular," nominally state-bearing nationalities, especially in higher education and employment. While such preferential treatment, under the name of *korenizatsiia* or "nativization," was an explicit policy of the Soviet center only in the 1920s and early 1930s, local patterns of preferential treatment for titular nationalities persisted, and were generally tolerated by the center. Definition of the republics as national states also legitimated the promotion of the language of the titular nationality – not at the expense of Russian, which the Soviet regime vigorously promoted as a union-wide lingua franca, but at the expense of the other non-Russian languages spoken by non-titulars living in the republic.

Despite their favored access to positions defined by the regime as "strategic" or "sensitive," and despite the privileges they enjoyed as a

---

families, followed by rigorous resocialization to Islamic and Ottoman dynastic norms" ("The Autonomy of Ethnic Identity: Historic Cleavages and Nationality Relations in the USSR," in Alexander J. Motyl, ed., *Thinking Theoretically About Soviet Nationalities* [New York: Columbia University Press, 1992], p. 39).

[44] For an authoritative statement of this point with respect to the Baltic republics, arguing that Baltic nations, far from being on the verge of extinction after a half-century of Soviet rule, as many Baltic nationalists asserted in the Gorbachev era, were much more firmly established and consolidated as nations than they had been in 1940, see Romuald J. Misiunas and Rein Taagepera, *The Baltic States: Years of Dependence, 1940–1980* (Berkeley: University of California Press, 1983), pp. 260–2. For a similar argument formulated in more general terms, but resting especially on research on Transcaucasia, see Ronald Grigor Suny, "Nationalist and Ethnic Unrest in the Soviet Union," *World Policy Journal* 11, no. 3 (1989), 507.

[45] Many border changes were in fact made, but typically in top-down fashion, for various political or strategic reasons, not in response to irredentist ethnopolitical mobilization. The closest thing to such mobilization, in the pre-perestroika era, involved Armenian campaigns, particularly during the Khrushchev thaw, for the transfer of the over-whelmingly Armenian Nagorno-Karabakh Autonomous Oblast from Azerbaijan to Armenia (Birch, "Border Disputes," 50–3).

result of the special union-wide status of the Russian language, the Russian (and, more broadly, Russophone) residents of non-Russian republics resented the affirmative action programs designed to further the educational and professional chances of titular nationalities.[46] At the same time, the titular nationalities resented the key positions reserved for Russian (and Russophone) immigrants and the key role accorded the Russian language.

These mutual resentments stemmed from the dual definition of nationhood – territorial-political and cultural-personal – and from two corresponding conceptions of national autonomy. Here we can extend and enrich the characterization given above by linking conceptions of nationhood to conceptions of national autonomy. On one view, the fundamental parameters of nationhood are territorial. Political territory provides the frame of the nation, fixes the arena of its autonomy, defines the domain of its dominance. The subject of autonomy, on this view, is a unit of territorial administration. Autonomy means that the territorial units "belong" to the nations whose names they bear. They can legitimately be "filled up" with a particular national language and culture. In effect, an updated version of the formula *cuius regio, eius religio* applies. That formula, which dates from the era of religious wars in post-Reformation Central Europe, permitted the rulers of principalities or territorial states (a great profusion of which existed in Central Europe) to determine the religion of their own territories, to "fill up" their territories with a particular religion. Persons of another confession could convert or emigrate. Religious pluralism was thus institutionalized in Central Europe, but religious monism was institutionalized within each territorial unit. Religion, in effect, was territorialized. Similarly, on the territorial view of nationhood, national-cultural pluralism finds legitimate expression in the differences between territorial polities, but national-cultural homogeneity should prevail within each territorial polity. The telos of the national territories is to become fully nationalized, i.e. filled up with a homogeneous national culture. The welter of national cultures adjusts to fit the fixed frame of territorial polities. Culture and territory eventually converge.[47]

On the alternative view, nations cannot be adequately encapsulated or defined by the fixed and more or less arbitrarily drawn frontiers of ostensibly national territories. Even if territorial frontiers could be

[46] See for instance Karklins, *Ethnic Russians in the USSR*, pp. 64–5, 96.
[47] For a powerful theoretical argument on the tendential convergence of culture and territory in industrial society, see Ernest Gellner, *Nations and Nationalism* (Ithaca, NY: Cornell University Press, 1983).

"correctly" drawn at a given moment, the momentary match between the division of territory and the distribution of persons would not endure. For nations are inherently mobile and dynamic; their spatial configuration changes over time with the migration of their members. Nations are fundamentally groups of persons, not stretches of territory. The proper subject of national autonomy is not a nominally national territorial polity but the nation itself, that is, a particular group of persons. Nationality is carried by persons, not inscribed in a territory; it is consequently portable, not territorially fixed. National autonomy requires not the convergence of territorial administration and national culture, but their independence; it requires cultural rights – in the sphere of education, cultural facilities, and the language of public life – for members of nations wherever they live.[48]

Elements of both models, as we have seen, were institutionalized in the Soviet Union. On the one hand, the land of the state was divided into national polities that were permitted, to some extent, to "fill up" their territories with a particular national culture. On the other hand, the population was divided into non-territorial national groups, whose nationality was independent of their place of residence. But neither model was realized in full. Territorial autonomy was not carried through because of the special role reserved by the center for Russians and the Russian language. Extra-territorial cultural autonomy was not carried through (except for Russians) because of the leeway afforded to national republics to "nationalize" their territories (with the exception noted for Russians and the Russian language). Moreover, neither principle could have been more fully realized without violating the other. To have instituted cultural autonomy for non-Russians living in republics other than "their own" would have alienated the titular elites of those republics and further infringed their ability to "fill up" their territories with their particular national culture. To have increased the territorial autonomy of the republics, allowing them to "nationalize" more fully their territories, would have eroded the extra-territorial cultural autonomy enjoyed throughout the union by Russians. Tension between territorial and ethnocultural nationhood, and between territorial and extra-territorial national autonomy, was endemic to the Soviet nationality regime.

---

[48] This conception of extra-territorial or personal national autonomy was first elaborated in 1851 by the Hungarian statesman Louis Kossuth in the aftermath of the Austro-Russian suppression of the incipient Hungarian Republic; it received its most thorough development a half-century later in the writings of the Austro-Marxists, above all in Otto Bauer's *Die Nationalitätenfrage und die Sozialdemokratie* (Vienna: I. Brand, 1907).

The successor states

Soviet disintegration: from breakdown to breakup

With the breakup of the Soviet Union, the legacy of its dual institutional crystallization of nationhood and nationality passed to the successor states. The breakup itself, it should be emphasized, was shaped by the territorial-political crystallization of nationhood, not by the ethnocultural definition. The key actors in the drama of disintegration – besides the fragmented political and military elites of the center – were the institutionally empowered elites of the national republics, including, crucially, from late 1990 on, those of the Russian republic.[49] Disintegration occurred through intensifying jurisdictional struggles between the center and the national republics,[50] in which the latter were increasingly emboldened by the deepening divisions within and immobilization of the former.

Not only the gradual breakdown of effective Soviet statehood, but the final breakup of the state into fifteen incipient, internationally recognized successor states, was crucially framed and structured by the territorial-political crystallization of nationhood in the form of national republics. That this paradigmatically massive state could disappear in so comparatively orderly a fashion, ceasing to exist as a subject of international law and withering away as a unit of administration, was possible chiefly because the successor units already existed as internal quasi-nation-states, with fixed territories, names, legislatures, administrative staffs, cultural and political elites, and – not least – the constitutionally enshrined right to secede from the Soviet Union (it is one of the many ironies of the Soviet breakup that it was decisively facilitated by what

---

49 See among many accounts Roeder, "Soviet Federalism and Ethnic Mobilization"; Vujacic and Zaslavsky, "Causes of Disintegration"; Zaslavsky, "Nationalism and Democratic Transition"; Alexander J. Motyl, *Sovietology, Rationality, Nationality* (New York: Columbia University Press, 1990); Gail Lapidus, "From Democratization to Disintegration: The Impact of Perestroika on the National Question," in Gail Lapidus and Victor Zaslavsky, eds., *From Union to Commonwealth: Nationalism and Separatism in the Soviet Republics* (Cambridge: Cambridge University Press, 1992); and Ronald Grigor Suny, *The Revenge of the Past: Nationalism, Revolution, and the Collapse of the Soviet Union* (Stanford: Stanford University Press, 1993), chapter 4.

50 I am concerned here only with the Union Republics, not with lower-level autonomous formations. The latter, locked in their own jurisdictional struggles with the Union Republics to which they belonged, tended to collude with the center against the Union Republics. See Ian Bremmer, "Post Soviet Nationalities Theory: Past, Present, and Future," in Bremmer and Ray Taras, eds., *New States, New Politics: Building the Post-Soviet Nations* (Cambridge: Cambridge University Press, forthcoming 1996).

regime leaders and Western commentators alike had long dismissed as a constitutional fiction).[51]

The dual role played by the Russian republic in the breakup is worth underscoring. On the one hand, the RSFSR was one national republic among others, formally coordinate with them, and allied with them in their jurisdictional struggles against the center. That alliance – dramatized by Yeltsin's trip to Tallinn in January 1991, immediately after the military crackdown in Vilnius, to condemn the attack and to appeal to Russian soldiers to refuse to fire on civilians – strengthened the position of the republics. On the other hand, because of its preponderant size and (by comparison with other national republics) its much weaker spatial, ethnocultural, and institutional differentiation from the Soviet center, the RSFSR represented (as the other national republics did not) a potential alternative center, rather than simply a peripheral contender for autonomy from the center. The high degree of overlap between the RSFSR and the Union – the fact that the great majority of key Union facilities and institutions were located on Russian territory (if not formally subject to Russian jurisdiction), and the fact that Soviet elites, in their great majority, were either Russian by nationality, or long-standing residents of the RSFSR, or both – made it relatively easy for central Soviet military and bureaucratic elites to reorient themselves to the RSFSR at pivotal moments, especially during and immediately after the coup attempt. The jurisdictional struggles of the RSFSR against the Soviet center were therefore two-sided, tactically oriented to *weakening* the center and distributing its powers to the national republics, but strategically oriented to *capturing* the center and taking over its powers.[52]

Contrasting sharply with the central role played by elites of the territorial-political nations – that is, the national republics – in the breakup of the Soviet state was the marginal role played by actors representing extra-territorial ethnonational groups. The center made some effort to mobilize them – especially the Russians living in the non-Russian republics – by emphasizing the ethnopolitical dangers of independence for those living outside "their own" national territory. Yet while the ethnocultural groups to whom such appeals were addressed were institutionally defined in national terms (by the legal institution of extra-territorial personal nationality and the associated social practices and

[51] Zaslavsky, "Nationalism and Democratic Transition," 106.
[52] *Report on the USSR* 3, no. 4 (1991), 28–9; Riina Kionka, "Russia Recognizes Estonia's Independence," *Report on the USSR* 3, no. 5 (1991), 14–16; Alexander Rahr, "Are El'tsin and Gorbachev Now Allies?," *Report on the USSR* 3, no. 27 (1991), 8; Stephen Foye, "The Soviet Armed Forces: Things Fall Apart," *RFE/RL Research Report* 1, no. 1 (1992), 15–16, 18.

Russian case

cultural attitudes), they were not institutionally organized or empowered. As a result, although some action (for example, strikes protesting republican language laws) occurred in the name of ethnonational communities, they were not capable of the kind of sustained, organized, institutionally framed and legitimated action that the national republics could undertake; and they remained marginal to the jurisdictional struggles that pitted elites of the republics – including, crucially, the Russian republic – against those of decaying central institutions.

Yet while the ethnocultural crystallization of nationhood, unlike the territorial-political crystallization, did not figure centrally in the jurisdictional struggles through which predefined, deeply institutionalized national territorial polities asserted claims to progressively higher degrees of "stateness" against a divided and immobilized center, the ethnocultural definition of nationhood will figure centrally, indeed already is figuring centrally, as the successor states move to consolidate the formally independent statehood to which they so suddenly acceded.

The national question in the successor states

The successor states to the Soviet Union – and to Yugoslavia and Czechoslovakia as well – are at this writing still incipient states. Their juridical independence has been secured, but their sociological "stateness" remains to be established. The form of their statehood, even the fact of their durable statehood, is not yet settled. They are states-in-the-making.

Questions of citizenship and nationhood, broadly understood, are among the core aspects of statehood that remain unsettled and vigorously contested. Among the still unsettled, and unsettling, questions are the following : Who "belongs," by formal citizenship, or in some other sense or status, to the state? What circle of persons comprises, or should comprise, the citizenry of the state? To what extent should citizenship depend on, and coincide with, ethnocultural nationality?[53] Are there others, outside the circle of formal citizens – for example, co-ethnics in other states – who have special claims on the state, and in whose fate the state takes a special interest? Conversely, are there some inside the circle of formal citizens who are not full members or citizens in a substantive sense? And what *kind* of citizenship will the state institutionalize? Will citizenship be held individually, or will it be mediated, in some form, by ethnic or national group membership? Will

[53] I have addressed the politics of citizenship in the post-Soviet setting in "Citizenship Struggles in Soviet Successor States," *International Migration Review* 26 (1992).

the rights of citizenship consist solely in individual rights, or will they include group or collective rights as well?[54]

A similar set of unsettled questions clusters around the issue of nationhood or nationality. In what sense is the new state to be a nation-state, or a national state? If the state is understood as the state of and for a particular nation, how is the nation in question defined? Is it understood as a civic nation, defined and delimited by the legal and political status of citizenship, and consisting of the sum of the citizens of the state? Or is it understood as an ethnocultural nation, defined independently of the state, and not necessarily coextensive with its citizenry? In the latter case, how is the principle of nationality or national self-determination, on which the successor states base their claims to legitimacy, to be reconciled with the practices of democratic citizenship, to the idea of which successor state elites make uniform obeisance?[55]

A comprehensive exploration of these questions would far exceed the scope of this chapter. Some of them are taken up, from different points of view, in later chapters. My discussion here will focus on the way in which the legacy of the dual Soviet institutional crystallization of nationality has shaped – and is likely to continue to shape – the national question in the emerging successor states. To keep the discussion manageable, I consider here only one aspect of the national question, albeit one that is central to its overall configuration in post-Soviet Eurasia. This is the pervasive tension between (1) incipient national – and nationalizing – states; (2) the national minorities in the new states; and (3) the external "homeland" states to which the minorities "belong" by ethnonational affiliation but not legal citizenship.

This triadic relation between incipient nation-state, national minority, and external national homeland is replicated in varying configurations throughout post-Soviet Eurasia. Here I consider only one class of cases, albeit a large and heterogeneous class: those involving Russian minorities, and Russia as external national homeland.[56] This class includes almost all the successor states, for all except Armenia have, or had, substantial Russian minorities (more than 5 percent of their population in 1989). There are evident reasons for focusing on Russia and the Russians.

---

[54] On group-differentiated citizenship rights, see Will Kymlicka, *Multicultural Citizenship: A Liberal Theory of Minority Rights* (Oxford: Oxford University Press, 1995).

[55] For a searching analysis of the tension between national and democratic claims, see Juan J. Linz and Alfred Stepan, *Problems of Democratic Transition and Consolidation: Southern Europe, South America, and Post-Communist Europe* (Baltimore and London: Johns Hopkins University Press, 1996), chapters 2, 19, and 20.

[56] In Chapter 3, I examine in more sustained fashion the core dynamics of the triadic relational nexus and apply this analysis to the breakup of Yugoslavia.

Representable by contenders for power as an unjustly truncated, humiliated Great Power, Russia is a potentially revisionist state. While other successor states, too, are potentially revisionist, and may be more likely than Russia to be drawn into wars with their neighbors, the presence of nearly 25 million Russians in non-Russian successor states, the enormous military power of Russia, and the uniquely radical decline in status experienced both by the new Russian minorities and by key segments of Russian elites in Russia would make a revisionist Russia a potentially much graver threat than the other successor states to regional and even global security.

In the dynamic interplay between these three elements – the newly nationalizing non-Russian successor states, their large Russian minorities, and the Russian state – the contingency inherent in political action, especially when the "very parameters of political action are in flux," will play a key role.[57] Yet without adopting a determinist stance, I want to specify the way in which the broad contours of this interplay will be structured by the institutional legacy of the Soviet nationality regime. Consider first the situation of the newly nationalizing successor states, ethnically heterogeneous yet conceiving themselves as nation-states. Clearly, their prior institutional incarnation as Soviet republics laid the foundations not only for their independent statehood but also for their self-understanding as specifically *national* states. Their explicit *raison d'être*, in the Soviet scheme, was to serve as the institutional vehicles for national self-determination. They were expressly defined as the republics *of* and *for* the nations for whom they were named.

Thus despite their ethnic heterogeneity – extreme, by comparison to Western European national states – the Soviet republics understood themselves, and were supposed to understand themselves, as national polities. But national in what sense? Here we can extend and refine the argument that the Soviet regime institutionalized both territorial-political and personal-ethnocultural models of nationhood as well as the tension between them. The Soviet territorial-political definition of nationhood not only, as I argued above, stood in *tension* with the personal-ethnocultural definition, but *presupposed* that alternative definition. The relation between the two institutional crystallizations

[57] For a sophisticated emphasis on contingency, see Guillermo O'Donnell and Philippe Schmitter, *Transitions from Authoritarian Rule: Tentative Conclusions about Uncertain Democracies* (Baltimore, MD: Johns Hopkins University Press, 1986), and William H. Sewell, "Three Temporalities: Toward an Eventful Sociology," forthcoming in Terrence J. McDonald, ed., *The Historic Turn in the Human Sciences* (Ann Arbor: University of Michigan Press). The quotation is from O'Donnell and Schmitter, p. 4.

was asymmetrical. Ethnocultural nationhood did not depend on the existence of national republics; but the national republics did depend on – indeed their very existence was predicated on – the existence of ethnocultural nations. The republics were defined as the polities of and for particular nations; these nations were explicitly understood as prior to and independent of the polities whose creation they legitimated. The national republics did not (as the strong territorial-political model of nationhood requires) *constitute* "their" nations; rather, independently existing nations were given "their own" territorial polities. Even the territorial-political crystallization of nationhood in the Soviet Union, therefore, presupposed the existence of ethnocultural nations defined independently of them, and imperfectly "contained" by them. There was indeed, as we argued earlier, a tension between the territorial-political and ethnocultural crystallizations of nationhood. But the latter was clearly the more fundamental concept in the Soviet scheme. That scheme began by recognizing, and crystallizing in institutional form, the existence of ethnocultural nationalities. Then the larger and more compact nationalities were endowed with their own national republics. The nationalities "possessed" their respective territorial republics rather than being constituted by them.

The Soviet regime, then, deliberately constructed the republics as national polities "belonging" to the nations whose names they bore. At the same time, it severely limited the domain in which the republics were autonomous. The regime institutionalized a sense of "ownership" of the republics by ethnocultural nations, but limited the political consequences of that sense of ownership.[58] Ethnocultural nations were given their own political territories, but not the power to rule them. With the collapse of the Soviet Union, the sense of ethnonational entitlement and ownership of national territory persists, but is now joined to substantial powers of rule. Successor state elites can use these new powers to "nationalize" their states by promoting the language, culture, demographic predominance, economic welfare, and political hegemony of the state-bearing nation. Such nationalizing policies and programs, oriented

[58] On the centrality of notions of "ownership" to ethnic conflict, see the sophisticated account in Donald L. Horowitz, *Ethnic Groups in Conflict* (Berkeley: University of California Press, 1985), esp. pp. 201ff. Walker Connor, too, has emphasized the "exclusive proprietary claim[s]" to ethnonational "homelands" that are characteristically made in the name of ethnonational groups; see for example his essay "The Impact of Homelands upon Diasporas," in Gabriel Sheffer, ed., *Modern Diasporas in International Politics* (London: Croom Helm, 1986), p. 18 and *passim*. The sense of ownership and entitlement felt by titular nationalities of non-Russian republics, which developed well before the Gorbachev era, is thoroughly documented by Karklins, *Ethnic Relations in the USSR*, pp. 51ff., 66, 96–7.

to an ethnocultural nation distinct from the total population or total citizenry of the state, are likely to be politically profitable – and in some cases politically irresistible – in the new states, in considerable part because of the institutionalized expectations of "ownership" that the successor states inherited from the Soviet nationality regime.

I do not mean to suggest that successor state politics will be uniformly driven or dominated by such programs of ethnic "nationalization." Internally, the appeal of nationalizing programs and policies will be variable. While this appeal has been strong in the Baltic states, for example, it has been quite weak in Belarus. Moreover, external incentives – offered, for example, by international organizations or by economically, politically, or militarily powerful states – may favor transethnic state- and nation-building strategies, oriented to the citizenry as a whole rather than to one ethnonationally qualified segment of that citizenry.

How powerful can we expect this "discipline" imposed by external audiences to be? No doubt its strength will vary greatly across successor states and over time and context. Western states and European organizations have greatest leverage on the westernmost successor states, seeking integration into European economic and security structures, but this leverage has already been substantially eroded by the disappointment of their hopes for major economic assistance. What about the discipline imposed by powerful neighboring states, above all by Russia? Will the anticipated sanctions, positive and negative, offered by Russia significantly shape the politics of citizenship and nationhood in the non-Russian successor states? Clearly, the proximity of the (potentially) enormously powerful Russian state, as well as the presence of large Russian minorities in the successor states, other things being equal, would lead prudent successor state elites to avoid alienating their Russian minorities (and provoking the Russian state) by an overzealous program of nationalization. Considerations of this sort are doubtless partly responsible for the restrained and only cautiously nationalizing stances adopted in Ukraine and Kazakhstan, whose Russian populations are not only by far the largest, in absolute numbers, among the successor states (11.4 million and 6.2 million respectively), but also the most deeply rooted, and the most significant from the point of view of the Russian state. But prudential considerations did not deter Estonia and Latvia from pursuing a restrictive politics of citizenship, although their diminutive size – as well as the presence until 1994 of Russian troops on their territories – makes them much more vulnerable than Ukraine or Kazakhstan. Nor is there any guarantee that such counsels of prudence will continue to guide elites in Ukraine and Kazakhstan. Indeed the presence of large Russian minorities, and the proximity of the powerful

Russian state, may – given the institutional legacy of Soviet nationality policy – work to exacerbate rather than attenuate successor state nationalisms.

Russians as a new national minority

To see how this might occur, let us shift our focus from the first to the second element of our tripartite scheme: from the incipient successor states to the national minorities within those states. The first point to underscore is that their quality as specifically *national* minorities is not an objective fact of ethnic demography, but a subjective precipitate of their self-understanding, as channeled and shaped by the national scheme of social classification that was so pervasively institutionalized in the Soviet Union. Ethnic minorities think of themselves as members of distinct nations or nationalities because this is the way they learned to think of themselves under the Soviet regime. This is not a merely terminological matter; it has political implications. Minority elites will tend to represent the minority as *belonging to a different nation* from the members of the "titular," nominally state-bearing nation amongst or alongside whom they live. This will tend to be true even where – as is the case in many instances – intermarriage and assimilation, from a sociological point of view, have blurred the boundaries between the nations that are represented as distinct.

Will this general tendency for ethnic minorities to define themselves in national terms hold for Russians in non-Russian successor states?[59] Will they too represent themselves as differing in nationality – rather than merely in language, culture, or sub-national ethnicity – from the "titular" nation or nationality? The answer is not obvious. On the one hand, despite – or precisely because of – the hegemony of Russians in and the pervasive "Russianness" of the Soviet Union as a whole, Russian nationality was in some respects less strongly institutionalized than other nationalities. Precisely because what was "Russian" about the Soviet Union was diffused throughout its entire territory and (to a certain extent) its entire population, "Russianness" could not be adequately

---

[59] For a comprehensive discussion of Russian minorities in Soviet successor states, see Paul Kolstoe, *Russians in the Former Soviet Republics* (London: Hurst, 1995). See also Nikolai Rudensky, "Russian Minorities in the Newly Independent States," pp. 58–77 in Roman Szporluk, ed., *National Identity and Ethnicity in Russia and the New States of Eurasia* (Armonk, NY and London: M. E. Sharpe, 1994), and Vladimir Shlapentokh *et al.*, eds., *The New Russian Diaspora* (Armonk, NY and London: M. E. Sharpe, 1994). For a Russian overview, see Sergei Savoskul, "Russkie novogo zarubezh'ia [Russians of the Near Abroad]," *Obshchestvennye nauki i sovremennost'* [Social Sciences and the Present] 5 (1994).

expressed in or contained by a delimited national territory or a distinct personal nationality. "Russianness" suffused the entire state; it was too big, too general to be encoded in the system of institutionalized nationality as one among many. Russianness, like "whiteness" in the US, was in a sense invisible; it was experienced not as a particular nationality but as the general norm, the zero-value, the universal condition against which other nationalities existed as particular, and particularist, "deviations."

Yet while Russians indeed occupied a peculiar place, at once central and invisible, in the Soviet nationality regime, one should not conclude from this that Russians in the successor states are (by comparison with other nationalities) uniquely unprepared or disinclined to define themselves in national terms. Other considerations suggest that they will define themselves in this way. In the first place, "Russianness" was a zero-value, an unthematized background condition chiefly for Russians in Russia (and in the other Slavic republics). Russians in non-Slavic republics, by contrast, were more conscious of their nationality, especially during the last two decades of the Soviet era, in response to increased assertiveness and ethnic self-awareness on the part of the titular nationalities. Moreover, Russians in the non-Russian republics were long accustomed to enjoying a public existence as Russians (or perhaps, more precisely, a public existence "in Russian," which served as a pervasive medium not only of public life but of culture, education, and urban life in general).[60] Except where emigration is rapidly depleting the Russian communities (mainly in Central Asia, excluding northern and eastern Kazakhstan), many Russians in the successor states will want to retain or re-establish this public status in some form. Accordingly, they will seek a form of citizenship that is mediated by nationality, that is by membership of an ethnocultural group. This tendency will be stronger to the extent that the successor states are nationalizing states. To the extent that there is a strong sense that the state belongs to or exists for the sake of a particular "core" nation or nationality conceived as distinct from the citizenry as a whole, Russians (and other minorities) – excluded from this state-owning core nation – will be more likely to define themselves oppositionally and contextually in national terms. In such conditions, Russians will be suspicious of liberal forms of citizenship, in which rights attach directly to individuals, and group membership has no public

---

[60] David Laitin has argued that a new "Russian-speaking" nationality, distinct from the Russian nationality, will emerge among successor state Russians and Russophones. See Laitin, "Identity in Formation: The Russian-Speaking Nationality in the Post-Soviet Diaspora," paper presented at the Annual Meeting of the American Political Science Association, September 1994.

significance; for they will see such formally liberal models as ideological masks for substantively nationalizing and ethnocratic forms of rule, as assuring the cultural predominance and political hegemony of the dominant, state-bearing nation.

Under the Soviet regime, the public status, linguistic privilege, and cultural facilities enjoyed by Russians throughout the Soviet Union meant that Russians tended to think of the entire Union rather than only the Russian republic as "their" territory. The Russian republic, in this sense, held less significance for Russians than the other national republics did for their corresponding nationalities. With the loss of this wider "home" territory, Russians living in territorially concentrated settlements in the successor states are likely to seek to redefine areas of the successor states in which they form a local majority or plurality as "their own" territories by demanding some form of territorial autonomy. These areas include, most significantly, northern and eastern Kazakhstan, Moldova east of the Dniester River, northeastern Estonia, and parts of eastern and southern Ukraine, notably Crimea; indeed movements for territorial autonomy have already occurred in Crimea and trans-Dniestrian Moldova, secured in the latter case by backing from the former Soviet 14th Army.[61]

These demands of Russian (and other) national minorities for collective public rights and (where plausible) territorial autonomy, both shaped by the institutional legacy of the Soviet nationality regime, directly challenge successor state elites' claims to unitary "ownership" of what they regard as "their own" polities and territories. Such demands are easily perceived by successor state elites as threatening and as fundamentally illegitimate, even if political prudence dictates that limited concessions be made to them. Minorities' demands for collective rights or territorial autonomy may render them vulnerable to charges of equivocal loyalty or even outright disloyalty. Although they belong, formally, to the citizenry of the state, they may be excluded, substantively, from taken-for-granted membership of the state-bearing nation. Minorities' self-definition as members of distinct nations, and their claims for public rights in that capacity, may thus reinforce the

[61] A politics of territorial autonomy is likely to have less support from local Russians in northeastern Estonia than in the other regions of heavy Russian concentration, for Estonian Russians, given the relative strength of the Estonian economy and the relatively bright prospects of some form of westward economic integration, can more plausibly opt for a competing strategy of accommodation, acculturation, and inter-generational assimilation, and indeed, as David Laitin has argued, may be driven to seek acculturation and intergenerational assimilation by competitive pressures. See Laitin, "Four Nationality Games," *Journal of Soviet Nationalities* 2, no. 1 (1991), 13ff.

"ethnicist" self-understanding and ethnocratic practices of successor state elites, may reinforce their tendency to define their own nations in ethnocultural rather than civic-territorial terms and to rule their states with the interests of that ethnocultural nation in mind. This can be true even where successor state elites formally define their statehood and citizenship in liberal terms; for as minorities correctly suspect, formally liberal and ethnically neutral definitions of statehood and citizenship may, in an ethnically heterogeneous state in which state-bearing majority and minority or minorities understand themselves as belonging to distinct ethnocultural nations, mask a substantively ethnocratic organization of public life.

Reconstructing Russia

If only by virtue of its proximity and power, Russia could not help but be implicated in the relations between nationalizing successor states and their Russian (and, more broadly, "Russian-speaking") minorities. But it is not only proximity and power that implicate Russia in these relations. More important are two further factors. First, the basic parameters of Russian statehood are unsettled and lack substantial legitimacy. Second, Russian elites see Russia as an external national "homeland" for the new Russian diaspora, as permitted, indeed obliged, to protect the interests of successor state Russians.[62] The dynamic interplay between this Russian "homeland" nationalism, the "nationalizing" nationalisms of the successor states, and the minority nationalism of the new Russian diaspora is more potentially destabilizing and explosive than any one or two of these nationalisms taken on their own.

The Russian Federation today, like the RSFSR in the Soviet era, is widely seen as an inadequate institutional embodiment of the Russian nation. Under the Soviet regime, the salient territorial and institutional frame "of" and "for" Russians – the territorial and institutional space in which they could live and work *as Russians* – was that of the Soviet Union as a whole, not that of the Russian Republic.[63] Union territory was "their" territory; union institutions were, in an important sense, "their" institutions. By contrast, Russians did not think of the territory or the institutions of the Russian republic as "their own." On the one hand, the Russian republic was institutionally underdeveloped: it lacked key

---

[62] On Russian homeland nationalism, see Chapter 5.
[63] Victoria Koroteyeva, in a personal communication, has suggested that this was true for Russians in the Russian republic as well as for the diaspora living in non-Russian republics.

institutions found in other Soviet republics. On the other hand, some Russians, despite their privileged position outside the Russian republic, paradoxically felt underprivileged inside Russia. Much of the vast territory of the Russian republic was formally allocated to non-Russian nationalities as their national homelands – sixteen "autonomous republics" and fifteen lower-level autonomous national formations in 1989, all designated as the national territories of and for particular non-Russian nationalities, and together comprising more than half of the territory of the RSFSR.[64] And some nationally minded Russians complained of Russian underrepresentation (especially *vis-à-vis* Jews) in what were nominally "their own" institutions, leading Russian nationalists to campaign in the final years of the Soviet regime on the slogan of proportional representation for Russians in the RSFSR![65]

In the Soviet era, then, Russians' national self-understanding was not firmly embedded in, or contained by, the territorial and institutional frame of the Russian republic. The Russian republic was not for Russians what other national republics were for their corresponding nationalities. Elites of other nationalities viewed "their own" national polities as broadly adequate territorial and institutional frames for national statehood, and pursued greater autonomy or outright independence within those frames. But significant segments of the Russian elite did not view the Russian republic as an even broadly adequate territorial and institutional frame for Russian national statehood. As a result, the core institutional parameters of the emerging Russian state – territorial boundaries, internal state structure, demographic composition – are in even greater flux, and even more vigorously contested, than those of most incipient non-Russian successor states.[66]

The mismatch between ethnocultural nation and citizenry is central to this unsettledness. Twenty-five million Russians lived, in 1989, in non-Russian Soviet republics. Despite a substantial migration to Russia since then, mainly from the Central Asian republics, the vast majority of these remain in the incipient successor states.[67] They are not Russian citizens; indeed the large majority (except in Estonia and Latvia) are, legally speaking, citizens of the emerging non-Russian successor states. But they

---

[64] Calculated from *Bolshaia sovetskaia entsiklopediia*, third edition, vol. XXII, pp. 212–13.

[65] I am indebted to Sergei Sibirtsev for pointing this out.

[66] On the pervasive uncertainty concerning the core parameters of Russian statehood, see Victoria Koroteyeva, "The Old Imperial Power or an Emerging Nation: Russian Responses to Ethnic Separatism," Paper presented at conference on "Nations, States and Ethnic Identity," European University Institute, Florence, May 1992.

[67] On migrations of ethnic unmixing involving Russians and other formerly dominant national groups in the aftermath of empire, see Chapter 6.

are considered by elites in Russia to belong, in some sense, to Russia; they are viewed as legitimate, even obligatory objects of concern on the part of the Russian state.

With the collapse of the institutional and territorial frame of the Soviet Union, and the sudden transfer of jurisdiction over 25 million Russians to non-Russian successor states, the fundamental parameters of Russian statehood are deeply contested. This is not chiefly a question – as it is in most non-Russian successor states – of nationalizing the "given" state territory and institutions, of making them more fully the territory and institutions of and for the dominant ethnocultural nation, in accordance with the institutionalized expectations of "ownership" that were discussed above. In the Russian case, the basic parameters of statehood lack even the minimal "givenness" that characterizes those of the non-Russian successor states.[68] It is a question, rather, of what the basic parameters of statehood should be in a situation in which the existing, provisional parameters defining the territory, citizenry, and internal ethnofederal structure of the state have little institutional weight or normative dignity in the eyes of Russians. They have little weight or dignity – little legitimacy – in part because they stand in no "adequate" relation to the far-flung Russian nation, because they conspicuously exclude, in particular, the 25 million Russians who found themselves residents and (formally) citizens of states that they did not feel were "their own."

The cross-border "homeland" nationalism of Russia is a response to this conspicuous exclusion. But this commitment by one state to protect the rights and promote the interests of citizens of another may be perceived by elites of the latter as a challenge to their sovereignty and a threat to their security; and they may be inclined to intensify rather than desist from the nationalizing practices to which Russian homeland nationalists object. Russian homeland nationalism, moreover, may encourage Russian minorities to adopt more intransigent stances than they would have been inclined to do without support from Russia. There is nothing inevitable about the interactive escalation of interlocking nationalisms; and as of this writing, it has not occurred in connection with the Russian minorities. As I argue in Chapter 3, however, precisely this did occur in the former Yugoslavia, and it remains a danger inscribed

68   On the givenness or "hegemony" of state boundaries, see David Laitin and Ian Lustick, "Hegemony and the State," *States and Social Structures Newsletter* 9 (1989); Lustick, "Becoming Problematic: Breakdown of a Hegemonic Conception of Ireland in Nineteenth-Century Britain," *Politics and Society* 18 (1990); Lustick, "Israeli State-Building in the West Bank and the Gaza Strip: Theory and Practice," *International Organization* 41 (1987).

in the structure of the triadic relational nexus between nationalizing successor states, Russian minorities, and Russia as external national "homeland."[69]

Conclusion

The Soviet nationality regime, with its distinctive and pervasive manner of institutionalizing nationhood and nationality, has transmitted to the successor states a set of deeply structured, and powerfully conflicting, *expectations of belonging*. Successor state elites, with their deeply institutionalized sense of political ownership and entitlement, see the polities that bear the names of their respective nations – above all the territory and institutions, but also, with some ambivalence, the population as well – as "their own," as belonging, in a fundamental sense, to them. National minorities, above all Russians, with their institutionally supported understanding of nationality as distinct from citizenship, see themselves as belonging, in a deep if not exclusive sense, to an "external" nation; this cannot help but color and qualify, even if it does not exclude, their belonging to the would-be nation-state in which they live, and of which they (or most of them) hold citizenship. Russian state elites, finally, whose national self-understanding was not in the Soviet period embedded in, and is now only very imperfectly contained by, the institutional and territorial frame of the Russian Federation, see the Russian minorities in the non-Russian successor states as belonging, in an ill-defined yet potent sense, to the emerging Russian state. These deeply rooted and powerfully conflicting expectations of belonging – interacting, of course, with conflicts of interest engendered by state-building, regime change, and economic restructuring – will make the dynamic interplay between non-Russian successor states, Russian minorities, and the Russian state a locus of refractory, and potentially explosive, ethnonational conflict in coming years.

[69] For an account of this danger in the relations between Russia and the new states of Central Asia, see Rajan Menon, "In the Shadow of the Bear: Security in Post-Soviet Central Asia," *International Security* 20, no. 1 (1995), esp. 170–4.

3   National minorities, nationalizing states, and external national homelands in the New Europe

Twice in this century, Central and Eastern Europe have undergone a massive and concentrated reconfiguration of political space along national lines. In the first phase of this reconfiguration (which actually began in the nineteenth century), the crumbling of the great "traditional" multinational land empires – the prolonged decay of the Ottoman Empire and the sudden collapse, in the First World War, of the Habsburg and Romanov empires – left in its wake a broad north–south belt of new states in East Central Europe, stretching from the Baltic littoral to the Balkan peninsula. In the second phase, the disintegration of the Soviet Union, Yugoslavia, and Czechoslovakia and the emergence of some twenty new states in their stead have resulted in the nationalization of political space on a much vaster scale, extending from Central and Eastern Europe eastward across the entire breadth of Eurasia.

Like the nationalizing settlement that followed the First World War, the most recent reconfiguration of political space along ostensibly national lines has conspicuously failed to "solve" the region's long-refractory national question. Yet while nationalist tensions have not been resolved, they have been restructured. This chapter addresses this new phase and form of the national question, focusing on the triadic nexus linking national minorities, nationalizing states, and external national "homelands," and illustrating its dynamically interactive quality with a discussion of the breakup of Yugoslavia.

A triadic configuration

The triadic relational nexus has been engendered, or given new urgency, by the new (or at least newly salient) mismatch between cultural and political boundaries. The massive nationalization of political space in the region has left tens of millions of people outside "their own" national territory at the same time that it has subjected the "national" quality of persons and territories to heightened scrutiny. Foremost among these nationally "mismatched" persons, as suggested in Chapter 2, are the

25 million ethnic Russians, abruptly transformed from state-bearing nationality in a vast and powerful state into vulnerably situated minorities of uncertain identity and loyalty in weak and struggling successor states. But many other groups have a similar, structurally ambivalent membership status, belonging by residence and (in most cases) by formal citizenship to one state and by putative ethnonational affinity to another. These include – to name only a few of the more important – some 3 million ethnic Hungarians in Romania, Slovakia, Serbia, and Ukraine, whose relations with Hungary, limited during the communist era, have multiplied and intensified in recent years; the 2 million Albanians in Serbia, Montenegro, and Macedonia, whose ties to neighboring Albania have been renewed and strengthened; the nearly 2 million Serbs living (before the war) in Croatia and Bosnia-Hercegovina, who, as Yugoslavia began to disintegrate, looked to Serbia as their external national homeland; the nearly one million Turks in Bulgaria; the Armenians in Azerbaijan, especially in Nagorno-Karabakh; the Uzbeks in Tajikistan and the Tajiks in Uzbekistan; and the Poles in Lithuania and other Soviet successor states.[1] All of these groups, as well as numerous smaller groups (or potential groups, since in many cases their "groupness" is more a political project than a social fact),[2] must contend not only with political and economic reconfiguration and dislocation but also with two mutually antagonistic nationalisms – the "nationalizing" nationalisms of the states in which they live, and the "homeland" nationalisms of the states to which they belong, or can be construed as belonging, by ethnocultural affinity though not (ordinarily) by legal citizenship. All are, therefore, inscribed in the triadic nexus linking the minority communities themselves, the states in which they live, and their external national "homelands."

[1] I provide numbers in the text only as a very rough indicator of the orders of magnitude involved. The figures are invariably contested; indeed disputes concerning the size of putative nations and national minorities have long been central to nationalist politics. It is an illusion – and one that contributes to the prevalence of ethnic nationalism – to think that one could somehow arrive at objectively "correct" figures. Nationality is not a fixed, given, indelible, objectively ascertainable property; and even subjective, self-identified nationality is variable across time and context of elicitation, and therefore not measurable as if it were an enduring fact that needed only to be registered.

[2] In sheer numbers, Ukrainians – that is, those who identified their nationality as such in the 1989 Soviet census – in Soviet successor states other than Ukraine are, at more than 6 million, more numerous than any of the other minority groups except Russians. But the "groupness" suggested by this distinct statistical existence is, from a sociological point of view, largely illusory. Both in the Russian Federation, where over 4 million self-identified Ukrainians lived in 1989, and in other successor states, Ukrainians have tended to assimilate linguistically to, and intermarry with, Russians. Although some political entrepreneurs have tried to mobilize Ukrainians as a national minority distinct from Russians, this "group-making" project is unlikely to succeed.

That relationship is not everywhere and always conflictual. In the case of the residual, though still large, German minority in Eastern Europe and the former Soviet Union,[3] for example, the triangular relationship has a unique and largely nonconflictual configuration. This contrasts starkly with the interwar period. Then, too, there was a dynamic triangular interplay between the huge German national minority, the newly nationalizing states of East Central Europe in which they lived, above all Poland and Czechoslovakia, and Germany as their external national "homeland." That relation was deeply conflictual, even in the Weimar period, and it became fateful after the Nazi seizure of power. Today, by contrast, guaranteed immigration and citizenship rights in a prosperous and stable external "homeland," together with the new freedom of exit from the countries of Eastern Europe and the former Soviet Union, act as a powerful solvent, and magnet, on German minority communities, causing their steady depletion through heavy emigration. Within a generation, these rights extended to ethnic co-nationals by the Federal Republic of Germany are likely to lead to a final dissolution of the centuries-old German presence in Eastern Europe.

In cases where the triangular relationship is more deeply conflictual, however, the new Europe, like interwar Europe, confronts a potentially explosive – and in some cases actually explosive – dynamic interplay between a set of new or newly reconfigured *nationalizing states*, ethnically heterogeneous yet conceived as nation-states, whose dominant elites promote (to varying degrees) the language, culture, demographic position, economic flourishing, or political hegemony of the nominally state-bearing nation; the substantial, self-conscious, and (to varying degrees) organized and politically alienated *national minorities* in those states, whose leaders demand cultural or territorial autonomy and resist actual or perceived policies or processes of assimilation or discrimination; and the *external national "homelands"* of the minorities, whose elites (again to varying degrees) closely monitor the situation of their co-ethnics in the new states, vigorously protest alleged violations of their rights, and assert the right, even the obligation, to defend their interests.

---

[3] It is difficult to give an even approximate estimate of the size of the German minority. The immigration and citizenship rights extended by Germany to Germans in Eastern Europe and the former Soviet Union have created a strong incentive for people with any familial connection to Germany or Germanness to identify themselves as German. In this way the large-scale migration of East European and ex-Soviet Germans to Germany, by inducing ethnonational reidentification as German, may for a time *increase* rather than *decrease* the size of the German minority in the region.

Since the last term is vulnerable to misunderstanding, I will characterize it a bit more fully. By "homeland" I do not mean the actual homeland of the minority, in the sense that they or their ancestors once lived there. That is not necessarily the case. Nor need the minority even think of the external state, or the territory of that state, as its homeland. External national homelands are constructed through political action, not given by the facts of ethnic demography. A state becomes an external national "homeland" for "its" ethnic diaspora when political or cultural elites define ethnonational kin in other states as members of one and the same nation, claim that they "belong," in some sense, to the state, and assert that their condition must be monitored and their interests protected and promoted by the state; and when the state actually does take action in the name of monitoring, promoting, or protecting the interests of its ethnonational kin abroad. Homeland politics takes a variety of forms, ranging from immigration and citizenship privileges for "returning" members of the ethnic diaspora, through various attempts to influence other states' policies towards its co-ethnics, to irredentist claims on the territory of other states.

National minorities, nationalizing states, and external national homelands are bound together in a single, interdependent relational nexus. Projects of nationalization or national integration in the new nation-states, for example, "exist" and exercise their effects not in isolation but in a relational field that includes both the national minority and its external national homeland. In this relational field, minority and homeland elites continuously monitor the new nation-state and are especially sensitive to any signs of projects of "nationalization" or "national integration." When they perceive such signs, they seek to build up and sustain a perception of the state as an oppressively or unjustly nationalizing state. And they might act on this perception. The minority might mobilize against the perceived projects of nationalization and might seek autonomy or even threaten secession. The homeland, claiming the right to monitor and protect the interests of its ethnic co-nationals abroad, might provide material or moral support for these initiatives and might lodge protests with the nationalizing state or with international organizations against the perceived projects of nationalization. This protest activity will react back on the nationalizing state, although it will not necessarily dissuade it from its nationalizing projects, and it might even lead to their intensification. The minority might be accused of disloyalty, the homeland of illegitimate interference in the internal affairs of the nationalizing state.

The dynamic interdependence linking national minorities, nationalizing states, and external national homelands in a single web of relations calls for analysis in its own right. This requires a reorientation in the study of nationalism. While the burgeoning corpus of work on nationalism includes large, if dated, literatures on national integration in new states and on national minorities, as well as a smaller, more recent literature on state intervention on behalf of co-ethnics in other states, these have remained isolated from one another. I know of no studies that develop an explicit analytical or theoretical account of the relational nexus linking national minorities, nationalizing states, and external national homelands.[4] Some studies of particular nationalist situations – especially historical ones – are sensitive to interactive dynamics of this sort,[5] but none, to my knowledge, has worked out an explicit model or provided a sustained analytical discussion of the relational field and its interactive dynamics. To begin to do so is the task of this chapter.

[4] Myron Weiner, "The Macedonian Syndrome," *World Politics* 23, no. 1 (1970), comes closest to developing such an account, outlining a "syndrome" of predictably covarying characteristics typically found when an irredentist state confronts an anti-irredentist neighboring state in connection with a border-straddling ethnic group. The account offered here differs from Weiner's chiefly in three respects. First, Weiner is concerned only with irredentist claims and disputed borders, while I am concerned with the broader field of homeland politics, in which irredentism is a limiting case. Second, Weiner is concerned with all border-straddling ethnic groups associated with border disputes, while I consider only national minorities whose co-ethnics are numerically or politically dominant in another state that can, for this reason, be construed as their "external national homeland." Third, while Weiner specifies a "syndrome" of covarying characteristics, I emphasize the contingency and variability of the relations between national minorities, nationalizing states, and external national homelands – contingency and variability that follow from treating each of these three "elements" as fields of struggle among competing positions or stances, and from seeing the relations between these three fields as closely intertwined with relations internal to the fields. More recently, an emergent literature on diasporas in international politics has begun to explore the triadic relation between diasporas, host states, and home states, but it focuses on migrant diasporas rather than consolidated national minorities, settled, in considerable part, in compact areas directly adjoining their respective national homelands. See Gabriel Sheffer, "A New Field of Study: Modern Diasporas in International Politics," in Sheffer, ed., *Modern Diasporas in International Politics* (London and Sydney: Croom Helm, 1986).

[5] For sophisticated studies of the national question in interwar Europe, alert to this dynamic, see Joseph Rothschild, *East Central Europe Between the Two World Wars* (Seattle: University of Washington Press, 1974); Ronald M. Smelser, *The Sudeten Problem, 1933–1938: Volkstumspolitik and the Formulation of Nazi Foreign Policy* (Folkestone, UK: Dawson, 1975); Rudolf Jaworski, *Vorposten oder Minderheit? Der sudetendeutsche Volkstumskampf in den Beziehungen zwischen der Weimarer Republik und der ČSR* (Stuttgart: Deutsche Verlags-Anstalt, 1977); C. A. Macartney, *National States and National Minorities* (London: Oxford University Press, 1934); and C. A. Macartney, *Hungary and Her Successors: The Treaty of Trianon and Its Consequences, 1919–1937* (London: Oxford University Press, 1937).

National minorities, nationalizing states, and external national homelands as arenas of struggle

To invoke, as I have done, a relationship between three terms might suggest that the terms themselves are fixed and given. They are, however, not fixed entities but variably configured and continuously contested *political fields*. Thinking of what we summarily call national minorities, nationalizing states, and external national homelands as political fields is a useful way of making explicit the fact that these are dynamic and relational concepts and should not be reified or treated in a substantialist fashion.

National minority

A national minority is not simply a "group" that is given by the facts of ethnic demography. It is a dynamic political stance, or, more precisely, a family of related yet mutually competing stances, not a static ethno-demographic condition. Three elements are characteristic of this political stance, or family of stances: (1) the public claim to membership of an ethnocultural nation different from the numerically or politically dominant ethnocultural nation;[6] (2) the demand for state recognition of this distinct ethnocultural nationality; and (3) the assertion, on the basis of this ethnocultural nationality, of certain collective cultural or political rights.

Nationality-based assertions of collective cultural or political rights, although similar in form, vary widely in their specific content. They range, for example, from modest demands for administration or education in the minority language to maximalist claims for far-reaching territorial and political autonomy verging on full independence. Other aspects of the stance of national minorities are also highly variable. While some favor full cooperative participation in the institutions of the host state, including participation in coalition governments, others may favor a separatist, noncooperative stance. And while some may shun overtures to external parties, believing it important to demonstrate their loyalty to

---

[6] This suggests why it is difficult to assert a status as national minority in states such as the United States that do not have clear dominant ethnocultural nations. If the nation that legitimates the state as a whole is not clearly an ethnocultural nation but a political nation open, in principle, to all, then the background condition against which the claim of national minority status makes sense is missing. Collective self-representation as a national minority presupposes a certain type of collective representation of the majority.

the state in which they live and hold citizenship, others may actively seek patronage or protection from abroad – whether from a state dominated by their ethnic kin or from other states or international organizations.

This variation in specific claims to collective rights, and in overall "stance," occurs not only between but within national minorities. The full range of stances just sketched could be found, for example, among the Sudeten Germans of interwar Czechoslovakia.[7] This variation in stances within a single national minority, this spectrum of related yet distinct and even mutually antagonistic stances adopted by different segments of "the same" ethnonational group, suggests the analytical usefulness of the notion of field. Using this notion, developed and employed by Pierre Bourdieu in an impressive variety of studies,[8] we can think of a national minority not as a fixed entity or a unitary group but rather in terms of the *field of differentiated and competitive positions or stances* adopted by different organizations, parties, movements, or individual political entrepreneurs, each seeking to "represent" the minority to its own putative members, to the host state, or to the outside world, each seeking to monopolize the legitimate representation of the group.[9]

Competition in the representation of the group may occur not only among those making different claims for the group *qua* national minority, but also between those making such claims and those rejecting the designation "national minority" and the family of claims associated with it. This is no mere academic possibility. Think, for example, of "Russians in Ukraine" (and bracket for the moment the difficulties inherent in the very expression "Russians in Ukraine" – the fact that this expression, with its clean syntax, designates something that does not in fact exist, namely a definite, clearly bounded group of Russians in

---

[7] On the 1920s struggle among Sudeten Germans between "activists," favoring cooperation with Czechoslovak parties and participation in coalition governments, and "negativists," rejecting these forms of cooperation, see Jaworski, *Vorposten oder Minderheit?;* and Johann Wolfgang Brügel, *Tschechen und Deutsche 1918–1938* (Munich: Nymphenburger, 1967). On competition among Sudeten Germans after the Nazi seizure of power in Germany, see Ronald M. Smelser, *The Sudeten Problem.*

[8] See Pierre Bourdieu and Loïc Wacquant, *An Invitation to Reflexive Sociology* (Chicago: University of Chicago Press, 1992), pp. 94ff., and the references cited there.

[9] Although Bourdieu has not written on national minorities as such, his essay on regionalism as well as a more general article on group-making contain suggestive formulations about the importance of representational struggles in the effort to make and remake groups. See Pierre Bourdieu, "L'identité et la représentation: éléments pour une réflexion critique sur l'idée de région," *Actes de la recherche en sciences sociales* 35 (1980), and "Social Space and the Genesis of Groups," *Theory and Society* 14 (1985).

Ukraine).[10] There are different ways of conceiving what it means to be a Russian in Ukraine, only some of which are consistent with conceiving Russians in Ukraine as a national minority. Thus Russians in Ukraine can be understood as persons of Russian ethnic origin, most of whom speak Russian as their native language, who nonetheless belong to the Ukrainian nation, understood as a political, territorial, or civic nation, as the nation of and for all its citizens, regardless of language and ethnicity, not as the nation of and for ethnic Ukrainians. Were this the prevailing self-understanding of Russians in Ukraine, there would be no Russian "national minority." There would be persons of Russian ethnic origin and persons speaking Russian as a native language, but they would not claim to be members of the Russian nation or nationality.[11] There is, of course, no chance of this view monopolizing the field of competing identities. Indeed, it may recently have been losing ground, as support for independent Ukrainian statehood among eastern Ukrainian Russians has waned with the rapid deterioration of the Ukrainian economy. But it does belong to the field of competing stances.

Where does this leave us? If we rethink the concept of national minority along the lines sketched here, the apparent clarity and simplicity of the concept dissolve. National minorities are not the internally unified, externally sharply bounded groups that our ordinary language suggests. I will continue to speak of "national minorities" for convenience, but it should be understood that this is a loose and imperfect designation for a field of competing stances, and that the "stakes" of the competition concern not only *what* stance to adopt as a national minority but *whether* the "group" (or potential group) in question should understand and represent itself as a national minority.

10 During the 1989 census, some 11.4 million residents of Ukraine identified their "nationality" (*natsional'nost'*) as Russian. A larger number – nearly 17 million – identified their native language as Russian. See Gosudarstvennyi komitet po statistike, *Natsional'nyi sostav naseleniia SSSR* (Moscow: Finansy i statistika, 1991), p. 78. There are no fixed identities here, but rather a fluid field of competing identities and identifications. One should be skeptical of the illusion of bounded groupness created by the census, with its exhaustive and mutually exclusive categories. For an argument suggesting that divisions of language are more significant in post-independence Ukraine than divisions of ethnic nationality, see Dominique Arel, "Language and Group Boundaries in the Two Ukraines," paper presented at a conference on "National Minorities, Nationalizing States, and External National Homelands in the New Europe," Bellagio Study and Conference Center, Italy, August 1994.

11 See Roman Szporluk, "Reflections on Ukraine after 1994: The Dilemmas of Nationhood," *The Harriman Review* 7, nos. 7–9 (1994).

Nationalizing state

A similar set of points can be made about the concept of "nationalizing state." I choose this term rather than "nation-state" to emphasize that I am talking about a dynamic political stance – or family of related yet competing stances – rather than a static condition.[12] Characteristic of this stance, or set of stances, is the tendency to see the state as an "unrealized" nation-state, as a state destined to be a nation-state, the state of and for a particular nation, but not yet in fact a nation-state (at least not to a sufficient degree); and the concomitant disposition to remedy this perceived defect, to make the state what it is properly and legitimately destined to be, by promoting the language, culture, demographic position, economic flourishing, or political hegemony of the nominally state-bearing nation.

Such a stance may be an avowed and expressly articulated "position." But it need not be avowed or articulated for it to be "real" in the sense that matters for this chapter, namely exercising a *real effect* on the minority and "homeland" political fields. This may be the case if policies, practices, symbols, events, officials, organizations, even "the state" as a whole are *perceived* as nationalizing by representatives of the national minority or external national "homeland," even if this characterization is repudiated by persons claiming to speak for the state. To ask whether such policies, practices, and so on are "really" nationalizing makes little sense. For present purposes, a nationalizing state (or nationalizing practice, policy, or event) is not one whose representatives, authors, or agents understand and articulate it as such, but rather one that is perceived as such in the field of the national minority or the external national homeland.

This raises a further complication. What does it mean for a state to be perceived as nationalizing in the political field of the national minority or that of the external national homeland? It is not sufficient for anyone who

---

[12] A nationalizing state is precisely not a nation-state in the widely used sense of an ethnoculturally homogeneous state, the very large majority of whose citizens belong to the same ethnocultural nation. Quite the contrary. Although it does not *presuppose* ethnocultural heterogeneity (for nationalizing projects can be, and have been, advanced even in ethnoculturally homogeneous settings), nationalizing states are ordinarily ethnoculturally heterogeneous. A further reason for preferring the term "nationalizing state" to "nation-state" is that the latter implies an achieved or completed condition, while the former usefully implies that this completed condition has *not* been achieved. A nationalizing state is one conceived by its elites as a specifically *unfinished* state (cf. the German conception, current in the Bismarckian period, of the *unvollendet* or "incomplete" nation-state). I discuss the concept of nationalizing state in more sustained fashion in Chapter 4, using interwar Poland as an example.

acts in those fields to perceive and characterize the state as nationalizing. The perception has to be "validated" or socially "sustained." The perception and characterization of the host state and its practices and policies are themselves crucial objects of struggle within the political fields of the national minority and the external national homeland.

A national minority – to return for a moment to this concept – is a field of struggle in a double sense. It is (as we saw earlier) a struggle to impose and sustain a certain kind of stance *vis-à-vis* the state; but at the same time it is a struggle to impose and sustain a certain vision of the host state, namely as a nationalizing or nationally oppressive state. The two struggles are inseparable: one can impose and sustain a stance as a mobilized national minority, with its demands for recognition and for rights, only by imposing and sustaining a vision of the host state as a nationalizing or nationally oppressive state. To the extent that this vision of the host state cannot be sustained, the rationale for mobilizing as a national minority will be undermined.

I do not want to give the impression that all that matters are the external perceptions of a host state's policies and practices as nationalizing. Such external perceptions – and the political stance they help justify and sustain – are indeed more important than the self-understanding of participants in the political field of the nationalizing state, but they are not independent of the political idioms used by participants in that field. When nationalization is an explicit project rather than merely a perceived practice, when host state policies and practices are expressly avowed and articulated as nationalizing, the perception of the state as a nationalizing state will be much more likely to prevail in the external fields – among the national minority or in the external national homeland.

Nor is it unusual for participants in the host state to articulate projects of nationalization, to conceive and justify policies and practices in a nationalizing idiom. Such an idiom is not only eminently respectable but virtually obligatory in some contexts. This is often the case in new states, especially those that, for historical and institutional as well as ethnodemographic reasons, are closely identified with one particular ethnocultural nation.[13] This is the case in almost all Soviet and Yugoslav

---

13 In the twentieth century, new states have been created in three great bursts – after World War I, when the territories of the great European and Eurasian multinational empires were divided and reconfigured; during mid-century decolonization, when new states were carved out from most of the overseas territories of the Western European colonial empires; and in the post-Cold War present, when, in a continuation of the process of national reconfiguration of political space begun in the nineteenth and early

successor states, thanks to the legacy of Soviet and Yugoslav nationality policy, which (as I argued in Chapter 2 with respect to the Soviet case) fixed and crystallized ethnocultural nations and endowed them with "their own" territorial "polities," that is, with polities (or pseudopolities) that were deliberately constructed as *belonging to* particular ethnocultural nations.

Whether we are talking about perceived nationalizing stances or openly avowed nationalizing projects, there is a great deal of variation among such stances and projects, not only between states, but within a given state. The notion of field can be useful here too. It brings into analytical focus the wide range of nationalizing stances within a single state, the spectrum of related yet distinct and even mutually antagonistic stances adopted by differently positioned figures in and around the

twentieth centuries, incipient nation-states have been formed from the territories of the multinational Soviet and Yugoslav states and binational Czechoslovakia. All of these states have been conceived by their dominant political and cultural elites as nation-states and, in a very broad sense, as nationalizing states. But there is an important difference between the new states that succeeded to multinational territorial states at the beginning and end of the twentieth century on the one hand, and most of those that were carved out of overseas empires – especially in sub-Saharan Africa – on the other. Almost every one of the former was conceived and justified, in the nationalist movements preceding their independent statehood as well as after statehood was achieved, as the state of and for a particular ethnonational group, which, though in no case coincident with the entire state population, in almost all cases constituted the majority, and usually the substantial (though seldom the overwhelming) majority of the state population. Why this was the case would require a lengthy historical excursus; that it was and is the case is clear. By contrast, most states carved out of overseas colonial empires were not conceived in the same way – before or after independence – as the states of and for particular ethnonational groups. Of course, in practice, some states – or portions of the state apparatus, such as the army – did come to "belong" to particular ethnonational groups (not always the same groups that had been favored by colonial administrators). See for example Donald Horowitz, *Ethnic Groups in Conflict* (Berkeley: University of California Press, 1985). But given the general discrepancy in scale between colonial units and ethnic groups, the rhetoric of anticolonial nationalism – the claims to nationhood made during anticolonial struggles – was framed in a territorial (and expressly supra-ethnic) rather than an ethnonational idiom. And leaders of newly independent states also framed their nationalizing projects in territorial and civic rather than ethnonational terms, hoping to build up a "modern" territorial national identity. See Anthony Smith, *State and Nation in the Third World: The Western State and African Nationalism* (New York: St. Martin's Press, 1983). In fact, of course, politicized ethnicity has flourished at least as much in postcolonial sub-Saharan Africa as elsewhere. But in large part because of the discrepancy in scale between political and ethnocultural units, state-backed nationalizing projects could not be as easily linked to one particular ethnonational group as was the case in the new states formed from the continental multinational empires. The point of this digressive footnote (a point I return to in Chapter 4) is to emphasize that nationalizing idioms – more precisely, idioms of *ethnic* or *ethnocultural* nationalization – were widely employed in the new states of interwar Europe, and they are widely employed in the new states of post-Cold War Europe.

complex inter- and intra-organizational network that we call, for convenience, "the state."

We can think of a nationalizing state not in terms of a fixed policy orientation or a univocal set of policies or practices but rather in terms of a dynamically changing field of differentiated and competitive positions or stances adopted by different organizations, parties, movements, or individual figures within and around the state, competing to inflect state policy in a particular direction, and seeking, in various and often mutually antagonistic ways, to make the state a "real" nation-state, the state of and for a particular nation.[14]

An example of competition among nationalizing stances might help make this a bit less abstract. Consider the question of language. Elites in all Soviet successor states believe it necessary and desirable to promote the language of the nominally state-bearing nation. This is a nationalizing stance that all share. Yet there have been vigorous struggles, in all successor states, about *how* this should be done. Should knowledge of the national language be required for citizenship or for certain types of employment? If so, what level of knowledge? How should the legacy of linguistic Russification be combated, and knowledge of the national language promoted, when a substantial fraction of the majority nationality does not speak the national language (as is the case, for example, in Ukraine and Kazakhstan)? In what circumstances should the use of other languages be permitted, or required, in public life, in the school system, or in the associational sphere of civil society? What mix of incentives and authoritative measures should be employed to promote the national language?[15]

External national homeland

Since the analytical points to be made are similar to those made about national minorities and nationalizing states, the concept of external national homeland can be treated more briefly. It, too, denotes a dynamic political stance – or, again, a family of related yet competing stances – not a static condition, not a distinct "thing." Common to

---

[14] This competitive field also includes stances that reject principles and programs of nationalization, for example, in favor of some form of cultural pluralism. But for the historical and institutional reasons alluded to above, successor state elites are strongly disposed to adopt nationalizing stances of one kind or another.

[15] On the politics of language in Soviet successor states, see the special issue of *Nationalities Papers* 23, no. 3 (1995), on "Implementing Language Laws: Perestroika and its Legacy in Five Republics."

"homeland" stances are the axiom of shared nationhood across the boundaries of state and citizenship and the idea that this shared nationhood makes the state responsible, in some sense, not only for its own citizens but also for ethnic co-nationals who live in other states and possess other citizenships. These shared assumptions and orientations define a "generic" homeland stance. But there is great variation among particular homeland stances, great variation in understandings of just what the asserted responsibility for ethnic co-nationals entails: Should ethnic co-nationals living as minorities in other states be given moral support, or also material support? What sorts of ties and relations with the homeland or mother country should be fostered? What sort of immigration and citizenship privileges, if any, should co-ethnics abroad be offered? What sort of stance should they be encouraged to take *vis-à-vis* the states in which they live? And what sort of stance should the homeland adopt toward those states? How forcefully should it press its concerns about their policies toward minorities? What weight should those concerns be given in shaping the homeland state's overall relations toward the states in which its co-ethnics live? And how forcefully should it press its concerns in the various international forums that monitor and set standards for policies toward minorities? These are all contested questions in homeland states.

The various homeland stances compete not only with one another but with stances that reject the basic premise of homeland politics, or at least set sharp limits on the permissible forms of homeland politics. According to these anti-homeland stances, which are more consonant with classical understandings of interstate relations and international law, a state may, indeed must, protect its own *citizens* even when they live in other states. But it cannot legitimately claim to protect its *ethnic co-nationals* who live in another state and hold the citizenship of that state. The field of struggle to inflect state policy is therefore constituted by struggles over *whether* and *how* a state should be a homeland for its ethnic co-nationals in other states.

The triadic nexus: a relation between relational fields

As I have argued, national minority, nationalizing state, and external national homeland should each be conceived not as a given, analytically irreducible entity but rather as a field of differentiated and competing positions, as an arena of struggle among competing stances. The triadic relation between these three "elements" is, therefore, a *relation between relational fields*; and relations *between* the three fields are closely intertwined with relations *internal to*, and *constitutive of*, the fields. The approach to the national question adopted here is consistently and radically *relational*.

A central aspect of the triangular relational nexus is reciprocal inter-field monitoring: actors in each field closely and continuously monitor relations and actions in each of the other two fields. This process of continuous reciprocal monitoring should not be conceived of in passive terms, as a registering or transcription of goings-on in other fields. Rather, the monitoring involves selective attention, interpretation, and representation. Often, the interpretation of other fields is contested; it becomes the object of *representational struggles* among actors in a given field.

Such struggles among competing representations of an *external* field may be closely linked to struggles among competing stances *within* the given field. Thus, the struggle to mobilize a national minority may be linked to a struggle to represent the host state as a nationalizing or nationally oppressive state. Conversely, proponents of nationalization may seek to represent the national minority as actually or potentially disloyal, or the homeland as actually or potentially irredentist. The breakup of Yugoslavia illustrates both linkages: efforts to mobilize the Serb minority in Croatia depended on efforts to represent Croatia as a dangerously nationalizing state, while nationalizing elites in Croatia sought to represent the mobilizing Serb minority as disloyal and Serbia as an irredentist homeland.

Perceptions and representations of an external field may be linked with stances within a field in two ways. On the one hand, the stances within a field may be prior and governing. In a strong sense, this occurs when a stance to which one is already committed "requires" a certain rep-resentation of the external field, and therefore generates efforts to impose or sustain it through deliberately selective interpretation or outright misrepresentation and distortion of developments in that external field. In a weaker but still significant (and very widespread) sense, it occurs when a particular stance to which one is already at least provisionally committed disposes one, in entirely "sincere" and noncynical fashion, through well-known mechanisms of selective (mis-)perception and (mis-)representation, to accept a particular representation of an external field, a representation congruent with one's own (already provisionally adopted) stance or position.

On the other hand, perceptions and representations of developments in an external field may strengthen or undermine existing stances or evoke or provoke new ones. In this case, instead of already committed stances governing perceptions and representations of the external field, commitments to stances emerge interactively, in response to perceived and represented developments in the external field.

Thus, stances may shape (and distort) perceptions and representations of an external field, or they may take shape in response to perceptions and representations of developments in that external field. The two processes, although analytically distinct, are often intertwined in practice. The Yugoslav case, for example, abundantly illustrates how strong initial nationalist dispositions or stances among some Serbs and Croats shaped and distorted perceptions and representations of the other, through both sincere selective perception and cynical misrepresentation; it also illustrates how others, initially indifferent to nationalism, came to adopt nationalist stances in reaction to perceptions and representations of seemingly threatening developments in other fields.

This dual linkage exemplifies three general features of the relational nexus with which we are concerned: (1) the close interdependence of relations *within* and *between* fields; (2) the *responsive* and *interactive* character of the triadic relational interplay between the fields; and (3) the *mediated* character of this responsive interplay, the fact that responsive, interactive stance-taking is mediated by representations of stances in an external field, representations that may be shaped by stances already provisionally held.

The triadic nexus and the breakup of Yugoslavia

Having sketched the triadic relational nexus in abstract terms, I would like to conclude with a more concrete illustrative discussion. Volumes have been written about the collapse of Yugoslavia, and many more are sure to follow. My aim here is not to provide even a summary account of the collapse, but rather to highlight its crucially triadic form and to indicate – if only programmatically – how the relational approach outlined above might illuminate its bloody dynamics. I limit my attention here to the first phase of the breakup, involving Croatian and Slovenian moves toward independence and culminating in the war in Croatia; I do not discuss the war in Bosnia.

The first phase of the Yugoslav collapse was presented in the American press as a dyadic struggle. On one side stood Serbia, determined to reassert centralized control (and therefore Serb hegemony) over Yugoslavia as a whole, or, failing that, to carve out a "greater Serbia" from the ruins of the state. On the other side stood Slovenia and Croatia, seeking autonomy and ultimately independence in the face of the Serbian push for hegemony.[16] Yet while the Slovenian issue was

---

[16] For a sophisticated statement of this view, see Branka Magaš, *The Destruction of Yugoslavia* (London: Verso, 1993).

indeed dyadic, the Croatian conflict was, from the beginning, fundamentally triadic, involving a tension-fraught dynamic interplay between an incipient national minority (Serbs in Croatia), an incipient nationalizing state (Croatia), and an incipient external national homeland (Serbia).

Seeing the core dynamic in this way is not simply a matter of "adding" the Croatian Serbs to the equation. Rather, it directs our attention to differing underlying processes. The dyadic view of the Serb–Croat conflict construes it as involving a push for Serb hegemony, a responsive Croatian secessionist movement, and a subsequent war of aggression against independent Croatia. The triadic view, by contrast, focuses on the complex interplay of three overlapping and mutually intensifying processes: the nationalization of the Croatian incipient state (both before and after independence was formally declared); the increasing disaffection, and nationalist mobilization, of Serbs in the ethnic borderlands of Croatia; and the development of a radical and belligerent "homeland" stance in the incipient Serbian state, leading eventually to the intervention of the increasingly Serb-dominated Yugoslav army in Croatia on the side of plans to salvage a "Greater Serbia" from the rubble of the federation.

The dyadic view rightly sees the Croatian drive for autonomy and independence as responding, in significant part, to Serbian nationalist assertiveness. Milošević's use of nationalist rhetoric to usurp leadership of the Serbian Communist Party in September 1987 and to mobilize mass support thereafter – especially his emphasis on Serb victimization in overwhelmingly Albanian Kosovo and on the need to reassert Serbian control over it by curtailing its constitutionally guaranteed autonomy – represented a fundamental and destabilizing challenge to the precarious national equilibrium constructed by Tito. The key to that equilibrium lay in the institutional restraints on the power of Serbia, preventing the Serbs from reacquiring the political dominance they had exercised, to disastrous effect, in the interwar Yugoslav state. The Serbian push to reassert control of Kosovo (and of the likewise formally autonomous Serbian province of Vojvodina) directly challenged those constraints and the fragile equilibrium built on them. While the resurgent Croatian nationalism of the late 1980s certainly had deep historical roots, and in many respects could be seen as reenacting (though going beyond) the Croatian nationalist movement of 1967–71, it was in crucial part a response to this destabilizing Serbian bid for hegemony within Yugoslavia.[17]

---

[17] For a lucid and sustained analysis of the resurgent Serbian nationalism of the 1980s, see Veljko Vujacic, "Communism and Nationalism in Russia and Serbia," Ph.D. dissertation, University of California at Berkeley, 1995.

While the dyadic view illuminates the causes and antecedents of the Croat drive for autonomy and independence, it obscures the nature and consequences of that drive. Construing it as a *secessionist* movement, the dyadic view obscures the extent to which it was also, and inseparably, a *nationalizing* movement — a movement to assert Croat "ownership" and control over the territory and institutions of Croatia, to make Croatia the state of and for the Croatian nation.

This was evident in the campaign rhetoric with which Franjo Tudjman, with strong financial backing from nationalist Croat émigrés, swept to victory in the spring 1990 elections, especially in his stress on the deep cultural differences between Serbs and Croats and the need to replace Serbs, heretofore overrepresented in key cultural, economic, and administrative positions in the republic, with Croats. It was evident in the iconography of the new regime, notably in the ubiquitous display of the red-and-white checkered armorial shield that had been an emblem of the medieval Croatian state but also of the murderous wartime Ustasha state (which the new leadership failed categorically and publicly to denounce). It was evident in the official, and ludicrous, "Croatization" of language. It was evident in the rhetoric of the new Croatian constitution, which claimed "full state sovereignty" as the "historical right of the Croatian nation" and symbolically demoted Serbs from their previous status as co-"owners" of the Republic. And it was evident, perhaps most significantly, in a substantial purge, concentrated in the state administration but extending beyond it as well, in which many Serbs lost their jobs.[18]

The significance of these and similar events, discourses, and practices lay not in themselves but in the representations and reactions they evoked among Croatian Serbs – especially village and small-town Serbs of the Krajina region – and in Serbia. The dynamic of nationalization, though partial and incipient, was real – and troubling – enough. But through varying mixes of selective appropriation, exaggeration, distortion, and outright fabrication, Serb nationalist politicians in Croatia

---

[18] See Misha Glenny, *The Fall of Yugoslavia: The Third Balkan War* (London: Penguin, 1992), esp. pp. 12–13, 77, 81–2; Leonard J. Cohen, *Broken Bonds: The Disintegration of Yugoslavia* (Boulder, Colo.: Westview Press, 1993), pp. 96–8, 208; Bette Denich, "Dismembering Yugoslavia: Nationalist Ideologies and the Symbolic Revival of Genocide," *American Ethnologist* 21, no. 2 (1994), 377–81; Robert Hayden, "Constitutional Nationalism in the Formerly Yugoslav Republics," *Slavic Review* 51, no. 4 (1992); Eugene A. Hammel, "The Yugoslav Labyrinth," in Eugene Hammel, Irwin Wall, and Benjamin Ward, *Crisis in the Balkans* (Berkeley: Institute of International Studies, University of California, 1993), pp. 16–17; and Bogdan Denitch, *Ethnic Nationalism: The Tragic Death of Yugoslavia* (Minneapolis: University of Minnesota Press, 1994), p. 45.

and in Serbia proper represented these nationalizing moves in a sinister light as heralding the establishment of an ultranationalist regime that threatened the liberties, livelihoods, and – if Croatia were to opt for full independence – even the lives of Croatian Serbs.

The cynical and opportunistic manipulation involved in the more extreme of these representations and misrepresentations, irresponsibly evoking the specter of the Ustasha regime to discredit every manifestation of Croatian nationalism, is often stressed. But the emphasis on elite manipulation cannot explain why representations of a prospectively independent Croatia as a dangerously nationalizing state were sufficiently resonant, and sufficiently plausible, among certain segments of the Krajina Serb population, to inspire genuine fear and induce militant mobilization, and eventually armed rebellion, against the Croatian regime.[19]

While the dyadic view treats Croatian and particularly Krajina Serbs as passive dupes, vehicles, or objects of manipulative designs originating in Serbia, the triadic view sees them as active participants in the intensifying conflict and as political subjects in their own right, construing (and misconstruing) the dangers of the present in the light of the atrocities of the past. The complex process through which representations of Croatia as a dangerously nationalizing, even protofascist, state emerged, took root, and became hegemonic among Serbs in certain parts of Croatia's ethnic borderlands cannot be reduced to a story of outside manipulation. Efforts by nationalist radicals in Serbia to mobilize grievances and fears among Croatian Serbs were indeed an important part of the process. But the bulk of the work of mobilizing grievances and fears was undertaken locally by Croatian Serbs. And the grievances and fears were there to be mobilized. Although representations of wartime atrocities – often greatly exaggerated – were indeed widely propagated from Belgrade, memories of and stories about the murderous wartime Independent State of Croatia, and especially about the gruesome fate of many Croatian and Bosnian Serbs (Bosnia having been incorporated into the wartime Croatian state), were not imports. They were locally rooted, sustained within family and village circles, and transmitted to the postwar generations, especially in the ethnically mixed and partly Serb-majority borderland regions where (outside of Bosnia) most atrocities against Serb civilians had occurred, and where (again excluding Bosnia) the main Partisan as well as the few Chetnik strongholds in Croatia had been located. It was among village and small-town Serbs in just these regions – and not, for example, among the

---

[19] Glenny, *The Fall of Yugoslavia* , p. 11; and Denich, "Dismembering Yugoslavia," 381.

cosmopolitan Serbs of Zagreb – that encounters with the incipient Croatian nationalizing state, interpreted through the prism of revived representations of wartime trauma, generated intransigent opposition to Croatian independence.[20]

These mutually alienating encounters between the nationalizing and increasingly independent Croatian state and the fearful and increasingly radicalized Serb borderland minority thus had their own destabilizing logic; they were not orchestrated from Belgrade. But Serbian "homeland politics" was crucial to the overall relational nexus. Homeland stances – involving identification with, assertions of responsibility for, and demands to support or even "redeem" and incorporate ethnic Serbs outside Serbian state territory – have a long tradition in Serbian politics.[21] The relation between the expansionist "small Serbia" (established as an independent kingdom, though still under nominal Ottoman suzerainty, in 1829 and recognized as fully independent in 1878) and the large Serb communities in the Ottoman and Austro-Hungarian empires was a burning issue in the decades before World War I, and one that touched off the war when a Bosnian Serb nationalist revolutionary assassinated Archduke Francis Ferdinand, heir to the Habsburg throne, in Sarajevo. With the formation of a Serb-dominated South Slav state after the war, incorporating the great majority of former Habsburg and Ottoman Serbs, the problematic of homeland politics receded. Nor did it reemerge openly after World War II in Tito's reconstructed (and more nationally equilibrated) Yugoslavia. Just as Russians viewed the Soviet Union as a whole (and not just the Russian republic) as "their" state, so Serbs viewed the Yugoslav state as a whole (and not just Serbia) as their own, regarding internal boundaries as insignificant or "merely administrative." Yet homeland politics revived in Serbia, and emerged in Russia, when the "nationalization" of constituent units of Yugoslavia and the Soviet Union eroded Serbs' and Russians' sense of being "at home" throughout the state.

The revival of Serbian homeland politics – of politicized concern with Serbs outside Serbia – centered initially on Kosovo. Although it was formally part of the Serbian Republic, its constitutional promotion to near-republic status in 1974, together with its gradual but thoroughgoing "Albanianization" (through differential fertility, Serb out-migration, and preferential treatment in cultural and administrative positions), were

---

[20] Denich, "Dismembering Yugoslavia"; Glenny, The *Fall of Yugoslavia*; and Denitch, *Ethnic Nationalism*, p. 33.

[21] Ivo Lederer, "Nationalism and the Yugoslavs," in Peter F. Sugar and Ivo John Lederer, eds., *Nationalism in Eastern Europe* (Seattle: University of Washington Press, 1994 [1969]).

perceived by Serb intellectuals as a "quiet secession" that had, in practice, stripped Serbia of its historic heartland.[22] The dwindling Serb community in Kosovo was represented as a physically and psychologically harassed national minority, forced increasingly to emigrate, subject to "genocide," in the scandalously hyperbolic language of the first major statement of the Serb nationalist revival.[23] Having again been "lost," Kosovo was in need of redemption, of reincorporation into a restored, strengthened, unitary Serbia – a program taken up, with great mobilizational success, by Milošević.

As Slovenia, Croatia, and later Bosnia-Hercegovina moved toward independence, Serbian homeland politics – as articulated by Milošević, by his even more radically nationalist opponents, and by the state-controlled broadcast media – was extended to, and came to focus increasingly on, Serb minorities in Croatia and Bosnia. Through the prevalence in the media and public discourse of what one anthropologist has called "narratives of victimization and of threat, linking the present with the past and projecting onto the future,"[24] the plight of Kosovo Serbs was represented in generalized terms as a threat to Serbs in minority positions everywhere. After the election of Tudjman, this threat was seen as particularly acute in Croatia, which was increasingly represented as a protofascist successor to the wartime Ustasha state. Croatian claims to self-determination and sovereign statehood were met with counterclaims that Serbs, too, had the right to self-determination, the right to a state of their own – if not Yugoslavia, then an enlarged Serbia. The secession of Croatia, Milošević bluntly warned throughout 1990 and the first half of 1991, would require the redrawing of its boundaries. Croatia's borderland Serbs were encouraged to take a stand of intransigent opposition to the new Croatian regime and to its bid for independence, and, as the crisis intensified, were provided with arms and logistical support.

The increasingly ominous tenor of Serbian homeland politics was doubly destabilizing, provoking both the Croatian government and Croatian Serbs to adopt more intransigent stances. Just as the reassertion

---

22 Dennison Rusinow, "Nationalities Policy and the 'National Question,'" in Pedro Ramet, ed., *Yugoslavia in the 1980s* (Boulder, Colo.: Westview Press, 1985), pp. 146–7. On the background to Serb concern about Kosovo, see Vujacic, "Communism and Nationalism," pp. 204–30.

23 This was the "Memorandum" of the Serbian Academy of Arts and Sciences, prepared in 1986. A French version has been published in Mirko Grmek *et al.*, eds., *Le nettoyage ethnique: documents historiques sur une idéologie serbe* (Paris: Fayard, 1993). On the memorandum, see Vujacic, *Communism and Nationalism*, pp. 257–67.

24 Bette Denich, "Unmaking Multi-Ethnicity in Yugoslavia: Metamorphosis Observed," *Anthropology of East Europe Review* 11, nos. 1–2 (1993), 51.

of central Serbian control over Kosovo, by upsetting the precarious national equilibrium in Yugoslavia, helped spark Croatian secessionism, so Serbian claims to speak for Croatian Serbs, by challenging Croatian sovereignty and reinforcing representations and fears of aggressive Serb hegemony, helped push the Croatian government toward a more uncompromising stance – toward the pursuit of full independence (rather than a restructured federal or confederal arrangement) and toward the more vigorous assertion of its authority in the rebellious borderlands (which occasioned armed clashes that led to the intervention of the army, initially as a peacekeeping force, but increasingly as an ally of local Serb forces). At the same time, the pan-Serb rhetoric, anti-Croat propaganda, and talk of border revisions emanating from Belgrade, together with the more uncompromising Croatian government stance, pushed Croatia's borderland Serbs toward greater intransigence – toward such steps as the formation of a "Serbian National Council" (July 1990), the holding of a referendum on autonomy for Croatian Serbs despite its prohibition by Croatian authorities (August 1990), the establishment of the "Serbian Autonomous Region of Krajina" (December 1990), and the proclamation of that region's "separation" from Croatia (February 1991).

It is not possible here to discuss in detail the interactive dynamic that led to the outbreak of a war pitting the heavily Serbianized "Yugoslav People's Army" and various Croatian Serb militias against the over-matched Croatian army, resulting in the occupation for several years of nearly a third of Croatian territory (including parts in which Serbs had been only a small minority) and sealing the final dissolution of Yugoslavia before spreading, with still more devastating consequences, to Bosnia-Hercegovina. I have had to limit my discussion to a general sketch of the interplay between the incipient Serb national minority in Croatia, the incipient Croatian nationalizing state, and the incipient Serbian homeland, locked in an intensifying spiral of mistrust, misrepresentation, and mutual fear. I have had to ignore not only the detailed interactive sequence of that interplay, but also the struggles among competing stances internal to the minority, nationalizing state, and homeland. Enough has perhaps been said, however, to suggest the potential fruitfulness of a relational, dynamic, interactive approach to nationalist conflict.

Conclusion

The fears and fault lines, the resentments and aspirations, the myths and memories that defined the national question in Yugoslavia have long been well known. But they did not foreordain the bloody breakup of the state. That was a contingent outcome of the interplay of mutually suspicious, mutually monitoring, mutually misrepresenting political elites in the incipient Croatian nationalizing state, the incipient Serb national minority in that state, and the incipient Serbian "homeland" state.

The relational and interactive perspective outlined in this essay, and illustrated with respect to the breakup of Yugoslavia, makes it possible to give due weight to both structure and contingency in the analysis of the national question in Eastern Europe and post-Soviet Eurasia. The relational field in which the national question arises is a highly structured one. In the post-Soviet case, for example, it was predictable – for the historical and institutional reasons analyzed in Chapter 2 as well as for conjunctural reasons linked to economic and political crisis – that nationalizing stances of some kind would prevail among successor state elites; that successor state Russians would tend to represent themselves as a national minority; and that Russian Federation elites would engage in "homeland" politics, asserting Russia's right, and obligation, to protect the interests of diaspora Russians. In the Yugoslav case, again for historical and institutional as well as conjunctural reasons, the emergence of nationalizing, minority, and homeland stances was similarly predictable. But what could not be predicted in these or other cases – and what cannot be retrospectively explained as structurally determined – was just what kind of nationalizing stance, what kind of minority self-understanding, what kind of homeland politics would prevail in the struggles among competing stances within these three relational fields, and just how the interplay between the three fields would develop. Here, social science and history must acknowledge, and theorize, the crucial causal significance of the contingency inherent in social and political action, without neglecting the powerful structuration of the relational fields in which action and struggle occur.

Part II

The old "New Europe" and the new

4 Nationalizing states in the old "New Europe" – and the new

Nationalism can be understood as a form of remedial political action. It addresses an allegedly deficient or "pathological" condition and proposes to remedy it. The discourse that frames, and in part constitutes, nationalist political action – and the subdiscursive sentiments which nationalist political stances seek to mobilize and evoke – can be conceived as a set of variations on a single core lament: that the identity and interests of a putative nation are not properly expressed or realized in political institutions, practices, or policies.

This allegedly deficient condition comes in two basic forms: a nation may be held to lack an adequate polity, or a polity may be held to lack an adequate national base. Two corresponding types of nationalism may be distinguished: *polity-seeking* or *polity-upgrading* nationalisms that aim to establish or upgrade an autonomous national polity; and *polity-based, nation-shaping (or nation-promoting)* nationalisms that aim to nationalize an existing polity.[1]

The literature on nationalism as a form of politics – leaving aside the broader literature on nationalism as an idea, or sentiment, or state of mind – has focused on polity-seeking nationalist movements, paying much less attention to the nationalization of existing polities. This chapter reverses the emphasis. It develops a framework for the analysis of what I call "nationalizing states." These are states that are conceived by their dominant elites as nation-states, as the states of and for particular nations, yet as "incomplete" or "unrealized" nation-states, as insufficiently "national" in a variety of senses to be explored below.

Almost all of the twenty-odd new states of post-Communist Eurasia

---

[1] This and the previous paragraph are based on my "East European, Soviet, and Post-Soviet Nationalisms: A Framework for Analysis," in Frederick D. Weil, ed., *Research on Democracy and Society*, vol. I (Greenwich, Conn.: JAI Press, 1993), p. 354. Since writing that article, I have discovered a similar distinction, between the "politicization of ethnicity" and the "ethnicization of the polity," in anthropologist Ralph Grillo's Introduction to *"Nation" and "State" in Europe: Anthropological Perspectives* (London: Academic Press, 1980), p. 7.

can be understood as nationalizing states in this sense, although there is a great deal of variation in the strength and forms of nationalizing policies and practices. Without directly analyzing developments in these incipient states – a difficult task when so much is still in flux – this chapter seeks to develop an analytical vocabulary for addressing contemporary projects and processes of "nationalization." It does so by way of a sustained examination of one particular nationalizing state – the newly resurrected Polish state – during the interwar period. The chapter begins, though, with a more general analytical discussion of nationalization.

Nation-building and nationalization

Although the literature on nationalist politics has focused on state-seeking nationalisms, one developed body of literature has addressed policies and processes of nationalization within the frame of existing states. This is the literature on "nation-building" and "national integration" that developed in the 1960s, stimulated by the emergence of new states in the former colonial territories of Asia and Africa. The central idea of this literature is that the population of the state – the citizenry – is progressively welded into a "nation" in the crucible of a bounded and relatively homogeneous transactional and communicative space, a space defined and delimited by the state and by state-wide social, political, economic, and cultural institutions and processes. In place of a welter of more parochial loyalties and identities, the citizenry is progressively united, through the gradually assimilative workings of these state-wide institutions, processes, and transactions, by a common "national" loyalty and identity.

Although analytically sophisticated in at least some of its variants, notably those developed by Karl Deutsch and Stein Rokkan and some of their followers,[2] much of this literature is flawed by a teleological model of development toward "full" national integration. Moreover – and particularly relevant for the present analysis – "nation" and "national" are conceived in this literature as definitionally coextensive with the citizenry and with the territorial and institutional frame of the state. The "nation" is simply the citizenry, to the extent that it becomes a unit of

---

[2] See among many other works Karl Deutsch, *Nationalism and Social Communication* (Cambridge, Mass. and New York: The Technology Press of the Massachusetts Institute of Technology and John Wiley, 1953); and Stein Rokkan, "Dimensions of State Formation and Nation-Building: A Possible Paradigm for Research on Variations within Europe," in Charles Tilly, ed., *The Formation of National States in Western Europe* (Princeton: Princeton University Press, 1975).

identity and loyalty – to the extent, that is, that citizens recognize one another as "belonging together" in a subjective, "internal" sense rather than as simply belonging to the state in a formal, external sense. Similarly, "national" is primarily a term of scale and scope: it often means no more than "state-wide." In this perspective, as a result, "nation-building" and "national integration" are axiomatically inclusive.

Articulated during the high noon of modernization theory, and deeply influenced by its assumptions, much of the early nation-building literature either ignored ethnicity or conceived it, like other local and particularistic attachments, as progressively attenuated by the multiple solvents of modernity, in particular by such universalizing, homogenizing, and thereby nationalizing social forms and forces as markets, bureaucracies, armies, cities, school systems, transportation and communication networks, and so on.[3] Nationhood, by contrast, was seen as strengthened, indeed constituted, by these modernizing forces. Ethnicity and nationhood were understood as definitionally antithetical, and as operating at different levels of social and political process. The resilience of ethnicity in modernizing contexts, to be sure, soon came to be widely appreciated; and a sophisticated literature on ethnic conflict in postcolonial states developed, culminating in major synthetic works by Crawford Young, Donald Horowitz, and others.[4] Yet the definitional opposition between ethnicity and nationhood persisted. Ethnicity could be understood as a potentially serious *impediment* to nation-building and national integration, but was not easily conceptualized as a major *component* of these processes.

This prevailing opposition, in studies of postcolonial states, between the definitionally state-oriented category of the "nation" and the definitionally sub-national category of ethnicity reflects the striking and consistent *territorialism* of anticolonial nationalisms and postcolonial states. Especially in African colonies, territorial boundaries – as established by the colonial powers, and accepted, for the most part, as legitimate by anticolonial nationalists – were not even approximately congruent with cultural boundaries. For this reason it has been nearly impossible to equate, even approximately, an ethnocultural group with a potentially sovereign "nation." The "nation" in the name of which sovereignty over those territories could be claimed by anticolonial

---

[3] For an influential critique of this modernizationist understanding of ethnicity, see Walker Connor, "Nation-Building or Nation-Destroying," *World Politics* 24 (1972).

[4] Crawford Young, *The Politics of Cultural Pluralism* (Madison: University of Wisconsin Press, 1976); Donald Horowitz, *Ethnic Groups in Conflict* (Berkeley: University of California Press, 1985).

nationalists was therefore almost universally conceived in territorial terms.[5]

In other settings, however, "ethnicity" (more precisely ethnolinguistically or ethnoreligiously embedded culture) is understood and experienced as constitutive of nationhood, not as opposed to it. In these cases, the dynamics of nationalization are quite different. Yet they have not been adequately explored. There is of course a large literature on ethnic nationalism; but it chiefly concerns polity-seeking nationalism, directed against the framework of existing states, rather than "nationalizing" nationalisms within the framework of an existing state. The literature on "nationalizing nationalisms," on the other hand, has focused on nationalization in a territorial rather than an ethnocultural mode, concentrating on two classes of cases: postcolonial states, and the "advanced" states and societies of northwestern Europe and North America, conceived (at least by the early wave of nation-building and national integration theorists) as models and exemplars for the postcolonial states.

This selective focus is understandable. It reflected the emergence of the nation-building literature in the early 1960s, at a moment of high political confidence in Western models of political development and their transferability to the developing world,[6] sustained by robust epistemological confidence in a generalizing style of social science capable of discovering universal patterns of social and political development and of validating policies aimed at promoting such development. At this forward-looking conjuncture, there was every reason to be interested in the territorial nation-building projects of the newly independent states of Asia and Africa, and to seek to analyze, and further, the "development" of those states along Western lines then widely accepted – in accordance with the intellectual and political spirit of the time – as normative for political development generally. There was, on the other hand, no reason to be especially interested in the more ethnocultural modes of nationalization prevalent in the earlier wave of new states that had emerged in the rubble of the great multinational land empires – Habsburg, Ottoman, and Romanov. To the extent that they were considered at all, these programs and practices of ethnocultural nationalization, together with so much else of interwar Europe, could be dismissed as marginal, as vestiges of a past peculiarly ridden with

---

5 For a succinct account of "territorialism" as one of the chief distinctive features of anticolonial nationalisms in Africa, see Anthony Smith, *State and Nation in the Third World* (New York: St. Martin's, 1983), pp. 50ff.

6 For this conjuncture and its subsequent eclipse, see Young, *The Politics of Cultural Pluralism*, pp. 7ff.

putatively ancient and singularly intractable ethnonational conflicts, or as pathological symptoms of the failure to modernize.

Today, however, the experience of the new nation-states of interwar Europe – itself, at the moment of its creation, a much-heralded "New Europe" – does not seem so marginal. As a point of comparative reference for the analysis of today's new nation-states – the twenty-odd states that have succeeded to the Soviet Union, Yugoslavia, and Czechoslovakia – the new states of interwar Europe seem far more relevant than the postcolonial states of midcentury or the old state-nations of Western Europe, on which the nation-building and national integration literatures have focused.

Far from being vestigial or unmodern, the dynamics of ethnocultural nationalization in the new nation-states of interwar Europe represented a distinctively modern form of politicized ethnicity, pivoting on claims made, in the name of a nation, to political control, economic well-being, and full cultural expression within "its own" national state. Similar claims are being made today. This chapter therefore approaches today's newly nationalizing states by way of a reconsideration of one of the newly nationalizing states of the interwar period – the newly reestablished Polish state.

The old "New Europe": nationalizing states in the interwar period

The new states that emerged from the decay and disintegration of the Ottoman, Habsburg, and Romanov empires were all created as nation-states, legitimated by their claim to be the states of and for particular nations. All, moreover, were not only nation-states but *nationalizing* states. The politics and processes of nationalization varied widely in form and intensity in these states, but they characteristically involved the following elements: (1) the existence (more precisely the conceived or understood or "imagined" existence) of a "core nation" or nationality, defined in ethnocultural terms, and sharply distinguished from the citizenry or permanent resident population of the state as a whole; (2) the idea that the core nation legitimately "owns" the polity, that the polity exists as the polity *of* and *for* the core nation; (3) the idea that the core nation is not flourishing, that its specific interests are not adequately "realized" or "expressed" despite its rightful "ownership" of the state; (4) the idea that specific action is needed in a variety of settings and domains to promote the language, cultural flourishing, demographic predominance, economic welfare, or political hegemony of the core nation; (5) the conception and justification of such action as remedial or compensatory, as needed to counterbalance and correct for previous discrimination against the nation before it had "its own" state to safeguard and promote its interests; (6) mobilization on the basis of these ideas in a variety of settings – legislatures, electoral campaigns, the press, associations, universities, the streets – in an effort to shape the policies or practices of the state, of particular organizations, agencies, or officials within the state, or of non-state organizations; and (7) the adoption – by the state, by particular state agencies and officials, and by non-state organizations – of formal and informal policies and practices informed by the ideas outlined above.

This sketch is deliberately drawn in broad and general terms. This is partly because it attempts to capture features common to a variety of nationalizing states. But it also reflects the fact that state-based, nation-promoting nationalisms – the post-independence nationalisms of nationalizing states – are inherently more diffuse than state-seeking nationalisms. Central to the latter are distinct movements with clear goals. Even where nationalisms are not unambiguously state-seeking but (as is often the case) split between movements for independence and movements for increased autonomy within an existing state, there are still distinct movements with definite, if contested, goals. "Nationalizing" nationalisms within the frame of independent states, by contrast, do not usually involve distinct movements with clear and specific goals. Consequently, it is harder to pinpoint what is specifically "nationalist" about politics in such states.[7] In such settings, nationalism becomes an "aspect" of politics – embracing both formal policies and informal practices, and existing both within and outside the state – rather than a discrete movement. It is that diffuse and pervasive yet nonetheless distinctive aspect of politics that I want to analyze here, by way of a discussion of the politics of nationalization in the region's most populous state, the newly reestablished Polish state.

Interwar Poland as a nationalizing state

The Polish state that was resurrected in the aftermath of the First World War differed radically from the old Polish Commonwealth that had

---

[7] As John Breuilly put it, "once a nationalist . . . opposition takes control of the state the specifically nationalist character of politics tends to diminish. Competing groups all proclaim their paramount concern with the 'national interest'. In such a situation nationalism as a specific form of politics becomes meaningless. Again, where all foreign policy is justified in nationalist language it is difficult to identify a specific form of foreign policy which could be called nationalist" (*Nationalism and the State* [Chicago: University of Chicago Press, 1985], p. 221).

disappeared from the map of Europe in the late eighteenth century after being thrice partitioned between Prussia, Austria, and Russia. The old Commonwealth had never been a nation-state or nationalizing state. It was a loosely integrated polity whose great ethnolinguistic heterogeneity was not seen as problematic. "The nation" in the old Commonwealth was defined by social and political status (membership in the ruling *szlachta* or gentry), not by language or ethnicity; it was conceptually located *above* non-privileged status groups (above all the Polish-speaking and non-Polish-speaking peasantry) in the same territory rather than *alongside* other coordinate nations.

During the century and a quarter of partition, however, Polish nation-hood was redefined in ethnolinguistic terms.[8] This redefinition had two aspects, which one might designate as "social deepening" and "ethnic narrowing" respectively. On the one hand, the eclipse of the status-bound notion of the "gentry nation" reflected the democratization or popularization or "social deepening" of the concept of nation throughout Europe that began in the late eighteenth and continued through the nineteenth century; everywhere "nation" was reconceived in a "populist" idiom that expressly included all social classes or strata. On the other hand, the increased salience of language as a nation-bounding diacritical marker reflected the experience of prolonged statelessness, which prevented the development of a state-oriented, state-framed, "civic" or "territorial" understanding of nationhood. This ethnonational self-understanding was reinforced by the prevailing narrative of the nineteenth-century Polish national movement, which presented this movement as the oft-martyred Polish ethnonation's heroic struggle for independence, and by the armed struggles of 1918–21 that accompanied the formation of the new state, pitting Poles against Germans in Poznania and Upper Silesia, Poles against Ukrainians in eastern Galicia, and Poles against the Red Army (represented by the Polish nationalist Right as a "Judeo-Bolshevik" force) in the eastern borderlands.[9]

The new Polish state, therefore, was conceived as the state *of* and *for* the ethnolinguistically (and ethnoreligiously) defined Polish nation, in part because it was seen as made *by* this nation against the resistance of Germans, Ukrainians, and Jews. A clear distinction was universally drawn between this Polish nation and the total citizenry of the state. By official count, which clearly overstated the relative predominance of

---

[8] Peter Brock, "Polish Nationalism," in Peter F. Sugar and Ivo J. Lederer, eds., *Nationalism in Eastern Europe* (Seattle: University of Washington Press, 1994 [1969]), p. 316.

[9] I am indebted for this last point to Dariusz Stola.

Poles, the citizenry included large numbers of Ukrainians (14% of the population in 1921), Belarusians (4%), Germans (4%), and Jews (8%).[10] Not that the boundaries of the Polish nation were thought to be fixed. Ukrainians – especially outside of Galicia – and Belarusians were considered candidates for membership in the Polish nation; policies toward them tended therefore to be assimilationist. The assimilation of Germans and Jews, however, was generally viewed as unlikely (in the case of Germans, especially those living in territories ceded by Germany after the war) or undesirable (in the case of Jews). Policies toward them were therefore more "dissimilationist" or "differentialist," based on differential treatment by ethnocultural nationality among citizens of the Polish state. Thus nationalizing policies and practices varied sharply. Broadly speaking, in eastern rural districts the aim was to nationalize the borderland East Slav population; in the cities and in the west, the aim was rather to nationalize the territory and economic life, by replacing Germans and Jews with Poles in key economic and political positions, and by encouraging their emigration.

Nationalizing the western borderlands

Ethnic Germans, particularly those in the long German-ruled western borderlands of the new state,[11] were trebly vulnerable to nationalizing programs and practices. To begin with, the borderland regions had for the preceding four decades been subjected to harsh, although ineffective, nationalizing policies by their Prussian and German rulers. These

---

[10] Joseph Rothschild, *East Central Europe Between the Two World Wars* (Seattle: University of Washington Press, 1974), pp. 34ff.; Antony Polonsky, *Politics in Independent Poland* (Oxford: Oxford University Press, 1972), pp. 35ff.

[11] The western borderlands had been ruled by Prussia since the late eighteenth-century partitions of Poland (in the case of East Upper Silesia since the mid-eighteenth century), and had belonged to the unified German state for half a century. Besides the perhaps 1.4 million ethnic Germans of these previously German-ruled western borderlands (a number soon sharply diminished by heavy emigration), there were some half million Germans living in the formerly Russian part of Poland and another hundred thousand in the formerly Austrian part. As Richard Blanke has argued, these are fundamentally different cases. Germans in the formerly Russian and formerly Austrian parts of Poland did not suffer so dramatic a reversal in status; they were not regarded as so dangerous by Poles; and they did not, consequently, bear the brunt of programs and practices of nationalization. I neglect them in this account. See Richard Blanke, *Orphans of Versailles: The Germans in Western Poland 1918–1939* (Lexington: University Press of Kentucky, 1993), pp. 3–4. On the size of the German population in interwar Poland, see *ibid.*, p. 31, and Walter Kuhn, "Das Deutschtum in Polen und sein Schicksal in Kriegs- und Nachkriegszeit," in Werner Markert, ed., *Polen* (Cologne and Graz: Böhlau, 1959), pp. 140–2.

policies had succeeded only in stimulating national solidarity and stiffening nationalist resistance among Poles. Nonetheless, the sustained (and openly acknowledged) German efforts to nationalize the German–Polish borderlands during the Kaiserreich provided a convenient rationale for analogous Polish measures after the First World War. It permitted such measures to be presented as remedial and compensatory, as needed to reverse the political, economic, cultural, and ethnodemographic legacy of the decades-long policy of Germanization.

Furthermore, Germans in the restored Polish state had the misfortune to "belong," by ethnocultural nationality, if not legal citizenship, to a powerful neighboring state with unconcealed revisionist ambitions.[12] Under the leadership of Gustav Stresemann, foreign minister from 1923 until his death in 1929, Weimar Germany achieved a *rapprochement* with Western powers, but it continued to make border revision in the east – albeit peaceful, negotiated border revision – a top foreign policy priority. The border with Poland, particularly the "Polish corridor" that cut off East Prussia from the rest of Germany, was universally viewed as an insupportable "national humiliation," unjustly imposed on a prostrate Germany.[13] Poles just as universally – and no doubt correctly – perceived borderland Germans as favoring, even if not actively supporting, a restoration of German rule in the borderlands. Thus Germans were perceived from the beginning as a dangerous "fifth column," stimulating, by their very existence, revisionist claims in Germany and unlikely, in any crucial test, to prove loyal to the Polish state.

Germans' third vulnerability lay in their preeminent economic position in the western borderlands – especially since this could be attributed to privileges they had enjoyed under a nationalizing German regime.[14] In Poznania and Pomerania, at the end of the period of German rule, Germans monopolized the civil service, held a disproportionate share of large landed estates and medium-sized farms, and were also disproportionately represented among professionals, merchants, and artisans. In Upper Silesia, Germans predominated among owners, managers, and workers of industrial enterprises.[15] This favorable economic position, like

---

[12] On interwar German homeland nationalism *vis-à-vis* ethnic Germans in western Poland, see Chapter 5.

[13] Detlev J. K. Peukert, *The Weimar Republic*, trans. Richard Deveson (New York: Hill and Wang, 1993), pp. 201ff.

[14] On "privilege" as a motif in Polish historiography, explaining German economic pre-eminence, and justifying remedial Polish nationalizing efforts, see Blanke, *Orphans of Versailles*, pp. 6–7.

[15] Blanke, *Orphans of Versailles*, pp. 51–3.

that alleged to be occupied by Jews, would be a focus of nationalist concern throughout the interwar period.[16]

These three features conditioned Germans' immediate vulnerability, in the new Polish nation-state, to a politics of nationalization. But what kind of nationalization? To characterize it, as is often done, as an effort at "Polonization" is insufficient. For Polonization can refer to two different, even antithetical processes. On the one hand, it can designate an attempt to remake the human material of the state, to nationalize the citizenry by turning Germans, and others, into Poles. In this sense, nationalization is a form of assimilation, that is, of "making similar": it involves making a target population similar to some reference population, whose putative characteristics are conceived as normative for the citizenry as a whole. On the other hand, nationalization can be directed at *spheres of practice* rather than *groups of people*. In this sense it involves *dissimilation* rather than *assimilation*. Far from seeking to make people *similar*, it prescribes differential treatment on the basis of their presumed fundamental *difference*. Instead of seeking to alter identities, it takes them as given. Assimilationist nationalization seeks to eradicate difference, while differentialist nationalization takes difference as axiomatic and foundational.

Vis-à-vis Germans, nationalization was dissimilationist rather than assimilationist. There was no attempt to transform Germans into Poles. Many Germans, to be sure, did acquire Polish *citizenship*, as most residents of the ceded territories were entitled to do by the Versailles Treaty.[17] But they did not understand themselves (nor were they understood by Poles) as having thereby acquired Polish *nationality*. Citizenship and nationality, legal membership of the state and ethnocultural membership of the nation, were seen as sharply distinct by Germans and Poles alike (and were indeed seen as sharply distinct throughout East Central and Eastern Europe). There was no attempt to transform Germans' nationality, to make Germans into Poles in an ethnocultural sense. This was viewed as unrealistic. Much cultural assimilation – in both directions – had indeed occurred over the centuries in the German–Slav borderlands. But by the late nineteenth century, a hardening

---

[16] On the economic dimensions of nationalizing states, Hans Jürgen Seraphim, "Wirtschaftliche Nationalitätenkämpfe in Ostmitteleuropa," *Leipziger Vierteljahrsschrift für Südosteuropa* 1, no. 4 (1937–38), is an analytically sophisticated statement.

[17] The entitlement to formal citizenship, granted to those who had been born in the ceded territories or had resided there since 1908, was not undisputed, for Poland construed the residence requirement as strictly as possible – in a manner ultimately invalidated by the Permanent Court of International Justice – so as to minimize the number of eligible Germans (Blanke, *Orphans of Versailles*, pp. 65–6).

national struggle in the eastern districts of Prussia, in the context of an overall increase in social mobilization, led to the intensification of national identifications on both sides, and to their extension to strata formerly indifferent to, or only tenuously aware of, nationality.[18] In this new context of struggle between mobilized nationalities, assimilation was much less likely to occur. It continued to occur in some regions outside the focus of the national struggle, for example among Poles who had migrated from eastern Prussia to the Ruhr industrial districts. And certain zones of mixed, fluid, and ambivalent national identification remained, notably Upper Silesia, where political orientation and language often did not coincide.[19] But on the whole the trend since the 1880s had been toward a sharper crystallization of boundaries between ethnonational groups. In this context it was implausible to think that the new Polish state might assimilate its German minority, highly mobilized and strongly conscious of its distinct ethnocultural nationality.

Nor was there a serious attempt to cultivate the political loyalty of Germans to the Polish state – to assimilate them politically while tolerating their ethnocultural Germanness. Such an attempt would have presupposed (1) an understanding of Germans' political loyalty and identity as open and contingent, and (2) an understanding of the Polish state as the state of and for all its citizens, not merely the state of and for Poles. But neither was forthcoming. Germans were widely perceived as unremittingly hostile to the Polish state and as sympathetic to German irredentism. And the Polish state was widely understood as "belonging" specifically to the Polish nation and existing to further its particular aims and interests. Given these prevailing understandings of German hostility towards, and Polish "ownership" of, the state, attempts to cultivate the political loyalty of Germans were condemned in advance as futile.

Policies and practices of nationalization thus were directed neither at the ethnocultural assimilation of Germans nor at turning them into loyal, if culturally unassimilated, citizens of the Polish state. They were directed at the nationalization not of Germans, but of Polish territory and of political, cultural, and economic life within it. They were differentialist, not assimilationist. By virtue of their distinct ethnic nationality – and in spite of their common citizenship – the ethnically German citizens of the new state were to be treated differently from ethnically Polish citizens. Nationalizing initiatives sought to build the Polish state as a specifically *Polish* state, that is, as a state that would embody and

[18] Geoff Eley, "German Politics and Polish Nationality: The Dialectic of Nation-Forming in the East of Prussia," *East European Quarterly* 18 (1984).
[19] See Blanke, *Orphans of Versailles*, p. 28; Kuhn, "Das Deutschtum in Polen," p. 143.

express the will and interests of the Polish nation. Such initiatives sought to Polonize the borderlands, the civil service, the professions, the industrial base of Upper Silesia, the school system, and so on, not by making Germans into Poles, but by displacing or excluding Germans from certain key positions and, more generally, by weakening Germans as an organized group, thereby preventing them from exercising undue influence over the political, cultural, or economic life of the new state.

The most visible form assumed by ethnic nationalization in the early years of the restored Polish state – indeed in anticipation of the restoration of Polish statehood – was a large-scale migration of ethnic unmixing, as Germans fled to Germany from the Prussian borderlands that were ceded to Poland.[20] Some two-thirds of the roughly 1.1 million ethnic Germans in these territories (not including Upper Silesia) had left by the mid-1920s, including 85 percent of the urban German population and 55 percent of rural Germans.[21] The main towns of Poznania and Pomerania, almost all majority German before the war, now contained only small German minorities. The exodus, to be sure, cannot be attributed solely, or even primarily, to the nationalizing policies of the new state. Some migration was to be expected, notably on the part of those civil servants and military personnel who had no roots in the borderland region and had been sustained there only by the Prussian and German state, and on the part of those who, regardless of the anticipated policies of the new Polish state, preferred to cast their lot with the more economically and politically powerful and culturally familiar German state. Furthermore, large-scale migration began before the new state was even established. Yet even this early migration – occurring in anticipation, rather than as a result, of the transfer of sovereignty – reflected a dynamic of nationalization: departing Germans anticipated (correctly) that the transfer of sovereignty would reverse the dynamic of nationalization, substituting Polonization for Germanization. Moreover, the migration was certainly welcomed, indirectly fostered, and on occasion explicitly demanded, by Polish officials.[22] Migration was also encouraged

---

20 For a comparative discussion of migrations of ethnic unmixing in the aftermath of empire, see Chapter 6.
21 Blanke, *Orphans of Versailles*, p. 49; Hermann Rauschning, *Die Entdeutschung Westpreussens und Posens* (Berlin: Reimar Hobbing, 1930), pp. 338ff., esp. 348–9
22 In 1919, for example, Stanisław Grabski, then chairman of the Sejm committee on foreign affairs, and later Minister of Culture, articulated the ruling National Democrats' view of the German–Polish borderlands: "We want to base our relationships on love, but there is one kind of love for countrymen and another for aliens. Their percentage among us is definitely too high; Poznania can show us the way by which the percentage can be brought from 14 percent or even 20 percent down to 1.5 percent. The foreign element will have to consider whether it will not be better off elsewhere;

by popular anti-German demonstrations, including some violence against Germans.[23] The most thorough, and most detached, recent study of the migration concludes that "Poland's basic policy, at least during the period of National Democratic influence to 1926, was simply to encourage as many Germans as possible to leave the country."[24] This does not mean that the migration was "forced," as many Germans claimed.[25] It does mean, however, that the anticipated and actual nationalization of life in restored Poland was a major cause of the mass migration (keeping in mind, of course, that this nationalization followed, and mirrored, two generations of rule by a nationalizing Prussian/German state).[26]

A less visible, but equally important, dimension of nationalization involved efforts to displace Germans from key positions in the economy. Central to economic nationalization throughout East Central Europe in the interwar period, for example, was land reform. By "expropriat[ing] ethnically 'alien' landlords," while sheltering landlords of the "correct" ethnic nationality from the brunt of agrarian reform, states sought to defuse an explosive social issue at minimal political cost.[27] Not only German but also Russian, Polish, Hungarian, Bulgarian and other landlords whose estates lay outside "their own" nation-state found themselves expropriated in this manner.[28] In Poland the most conveniently expropriable "alien" landlords were Germans in the western borderlands (though there were also some Russian as well as a few Ukrainian and Lithuanian estate owners in the eastern borderlands). Although policies formally applied to estates owned by Poles as well as to those owned

Polish land for the Poles!" (quoted in Blanke, *Orphans of Versailles*, p. 63 and in Rauschning, *Die Entdeutschung Westpreussens und Posens*, p. 45). See also Blanke, *Orphans of Versailles*, pp. 63–5.

23 Although violence is generally a crucial determinant of migrations of ethnic unmixing (see Chapter 6), it does not appear to have been central in this case. Violence between Germans and Poles was much greater in Upper Silesia in 1919–21 than in Poznania and Pomerania; yet emigration was heavier from the latter regions. One reason for the lesser migration from Upper Silesia is that the disposition of this territory was not settled until October 1921, when the territory was divided between Germany and Poland following a plebiscite in March of that year in which 60% (including a substantial fraction of Polish-speakers) had voted for the territory to remain with Germany. On the immediately postwar years in Upper Silesia, see Bogdan Koszel, "Nationality Problems in Upper Silesia," in Paul Smith, ed., *Ethnic Groups in International Relations* (Aldershot, UK and New York: Dartmouth Publishing Company and New York University Press, 1991); and Blanke, *Orphans of Versailles*, pp. 26–31.

24 Blanke, *Orphans of Versailles*, p. 64.

25 On the limited analytical usefulness of the concept of forced migration, see the discussion in Chapter 6, esp. pp. 168, 171.

26 Blanke, *Orphans of Versailles*, pp. 40–3, 63–5.

27 Rothschild, *East Central Europe Between the Two World Wars*, p. 15.

28 Seraphim, "Wirtschaftliche Nationalitätenkämpfe in Ostmitteleuropa," pp. 47–50.

by members of national minorities, in practice land reform was implemented most vigorously *vis-à-vis* Germans.[29] Distribution of the expropriated land, too, was guided by ethnopolitical considerations – a point that especially aggrieved the desperately poor Ukrainian and Belarusian peasants in the east, who saw Poles resettled on lands expropriated from Russian estate owners. Apart from land reform, state officials used administrative discretion to pursue a nationalizing agenda through such techniques as the selective denial of licenses required to practice certain professions, the exclusion of German firms from state contracts, the nationalization of the civil service, and pressure on industrial firms (especially in the strategically crucial heavy industrial district of Upper Silesia) to Polonize their managerial staffs and their labor force.[30]

A final dimension of nationalization can be broadly characterized as cultural, although in this sphere too specifically cultural concerns were intertwined with geopolitical and security concerns and with economic interests. Here questions of language were central. Polish was made the sole official language of the state. From 1924 on, Polish officials were instructed not to accept any communications in German, and postal authorities would not deliver mail using the German spelling of place names.[31] But the main arena of language politics – and of cultural nationalization in general – was the school system. The Minority Protection Treaty obliged Poland (like other East Central European states) to provide elementary education in minority languages where minorities formed a "considerable proportion" of the population.[32] The latitude allowed governments in interpreting these provisions, coupled with a cumbersome and ineffective enforcement procedure, made them easy to circumvent. The number of German-language schools dropped

---

[29] A confidential memorandum of 1929 from the *wojewode* of the Polish province of Pomorze clearly indicated the underlying ethnopolitical rationale of land reform. In undertaking land reform, he argued, one must consider the "loyalty of the affected citizens, their nationality, their religion, and their general attitude toward the vital interests of the state." Especially the strategically vital "Polish corridor," the main target of German irredentism, "must be cleansed of larger German holdings" and "settled with a nationally conscious Polish population" (quoted in Blanke, *Orphans of Versailles*, p. 113).

[30] Blanke, *Orphans of Versailles*, pp. 116–20. The initiative did not always come from the state. Nationalist associations in the borderlands, drawing their membership heavily from such state-dependent groups as teachers and civil servants, "staged anti-German rallies, organized boycotts of German businesses, [and] pressured employers to give preference to ethnic Poles" (*ibid.*, p. 94).

[31] *Ibid.*, p. 67.

[32] C. A. Macartney, *National States and National Minorities* (London: Oxford University Press, 1934), p. 505.

sharply, even after the end of mass German out-migration, declining in Poznania and Pomerania from 1250 in 1921–22 to 254 in 1926–27 (by which time mass emigration had ended) to 60 in 1937–38.[33] In the German schools that remained, the administration and teaching staff as well as the curriculum were increasingly Polonized. These measures seem to have aimed less at assimilating German schoolchildren than at preventing Germans from controlling – and from using toward ends inimical to the Polish nation-state – the powerful organizational and ideological resources of "their own" school system. In this respect Polish school policy reinforced other measures aimed at inhibiting, hindering, or controlling the associational and organizational life of Germans, and thereby at hindering the organizational articulation and expression of specifically German interests.

Nationalizing the urban economy

Toward Jews, as toward Germans, the nationalizing policies and practices of interwar Poland were dissimilationist rather than assimilationist. Yet while the dissimilationist stance toward Germans reflected the general belief that Germans *could* not be assimilated, the dissimilationist stance toward Jews reflected the prevailing view that Jews *should* not be assimilated. Rather than seeking to assimilate Jews, or to cultivate the loyalty of acculturated though unassimilated Jews, policies and practices of nationalization sought on the whole to displace Jews from their all-too-visible positions in the urban economy and, especially after the Nazi seizure of power in Germany, to encourage their emigration.

The identities of Jews – their religious, cultural, and political self-understandings – were exceedingly varied and intensely contested among Jews themselves in interwar Poland. There were deeply rooted political, cultural, economic, and demographic differences between Jews of Galicia, Congress Poland, and the eastern borderlands. And throughout Poland, Jews were torn between the Yiddish, Polish, and Hebrew languages, between religious and secular identities, between socialist and antisocialist ideologies, between Zionists and their opponents (both secular and religious). Consequently, generalizations about Polish Jews as a whole are exceedingly hazardous. Still, it seems safe to suggest that unlike Germans, and precisely because of the great flux in Polish Jewish self-understandings, a substantial minority of Jews were potentially "available" as members of the Polish nation during the interwar period, and more would have been or become available if the new Poland had

[33] Blanke, *Orphans of Versailles*, p. 79; Kuhn, "Das Deutschtum in Polen," p. 147.

not been the "most anti-Semitic state in Europe" at the beginning of the interwar period.[34]

Most Jews, to be sure, were linguistically and culturally unassimilated when the Polish state was reestablished. But this was a period of great mobilization, rapid acculturation, and linguistic assimilation, especially for the younger generation. Even at the beginning of the period, about a quarter of those who identified their religion as Jewish in the 1921 census identified their nationality as Polish rather than Jewish.[35] Yet apart from the Polish Left, which favored the assimilation of Jews, Poles generally did not encourage assimilation. While the Left remained a strong oppositional force throughout the interwar years (distinguishing Poland from most other East European countries), the predominant nationalizing policies and practices in interwar Poland were emphatically not those of the Left. So while a substantial fraction of Poland's Jewish population either already identified with Polish nationality or might have come to identify with it, Jews were excluded from that nationality by prevailing Polish understandings of nationhood and practices of nationalization (and of course also tended to exclude themselves from that nationality in *response* to those understandings of nationhood and practices of nationalization).

Germans in the west and Ukrainians and Belarusians in the east were *borderland* minorities. All were concentrated in areas adjacent to neighboring states that contained large populations of their ethno-national kin, that claimed (across the boundaries of state and citizenship) to protect and represent their interests, and that harbored unconcealed

---

[34] The quotation is from Ezra Mendelsohn, the leading historian of European Jews in the interwar period; see Mendelsohn, "A Note on Jewish Assimilation in the Polish Lands," in Bela Vago, ed., *Jewish Assimilation in Modern Times* (Boulder, Colo.: Westview, 1981), p. 145.

[35] Ezra Mendelsohn, *The Jews of East Central Europe Between the Two World Wars* (Bloomington: Indiana University Press, 1983), pp. 23, 29. These figures for self-identified nationality of Jews are suggestive, and reveal strong regional variation in Jewish identification with Polish nationality (this being strongest in Galicia, where Jewish assimilation to the dominant Polish language and culture had been strong under Habsburg rule, and weakest in the eastern borderlands). However, the artifactual character of these figures must be borne in mind. The 1921 census obliged all respondents to identify their nationality, regardless of whether nationality was a mean-ingful category of self-understanding for them. Clearly, for many Jews, nationality was not a meaningful category: many Jews, perhaps the majority, identified *neither* with Polish nationality *nor* with Jewish nationality; they defined their Jewishness not in national terms but in traditional religious terms. But my point here is that this traditional, non-national self-understanding was eroding and in flux as a result of pervasive processes of mobilization and acculturation, and that this process of reidentification in national terms created the potential for membership in the Polish nation.

irredentist designs on the borderland territories they inhabited. Polish nationalizing stances toward these borderland minorities were determined by the felt need to Polonize (though in different ways, dissimilationist in the west, assimilationist in the east) the ethnic borderlands and thereby secure them against the irredentist designs of Germany and the Soviet Union.[36]

This, of course, was not the case of Jews, whose external national homeland – for those who considered it such – was still in the making, a homeland distant not only in space but also (given British limits on Jewish immigration to Palestine) in time. The absence of a proximate, putatively irredentist homeland, to be sure, did not prevent Polish nationalists from questioning the loyalty of Jews. Indeed, suspicions of Jewish disloyalty were behind the outbreaks of anti-Semitic violence, including several major pogroms, that accompanied struggles against Ukrainian nationalists, the incipient Lithuanian state, and the Red Army over contested borderland regions of the new state in 1918–20.[37] But the *territorial* dimension of nationalizing policies and practices, so pronounced in the case of borderland minorities, was missing in the case of the Jews. *Vis-à-vis* territorially concentrated, rooted, homeland-linked Germans and East Slavs, Poles sought to nationalize the ethnic borderlands; *vis-à-vis* Jews, they sought instead to nationalize the urban commercial and professional economy.[38]

Jews were indeed prominent in Polish cities, and predominant in commerce and certain professions. In terms of demography and socio-economic structure, the contrast with the population as a whole was sharp. Jews constituted nearly a third of the urban population of Poland in 1921, and half of the urban population in the backward eastern borderlands, while comprising just over 10 percent of the population as a whole. While 60 percent of the total population depended on agriculture for their livelihood in 1931, this was true of only 4 percent of Jews. In 1921, Jews comprised over 60 percent of those employed in

---

[36] This is an instance of the triadic relational nexus, analyzed in Chapter 3, between nationalizing states, national minorities, and the external national "homelands" to which the minorities belong by shared ethnic nationality though not by legal citizenship. This relation is examined from the point of view of the German "homeland" in Chapter 5.

[37] Mendelsohn, *The Jews of East Central Europe Between the Two World Wars*, pp. 40–1.

[38] By emphasizing here Polish efforts to "nationalize" the urban and commercial economy, I am not suggesting that Polish anti-Semitism was somehow essentially economic. Indisputably, it had deep cultural roots; but they are beyond the scope of this discussion, which is concerned not with the origins of anti-Semitism but with the nature of interwar nationalizing practices and policies.

commerce; in 1931, they accounted for more than half of the doctors, a third of the lawyers, and substantial shares of other professions. In fact, the large majority of Polish Jews were very poor, and the single most striking economic fact about Polish Jews in the interwar period was their progressive pauperization. Nearly four-fifths of Jews active in commerce were self-employed, and did not employ other workers: "the typical Jewish 'merchant' was a small shopkeeper, or owner of a stall in the local market, working alone or with the help of his family." Yet the visible ethnic division of labor and statistics such as those given above "were interpreted by Polish anti-Semites as proof that Polish cities were dominated by 'foreigners,' against whom a holy war must be waged by the native middle class."[39]

Economic nationalization *vis-à-vis* Jews was both governmental and extra-governmental. Jews were systematically excluded from state-controlled sectors of the economy. They were not hired in the civil service, municipal administration, state hospitals, schools, or universities (where, even without an official *numerus clausus*, the proportion of Jewish students declined by two-thirds). Credit and work licenses were distributed differentially. Sunday work was forbidden, putting religious Jews who could not open their shops Saturdays at a competitive disadvantage. Governmental anti-Semitism was checked in the late 1920s under Piłsudski, but pressure on Jews intensified again with the onset of the Great Depression. After Piłsudski's death in 1935, the government, declaring it only "natural that Polish society should seek economic self-sufficiency," and openly endorsing "economic struggle [against the Jews]," renewed its campaign of economic nationalization. Governmental nationalization from above was complemented by extra-governmental nationalization from below. Right-wing students harassed, humiliated, and physically attacked Jews in universities. Centrist as well as right-wing parties campaigned against the economic position of Jews. The centrist Peasant Party, for example, even while rejecting violence and professing to endorse equal rights for Jews, blamed Jews – an unassimilable, "consciously alien nation within Poland" – for the alleged fact that "the Poles have no middle class of their own," and concluded that it was vital that "these middle-class functions shall more and more pass into the hands of the Poles." In the second half of the 1930s, a large-scale boycott of Jewish businesses was organized; and direct violence,

[39] Mendelsohn, *The Jews of East Central Europe Between the Two World Wars*, pp. 23–9 (the quotations are from pp. 28 and 23 respectively); Joseph Marcus, *Social and Political History of the Jews in Poland, 1919–1939* (Berlin: Mouton, 1983), pp. 29–31; Polonsky, *Politics in Independent Poland*, pp. 42–4.

unchecked by the state, was increasingly employed against Jewish shop-keepers and craftsmen.[40]

If nationalizing policies and practices *vis-à-vis* Jews sought in the short term to exclude them from the professional and commercial economy, the long-term aim was to promote Jewish emigration. Here the Polish government and right-wing nationalists made common cause with Zionist organizations. "If Zionism meant Jewish emigration to [Palestine], no one was more Zionist than Poland's leaders in the late 1930s." And as both economic crisis and anti-Semitism intensified, many Jews were willing to emigrate. Precisely in the late 1930s, however, the British government sharply curtailed Jewish immigration to Palestine, the number of Polish Jews immigrating dropping from a peak of 30,000 in 1935 to about 4,000 per year in the late 1930s. It was thus, ironically, against the wishes of Poland's virulently anti-Semitic govern-ment that the vast majority of Polish Jews remained in Poland to face the unimaginable catastrophe that would soon follow.[41]

Nationalizing the eastern borderlands

The eastern borderlands presented yet another picture. To the east, the territory of the Polish state extended far beyond that of the Polish language, including a nearly 200-mile-wide strip in which the language of the countryside was Belarusian (in the northeast) and Ukrainian (in the southeast).[42] Outside the cities, Belarusians and Ukrainians com-prised large local majorities in these borderlands, and they formed over 20 percent of the population of the state as a whole.[43]

---

[40] Mendelsohn, *The Jews of East Central Europe Between the Two World Wars*, pp. 42–3 and 69–74 (the quotations are from pp. 71 and 72); Rothschild, *East Central Europe Between the Two World Wars*, pp. 40–1; Polonsky, *Politics in Independent Poland*, pp. 465ff.

[41] Mendelsohn, *The Jews of East Central Europe Between the Two World Wars*, pp. 71, 79–80 (the quotation is from p. 71); Polonsky, *Politics in Independent Poland*, pp. 467–8.

[42] Paul Robert Magocsi, *Historical Atlas of East Central Europe* (Seattle: University of Washington Press, 1993), p. 131. What constituted a "language" rather than a "dialect" was of course a matter of dispute. The prevailing Polish view (like the prevailing pre-Revolutionary Russian view) was that Ukrainian and Belarusian were dialects rather than languages, and that the speakers of these dialects did not constitute distinct nations but were rather a kind of "ethnographic raw material" capable of being molded into Poles (or Russians). See Jerzy Tomaszewski, *Rzeczpospolita wielu narodów* (Warsaw: Czytelnik, 1985), p. 96.

[43] Rothschild, *East Central Europe Between the Two World Wars*, p. 36. Census figures for 1921 on religion showed 21.7 percent of the population were Uniate or Orthodox, almost all of whom were East Slavs; in addition, some Belarusians were Catholic. Census figures for 1921 by nationality showed the Ukrainians as more than three times as numerous as Belarusians, but this almost certainly exaggerated the disparity of size between the groups, since Catholic Belarusians were classified as Polish by nationality.

The economic and social condition of Belarusians and Ukrainians contrasted sharply with that of Germans and Jews. While Jews were 80 percent urban, the East Slavs were almost 95 percent rural (Germans were initially mixed but became heavily rural as a result of disproportionately heavy urban emigration).[44] Belarusians and Ukrainians occupied no desirable economic or political positions from which there was any interest in excluding them. They were recognized – while Germans and Jews were not – as autochthonous; no one sought to encourage them to emigrate.

As territorially concentrated borderland minorities, linked to large populations of co-ethnics in neighboring states, the East Slavs did of course share certain features with the Germans. But the national question in Poland's eastern borderlands was more complex than it was in the west. In the west, Germans and Poles faced one another as mobilized and opposed nationalities. There were, to be sure, zones of mixed settlement and others of uncertain national identity. But the contending identities were clearly profiled and deeply rooted even well before the reestablishment of Polish statehood.

In the eastern borderlands, the contours of national identity were more indeterminate. Between the Poles and Russians lay a vast zone extending from the Baltic to the Black Sea where national movements had developed only in the last few prewar decades, and where incipient national identities, articulated and propagated by a small urban intelligentsia, had yet to acquire a substantial social base among the still overwhelmingly peasant populations.

The major exception to this eastern pattern was in eastern Galicia. Unlike the rest of this zone, which had belonged to the Russian Empire, Galicia had been a Habsburg province, with Poles predominating in its western, Ukrainians in its eastern half. There, for half a century before the First World War, conditions for cultural and even political nationalist mobilization were much more favorable than they were in the more authoritarian Romanov territories. Consequently, a strong Ukrainian nationalist movement developed, led, as everywhere, by an urban intelligentsia, but mobilizing the peasantry as well, and generating, by the outbreak of the First World War, a more deeply rooted sense of national identity.

The collapse of Romanov, Habsburg, and Hohenzollern empires in the First World War as well as the postwar turmoil associated with the

---

[44] Ewald Ammende, ed., *Die Nationalitäten in den Staaten Europas: Sammlung von Lageberichten* (Vienna: Wilhelm Braumüller, 1931), p. 57, reporting results of the 1921 census.

Russian Revolution and subsequent civil war left the political fate of these regions radically uncertain. These turbulent years witnessed a welter of competing political projects for the region, sponsored by Germans, Poles, Bolsheviks, and various native intelligentsias, supported or undermined by a succession of armies, and ranging from creation of new sovereign states through various federalist and confederalist schemes to proposals for outright incorporation by larger powers.[45]

In the immediate postwar years, there were two contending Polish visions of the eastern borderlands. One, associated with Piłsudski and the Left, favored an expansive federal Poland that would incorporate the extensive eastern territories of the historic Commonwealth, grant their incipient nationalities wide autonomy, and encourage them to develop their national individuality – all as a buffer against Russia, presently prostrate, but likely, on this view, to revive and constitute the main future threat to Poland. The second vision, associated with Dmowski and the rightist National Democrats, favored a more compact state (though still one extending well beyond ethnographically Polish territory) whose East Slav-inhabited territories (albeit less extensive than those envisioned by Piłsudski) would be incorporated into a unitary Polish state, and whose East Slav inhabitants would be expected to assimilate.[46]

It was the latter, nationalizing approach to the eastern borderlands that prevailed.[47] Piłsudski's federalist scheme came to naught, as Lithuania insisted on – and was able to sustain – full independence and as the Belarusian–Ukrainian borderlands, following the Polish–Soviet War of 1920, were partitioned, their western parts incorporated integrally into the Polish state. East Galicia too, which Polish troops had occupied in 1918–19, crushing the "West Ukrainian People's Republic" that had been proclaimed in November 1918 and driving out its army, was

---

[45] On the Ukrainian lands, see Geoff Eley, "Remapping the Nation: War, Revolutionary Upheaval, and State Formation in Eastern Europe, 1914–1923," in Howard Aster and Peter J. Potichnyi, eds., *Ukrainian–Jewish Relations in Historical Perspective*, 2nd edn (Edmonton: Canadian Institute of Ukrainian Studies, University of Alberta, 1990). On the mobilization of Ukrainian ethnic identity under conditions of war, revolution, and imperial collapse, see Mark von Hagen, "The Great War and the Mobilization of Ethnicity in the Russian Empire," manuscript (1995).

[46] On the historical background of these competing visions of the eastern lands of historic Poland, see Brock, "Polish Nationalism."

[47] More generally, the National Democrats established the basic parameters of interwar Poland's nationalizing policies and practices. Piłsudski himself, to be sure, returned to power in a 1926 coup and remained in power until his death in 1935. Yet although he made certain conciliatory gestures towards minorities, he did not depart from the nationalizing course set by the National Democrats. See for example Pawel Korzec, "The Minority Problem of Poland, 1918–1939," in S. Vilfan, ed., *Ethnic Groups and Language Rights* (Aldershot, UK and New York: Dartmouth Publishing Company and New York University Press, 1993), pp. 205, 210.

incorporated in unitary fashion into Poland, despite the autonomy that had been promised by the Polish legislature in order to win Allied approval for Polish claims to sovereignty there.[48]

While it was widely believed that Germans could not and Jews should not be assimilated, the assimilation of Belarusians and Ukrainians was seen as both possible and desirable, even as necessary. As leading National Democrat Stanisław Grabski put it, referring to the eastern borderlands, "the transformation of the state territory of the Republic into a Polish national territory is a necessary condition of maintaining our frontiers."[49] Outside eastern Galicia, where Ukrainian national consciousness was strong, the prospects for assimilation in the eastern borderlands were indeed relatively favorable. These areas were extremely underdeveloped economically and culturally. Under tsarist rule, they had lacked nearly completely the educational and cultural facilities that could support a public sphere through which national consciousness could develop and diffuse.[50] The nationalist intelligentsia was tiny and lacked any substantial constituency. The Belarusian and Ukrainian inhabitants were overwhelmingly rural; their concerns were overwhelmingly economic, not national. Their identities were seldom, and then only weakly, articulated in national terms. Some identified themselves simply as *tuteshni* ("from here"). Others – notably Catholic Belarusian speakers in the area around Wilno (Vilna, Vilnius) – already identified themselves as Poles.

Yet far from furthering the assimilation or even securing the loyalty of borderland East Slavs, Poland's inept nationalizing policies and practices in the interwar period had just the opposite effect, producing by the end of the period what had not existed at the beginning: a consolidated, strongly anti-Polish Belarusian and – to an even greater extent – Ukrainian national consciousness. This happened through heavy-handed efforts to nationalize the land, the schools, and the churches of the region, and through the harsh repression of Belarusian and Ukrainian nationalist and social-revolutionary movements.

Although it had assimilationist aims, the new state's land policy in the eastern borderlands employed differentialist, discriminatory means. Just

---

[48] Hans Roos, "Polen zwischen den Weltkriegen," in Markert, ed., *Polen,* pp. 22–30; Pawel Korzec, "The Ukrainian Problem in Interwar Poland," in Paul Smith, ed., *Ethnic Groups in International Relations.*

[49] Quoted in Jerzy Tomaszewski, "The National Question in Poland in the Twentieth Century," in Mikulas Teich and Roy Porter, eds., *The National Question in Europe in Historical Context* (Cambridge: Cambridge University Press, 1993) p. 229.

[50] Eley, "Remapping the Nation," pp. 211, 226–7.

as the nationalizing German Kaiserreich had sought to Germanize the lands of its predominantly Polish eastern borderlands by promoting ethnically German at the expense of ethnically Polish landowners – through state sponsorship of what was forthrightly called "colonization" and state control over land sales – so the nationalizing Polish state pursued similar policies *vis-à-vis* Belarusians and Ukrainians, settling soldiers and other Poles from western territories on estates in the eastern borderlands; indeed Poles were well aware of the parallels between the national struggles in the German–Polish and those of the Polish–East Slav borderlands.[51] Yet just as the German colonization program provoked sustained Polish opposition (and was in any event ineffective), so too the Polish colonization efforts, while only marginally affecting ethnic demography and land ownership, powerfully antagonized the local, land-starved Belarusian and Ukrainian peasants.[52] This antagonism was compounded by the failure of the Polish state to carry out a radical land reform; but such a reform was unthinkable, for it would have meant expropriating Polish landlords (who held the great majority of large estates in the eastern borderlands) for the benefit of non-Polish peasants – precisely the reverse of the situation that made radical land reform politically profitable (and a perfect instrument of nationalization) elsewhere in East Central Europe, where ethnically alien landlords could be expropriated for the benefit of "national" peasantries.[53] The embittered agrarian situation allowed Belarusian and Ukrainian agitators to interpret economic grievances in national terms, and thereby contributed to the "nationalization" of the East Slav populations – but in a sense opposite to that intended by the Poles.

In the spheres of education, culture, and religion, policies toward the two East Slav nationalities initially differed. Before the war, the Belarusian national movement had been directed against Russia and Russification, while the most vigorous part of the Ukrainian national movement (in Austrian eastern Galicia) had been directed against Poles (who were dominant in Galicia as a whole). At first (before the triumph of the unitarist, assimilationist National Democrats), the new state sought to take advantage of this anti-Russian orientation of Belarusian nationalism. It therefore not only tolerated but actively supported Belarusian school and cultural institutions, seeking to further the sense of Belarusian distinctiveness from Russia and thereby to secure the

[51] Brock, "Polish Nationalism," p. 344.
[52] Polonsky, *Politics in Independent Poland 1921–1939*, p. 140; Rothschild, *East Central Europe Between the Two World Wars*, pp. 42–3; Ammende, ed., *Die Nationalitäten in den Staaten Europas*, pp. 62–3, 134–5.
[53] Rothschild, *East Central Europe Between the Two World Wars*, pp. 12–13, 67.

loyalty of the Belarusian population. Within a few years, however, this support was withdrawn and assimilationist policies were adopted throughout the eastern borderlands. Belarusian and Ukrainian schools were replaced with nominally bilingual but in fact predominantly Polish ones, and the activities of Belarusian and Ukrainian cultural organizations were restricted in a variety of ways. The Ukrainian university that had been envisioned when Poland was seeking Allied approval of its claims to Galicia was not established, and the existing Ukrainian-language chairs at Lwów (Lviv) University were abolished. In the 1930s, attempts were made, sometimes with force, to convert Orthodox Ukrainians (i.e. those living outside Galicia, where Ukrainians were Uniate Catholics) to Roman or Uniate Catholicism, and numerous Belarusian and Ukrainian Orthodox churches were closed down, or pressed to use Polish liturgical texts.[54]

In terms of their own objectives, the exclusionary, dissimilationist nationalizing policies and practices of interwar Poland towards Germans and Jews can be said to have "succeeded," at least in part. By contrast, the assimilationist nationalizing stance towards Belarusians and Ukrainians failed conspicuously on its own terms. Far from being absorbed into the Polish nation, Belarusian and Ukrainian speakers in the Polish borderlands developed much stronger Belarusian and Ukrainian national identities during the interwar period. Worse still, from the Polish point of view, whatever feelings of loyalty they might have had, or developed, toward the Polish state were replaced by hostility. When Poland was partitioned in 1939 between Germany and the Soviet Union, few Belarusians or Ukrainians regretted the end of Polish rule, though worse, by far, was in store for them under Soviet rule, and though the attractiveness of the Belarusian and Ukrainian national "republics" within the Soviet Union – considerable in the 1920s, when Belarusification and Ukrainization were vigorously promoted – had long since been spoiled by news of the purges, collectivization, and famine of the 1930s.

This draining of loyalty from the borderland population, to be sure, cannot be blamed solely on Poland's nationalizing policies and practices. More important, probably, was the government's harshly repressive response to the strong social-revolutionary and radical nationalist movements that developed in the borderlands; for the repression touched not

---

[54] Nicholas P. Vakar, *Belorussia: The Making of a Nation* (Cambridge, Mass.: Harvard University Press, 1956), pp. 121ff., 128–32; *Encyclopedia of Ukraine*, ed. Volodymyr Kubijovyc, 5 vols. (Toronto: University of Toronto Press, 1984–93), vol. IV, pp. 81, 108, 248–50; vol. V, p. 633.

only the extremists, who openly espoused and practiced terror against Polish officials, but fell heavily on moderate nationalists and apolitical villagers as well.[55] But the state's nationalizing policies and practices were crucial in generating and aggravating the grievances that provided a fertile seedbed for borderland militancy.

Coda: nationalizing states in the new "New Europe"

Can the model of a nationalizing state sketched above, and illustrated with reference to interwar Poland, help us think about today's new nation-states, the incipient successor states to the Soviet Union, Yugoslavia, and Czechoslovakia? A sustained discussion of this question is beyond the scope of this chapter. But a few general observations can be offered.[56]

A caveat is required at the outset. I do not try here to draw lessons from the Polish case. As has been shown in detail, Polish nationalizing policies and practices were shaped by the specific (and internally varied) political, geopolitical, economic, and cultural contexts that framed the relations between Poles and minorities. To say anything specific about nationalizing policies and practices in the new states, and about how they might resemble or differ from those of interwar Poland, would require sustained attention to *their* formative contexts – contexts that differ sharply from those that shaped nationalizing stances in interwar Poland (and that vary considerably from one new state to the next). To address these varied contexts is impossible here. My concluding remarks are necessarily on a much more general level, and take as their point of departure not the detailed discussion of Poland but the general model of the nationalizing state presented toward the beginning of the chapter.

A nationalizing state, I have suggested, is one understood to be the state *of* and *for* a particular ethnocultural "core nation" whose language, culture, demographic position, economic welfare, and political hegemony must be protected and promoted by the state. The key elements here are (1) the sense of "ownership" of the state by a particular ethnocultural nation that is conceived as distinct from the citizenry or permanent resident population as a whole, and (2) the "remedial" or

[55] Vakar, *Belorussia*, pp. 125ff.; Roos, "Polen Zwischen den Weltkriegen," pp. 42, 51.
[56] For initial appraisals of nation-building in the Soviet successor states, see Ian Bremmer and Ray Taras, eds., *New States, New Politics: Building the Post Soviet-Nations* (Cambridge: Cambridge University Press, forthcoming 1996); Juan J. Linz and Alfred Stepan, *Problems of Democratic Transition and Consolidation: Southern Europe, South America, and Post-Communist Europe* (Baltimore and London: Johns Hopkins University Press, 1996), especially chapters 2, 19, and 20; and Paul Kolstoe, "Nation-Building in Eurasia," forthcoming in *Journal of Democracy* (1996).

"compensatory" project of using state power to promote the core nation's specific (and heretofore inadequately served) interests.

In the new states of Eastern Europe and the former Soviet Union, these key elements are clearly present. The new states (with the partial and ambiguous exceptions of Bosnia-Hercegovina, rump Yugoslavia, and the Russian Federation) are closely identified with particular ethnocultural nations. This is the legacy of their prior incarnation as the major ethnoterritorial units of nominally federal multinational states, in which they were already defined as the (nominally sovereign) states of and for the particular ethnocultural nations whose names they bore. The Soviet regime, as I argued in Chapter 2, deliberately constructed its constituent republics as national polities "belonging" to their respective eponymous nations, while at the same time severely limiting their powers of rule; the Yugoslav and (to a lesser extent) Czechoslovak regimes, following the Soviet model, did the same. Today, the institutionalized sense of ownership and ethnonational entitlement persists, but is now coupled with substantial powers of rule. Successor state elites can use these new powers to "nationalize" their states, to make them more fully the polities of and for their core nations.

In almost all of the new states, the ethnoculturally defined, state-"owning" core nation is sharply distinct from the citizenry as a whole;[57] and the core nation has been represented by its elites – or at least an important segment of its elites – as weakened and underdeveloped as a result of previous discrimination and repression. Even the dominant nations in the preceding multinational states, Russia and Serbia, have been represented in this light. To compensate for this, the new state is seen as having the right, indeed the responsibility, to protect and promote the cultural, economic, demographic, and political interests of the core nation.

Indisputably, then, the conceptual and ideological foundations for programs and policies of nationalization are in place. To be sure, alternative models of the state are available as well. There are three principal alternative models in circulation. First, there is the model of the

---

[57] Exceptions include the Czech Republic, Slovenia, and Armenia, where the over-whelming majority of the population belongs to the core nation; and Belarus and Ukraine, where the boundary between the respective core nations and Russians, who comprise the largest minority in both states, is blurred. In Estonia (and to a lesser extent in Latvia), the citizenry is relatively homogeneous, but the total population of the state is not; this discrepancy is the *product* of a politics of nationalization that, in the name of protecting the interests of the core nation, has so far excluded the bulk of the non-Estonian and non-Latvian population from citizenship. I have addressed the question of citizenship in "Citizenship Struggles in Soviet Successor States," *International Migration Review* 26 (1992).

"civic" state, the state of and for all of its citizens, irrespective of their ethnicity. Second, there is the model of binational or multinational states, understood to be the states of and for two or more ethnocultural core nations. Note that these alternative models differ sharply from one another: ethnicity or ethnic nationality has no public significance in the former, yet major public significance in the latter; the constituent units of the polity are individuals in the first case, ethnonational groups in the second. Finally, there is the hybrid model of minority rights: the state is understood as a national, but not a nationalizing, state; members of minority groups are guaranteed not only equal rights as citizens (and thus protected, in principle, against differentialist nationalizing practices) but also certain specific minority rights, notably in the domain of language and education (and are thus protected, in principle, against assimilation-ist nationalizing practices).

In my view, neither the civic nor the binational-multinational model has much chance of prevailing in the new states of Eastern Europe and the former Soviet Union. The civic model has considerable international legitimacy; as a result, civic principles have been incorporated into some constitutional texts and evoked in some public declarations (especially those directed towards international audiences). But these civic prin-ciples remain external. It is hard to imagine a civic self-understanding coming to prevail given the pervasively institutionalized understandings of nationality as fundamentally ethnocultural rather than political, as sharply distinct from citizenship, and as grounding claims to "owner-ship" of polities (which, after all, were expressly constructed as the polities of and for their eponymous ethnocultural nations). For the same reason, it is hard to imagine a binational or multinational understanding of the state coming to prevail. Ironically, the civic model – where ethnicity and nationality are not supposed to have any public significance – may have the best chances of working in the states that most closely approximate ethnically homogeneous nation-states, notably in the Czech Republic and Slovenia. The best chance for the binational or multi-national model would occur if two or more successor states were to merge into a wider federal or confederal state, defining the new unit as binational or multinational, but preserving their own "national" character internally.

The prospects of the minority rights model might seem better. It has even greater international legitimacy than the civic model, and inter-national organizations such as the Council of Europe, the European Union, and the Organization for (formerly Conference on) Security and Cooperation in Europe have pressed the new states to adopt and implement minority rights legislation. As a result, all new states are formally committed to nondiscrimination and to protecting minority rights. But this was true of the new states of interwar Europe as well, all of whom were subject to League of Nations Minorities Treaties that expressly required equal treatment, protected the use of minority languages, and obliged the state to provide minority-language primary education in regions with substantial minority populations. These treaties did little to hinder the dynamic of nationalization; formal guarantees of minority rights failed to impede substantive nationaliz-ation. It remains to be seen whether internationally sponsored minority rights regimes will be more successful today.

Almost all of the new states, in my view, will be nationalizing states to *some* degree and in *some* form. Already, various nationalizing policies, practices, and stances have been adopted in domains such as language policy, education, mass media programming, constitutional symbolism, national iconography, migration policy, public sector employment, and citizenship legislation; significant elements of nationalization can be found even in states that have presented themselves as models of interethnic harmony, notably Ukraine and Kazakhstan.[58] But this does not mean that the new states will be as consistently, or counter-productively, nationalizing as was interwar Poland. There is and will continue to be great variation between states – and within states (over time, among parties, across regions, between sectors of the government, and so on) – in the extent to which and the manner in which nationalizing agendas are articulated and implemented. Moreover, in all states nationalizing agendas must compete with other social, political, and economic agendas for attention, support, and commitment – not so much with agendas that repudiate nationalization as with those that bypass or ignore it and thereby make it seem less urgent, compelling, or relevant to the problems of the day. The question is therefore not *whether* the new states will be nationalizing, but *how* they will be nationalizing – and *how nationalizing* they will be.

[58] See Dominique Arel, "Language and Group Boundaries in the Two Ukraines," and Ian Bremmer, "Russians as Ethnic Minorities in Ukraine and Kazakhstan," both pre-sented at the conference on "National Minorities, Nationalizing States, and External National Homelands in the New Europe," Bellagio Study and Conference Center, Italy, August 1994; Anatoly Khazanov, *After the USSR* (Madison, Wis.: University of Wisconsin Press, 1995), chapter 5; and Robert Kaiser and Jeff Chinn, "Russian–Kazakh Relations in Kazakhstan," *Post-Soviet Geography* 36 (1995). Nationalizing stances have been weakest in Belarus, where, in a May 1995 referendum, large majorities favored increasing economic integration with Russia, making Russian a "state language" alongside Belarusian, and restoring Soviet state symbols; see Ustina Markus, "Lukashenko's Victory," in *Transition* 1, no. 14 (1995), 77–8.

5   Homeland nationalism in Weimar Germany and "Weimar Russia"

In interwar Europe, one of the most dangerous fault lines was that along which the domestic nationalisms of ethnically heterogeneous nationalizing states collided with the transborder nationalisms of neighboring "homeland" states, oriented to co-ethnics living as minorities in the nationalizing states. The clash between the nationalizing nationalism of interwar Poland and the homeland nationalisms of Germany and the Soviet Union,[1] between the nationalizing nationalism of Czechoslovakia and the homeland nationalisms of Germany and Hungary, between the nationalizing nationalism of Romania and the homeland nationalisms of Hungary and Bulgaria[2] – to name only a few – generated both chronic tensions and acute crises, tensions and crises that were

---

[1] Since large Belarusian and Ukrainian populations were included in the interwar Polish state, the Soviet Union – having established nominally sovereign Belarusian and Ukrainian Soviet Republics, granted them considerable cultural autonomy during the 1920s, and even encouraged them to embark on "nationalizing" programs – could represent itself (with a certain plausibility during the 1920s) as the external national homeland for co-nationals in the eastern borderlands of Poland.

[2] Like Germany, Hungary and Bulgaria lost substantial territories and large numbers of co-nationals in the post-World War I settlement. More than 3 million Hungarians were stranded as minorities mainly in Romania, Czechoslovakia, and Yugoslavia, while Bulgarian nationalists, identifying the much-disputed nationality of all Slav inhabitants of Macedonia as Bulgarian, claimed that the post-war settlement had left a third of all Bulgarians in other states. Concern to recover lost territory and redeem ethnic kin dominated Hungarian and Bulgarian politics in the interwar era and led both states into wartime alliance with Nazi Germany. On interwar Hungary, see C. A. Macartney, *Hungary and Her Successors: The Treaty of Trianon and its Consequences, 1919–1937* (London: Oxford University Press, 1937); and Joseph Rothschild, *East Central Europe Between the Two World Wars* (Seattle: University of Washington Press, 1974), chapter 4. On Bulgaria, see *ibid.*, chapter 7, esp. pp. 325–6; and Myron Weiner, "The Macedonian Syndrome: An Historical Model of International Relations and Political Development," *World Politics* 23, no. 1 (1970), esp. 671. On the nationalizing nationalism of interwar Romania, see Irina Livezeanu, *Cultural Politics in Greater Romania: Regionalism, Nation Building, and Ethnic Struggle, 1918–1930* (Ithaca, NY and London: Cornell University Press, 1995).

bound up with the background to and the outbreak of the Second World War.[3]

Analogous collisions along the same fault line threaten the stability and security of the region today. In some cases they have already led to war. As I argued in Chapter 3, the interplay between the nationalizing nationalism of Croatia and the homeland nationalism of Serbia (along with the minority nationalism of Croatia's borderland Serbs) led to the breakup of Yugoslavia. Similarly, the interplay between the nationalizing nationalism of Azerbaijan and the homeland nationalism of Armenia (initially sparked by the minority nationalism of Karabakh Armenians) led to the war over Nagorno-Karabakh. Many other collisions or potential collisions along this fault line, while they have yet to generate large-scale violence, remain potentially destabilizing. The nationalizing nationalisms of Romania and Slovakia have clashed with the homeland nationalism of Hungary.[4] The nationalizing nationalisms of Serbia and Macedonia confront the incipient homeland nationalism of Albania.[5] The nationalizing nationalism of Bulgaria faces the potential homeland nationalism of neighboring Turkey.

The most important – and potentially the most dangerous – clash along this fault line today is between the nationalizing nationalisms of Soviet successor states and the homeland nationalism of Russia. The nationalizing policies and politics of Estonia and Latvia, especially their restrictive citizenship policies toward their large Russian minorities, have met with harsh Russian condemnations of "apartheid" and "ethnic cleansing" and repeated assertions of Russia's right to protect Russians against allegedly massive human rights violations. Chronic tensions between Ukraine and Russia over Russian-dominated Crimea flared up in 1994 when the Crimean Russian leadership declared itself virtually

[3] On conflicting national claims in interwar East Central Europe, see the splendidly concise overview in Rothschild, *East Central Europe Between the Two World Wars*, pp. 3–14. On national tensions and the background to World War II, see A. J. P. Taylor, *The Origins of the Second World War* (New York: Atheneum, 1961), especially chapter 8 on the Sudeten crisis. For an account of the complex relation between Nazi Germany, Sudeten German organizations, and the Czechoslovak state in the making of the Sudeten crisis and the Munich agreement, see Ronald Smelser, *The Sudeten Problem, 1933–1938* (Folkestone, UK: Dawson, 1975).

[4] Nationalizing nationalisms may be found in established as well as new states. On the nationalizing practices of post-Ceauşescu Romania, see Vilmos Táncos, "Kettős hatalmi szerkezet a Székelyföldön" ("The Dual Structure of Power in the Szekler Lands"), manuscript (1994). On the background to contemporary Hungarian homeland nationalism, see László Neményi, "The Dynamics of Homeland Politics: The Hungarian Case," paper presented at conference on "National Minorities, Nationalizing States, and External National Homelands in the New Europe," Bellagio Study and Conference Center, Italy, August 1994.

[5] Serbia exemplifies both homeland and nationalizing nationalisms; see n. 12 below.

independent of central Ukrainian authority and sought closer ties to Russia.[6] Tensions between Kazakhstan and Russia, too, have increased over the hardening nationalizing policies applied by the Kazakh regime in the Russian-dominated north.[7] And a limited war broke out in trans-Dniestrian Moldova in summer 1992 between the initially strongly nationalizing Moldovan state and the secessionist, Russian- and Ukrainian-led "Dniester Republic," backed by the Russian 14th army, acting with the tacit acquiescence, if not the active direction, of Moscow.[8]

Having addressed nationalizing states in Chapter 4, I turn in this chapter to the transborder nationalisms of external national homelands. Homeland nationalisms, too, have been neglected – indeed to an even greater extent than nationalizing nationalisms – in the literature on nationalist politics. One symptom of this is that there is no generally accepted analytical vocabulary for discussing – or even for identifying – what I have called "homeland nationalism." Particular instances of this kind of nationalism have, of course, been studied. The most substantial literature concerns interwar Germany. Even that literature – comprising only a few specialized books and a handful of articles, almost exclusively in German – is minimal by comparison with the huge literature on other aspects of German nationalism. Written overwhelmingly by historians, moreover, that literature has been highly particularizing, oriented to the details of one particular situation, indeed in most cases to one or another aspect of the interwar German concern with ethnic Germans in neighboring states. Its key concepts – *Deutschtumspolitik*, *Volkstumspolitik*, *Deutschtumsarbeit*, *Deutschtumspflege*, all denoting an active concern with ethnic "Germandom"(*Deutschtum*) – have been tied specifically to that historical situation; it has been little concerned to develop wider theoretical or comparative perspectives.[9]

---

[6] It should be noted, however, that while Russian nationalists have asserted that Crimea belongs to Russia, and have contested the validity of its 1954 transfer from the RSFSR to the Ukrainian SSR, the Russian government has not, as of this writing, encouraged Crimean Russian separatism.

[7] Ian Bremmer, "Nazarbaev and the North: State-Building and Ethnic Relations in Kazakhstan," *Ethnic and Racial Studies* 17, no. 4 (1994).

[8] See Paul Kolstoe and Andrei Edemsky, "The Dniester Conflict: Between Irredentism and Separatism," *Europe-Asia Studies* 45, no. 6 (1993); Jeff Chinn and Steven D. Roper, "Ethnic Mobilization and Reactive Nationalism: The Case of Moldova," unpublished manuscript (1994).

[9] *Volkstum* theorist Max Hildebert Boehm's sketch of "co-nationalism" – that is nationalism directed towards ethnic co-nationals living in other states – is an exception; but Boehm's discussion, to my knowledge, has not been taken up elsewhere in the literature. See Max Hildebert Boehm, *Das eigenständige Volk* (Göttingen: Vandenhoeck and Ruprecht, 1932), pp. 177ff.

As for the generalizing literature on ethnicity and nationalism, while it has addressed irredentism and external intervention in ethnic conflict, it has not focused sustained analytical attention on external national homelands or homeland nationalism as such. Irredentism – a movement to incorporate *irredenta*, that is, lands or peoples represented as "unredeemed" because stranded under "alien" rule – is indeed an instance of homeland nationalism, but it represents an extreme limiting case, not the field of homeland politics as a whole. And the problematic of "external intervention" cuts across that of homeland politics. On the one hand, it casts a broader net, including intervention by any external power, whether an external national homeland, another state, or a transnational or international organization. On the other hand, "intervention" is usually conceived narrowly as armed or at least coercive intervention, while the multifarious actions constitutive of homeland politics involve the use or threat of force only as a limiting case.[10]

To address this undertheorized form of nationalism, this chapter, like its predecessor, adopts an historical approach. The major part of the chapter is devoted to the analysis of one particular – and particularly relevant – case of homeland nationalism: that of Weimar Germany. Weimar homeland nationalism invites our attention not only for its intrinsic interest, and not only because its themes and methods were appropriated by the Nazis, but also because of the striking similarities between Germany after the First World War and Russia after the collapse of the Soviet Union – similarities that have led some commentators to speak of "Weimar Russia."[11] Accordingly, the final section of the

[10] On irredentism, see Donald Horowitz, *Ethnic Groups in Conflict* (Berkeley: University of California Press, 1985), chapter 6, and Naomi Chazan, ed., *Irredentism and International Politics* (Boulder and London: Lynne Rienner and Adamantine Press, 1991). From the burgeoning literature on external intervention in ethnic conflict – and, more generally, on the international dimensions of ethnic conflict – see for example Weiner, "The Macedonian Syndrome"; Astri Suhrke and Lela Gardner Noble, eds., *Ethnic Conflict in International Relations* (New York: Praeger, 1977); Joseph Rothschild, *Ethnopolitics: A Conceptual Framework* (New York : Columbia University Press, 1981), chapter 6; Gabriel Sheffer, ed., *Modern Diasporas in International Politics* (London and Sydney: Croom Helm, 1986); Alexis Heraclides, "Secessionist Minorities and External Involvement," *International Organization* 44, no. 3 (1990); Paul Smith, ed., *Ethnic Groups in International Relations* (Aldershot, UK and New York: Dartmouth Publishing Company and New York University Press, 1991); Robert Cooper and Mats Berdal, "Outside Intervention in Ethnic Conflicts," in Michael Brown, ed., *Ethnic Conflict and International Security* (Princeton: Princeton University Press, 1993). In this literature, Paul Smith's brief discussion of the relation between ethnic groups and their "external motherlands" perhaps comes closest to articulating the specific phenomenon of homeland nationalism that I address in this chapter; see *Ethnic Groups in International Relations*, p. 8.

[11] In the US, Stephen Sestanovich was an early exponent of this concept. See for example Bill Keller, "Gorbachev's Grand Plan," *The New York Times*, December 5,

chapter addresses the emergent homeland nationalism of post-Soviet Russia, comparing it with that of Weimar Germany.

Nationalizing and homeland nationalisms

Nationalizing and homeland nationalisms are diametrically opposed and directly conflicting: nationalizing nationalisms (like that of interwar Poland) are directed "inward" by states toward their own territories and citizenries, while homeland nationalisms (like that of interwar Germany) are directed "outward" by neighboring states, across the boundaries of territory and citizenship, toward members of "their own" ethnic nationality, that is toward persons who "belong" (or can be claimed to belong) to the external national homeland by ethnonational affinity, although they reside in and are (ordinarily) citizens of other states. Since these latter states are ordinarily nationalizing states (or are at least so represented by the external homeland), homeland and nationalizing nationalisms typically collide head-on.

Nationalizing states and external national homelands advance competing jurisdictional claims over the same set of persons. These are persons who "belong," or can be represented as belonging, to both states – to the nationalizing state by citizenship, to the homeland by putative ethnocultural nationality. The nationalizing state, appealing to norms of territorial integrity and sovereignty, asserts that the status and welfare of its citizens, whatever their ethnocultural nationality, is a strictly internal matter over which it alone has legitimate jurisdiction. The external national homeland, rejecting this view, asserts that its rights and responsibilities *vis-à-vis* "its" (transborder) nation cut across the boundaries of territory and citizenship, that it has the right, even the obligation, to monitor, promote, and, if necessary, protect the interests of "its" ethnic co-nationals even when they live in other states and possess other citizenships. Precariously situated between these competing claims are the national minorities themselves – sharing citizenship but not (ethnocultural) nationality with the nationalizing state, and sharing nationality but not citizenship with the external national homeland.

Yet despite their directly opposed orientations, homeland and nationalizing nationalisms share one key similarity: both are oriented to a "nation" distinct from the citizenry of the state. In nationalizing states, this nation is smaller than the citizenry; for external national homelands,

1988. For a critical discussion of the Weimar analogy, see Jack Snyder, "Nationalism and the Crisis of the Post-Soviet State," *Survival* 35, no. 1 (1993), 6.

it is larger, extending beyond the citizenry – and beyond the territory of the state – to include citizens and residents of other states.[12] Both nationalizing and homeland nationalisms therefore reveal, although in differing ways, a deep tension inherent in the nation-state as a model of political organization – a tension between the "conceived order" or "imagined community" of the "nation"[13] and the territorially framed organizational reality of the state.

The dominant "Western" understandings of the nation-state, whether in their English, American, or French variants, provide no analytical purchase on this tension, for in these traditions (important differences among them notwithstanding) "nation" is seen as subsumed under, congruent with, and framed by the state. (Even in the American tradition, with its weak sense of stateness, "nation" is seen as congruent with if not as subsumed under the state.) Yet where "nation" is understood (in however imprecise a fashion) not as a coincident but as an *alternative* reference, cross-cutting rather than reinforcing the territorial and institutional frame of the state, the flattened, "Western" conception of the nation-state, collapsing nation and state into fully congruent categories, is inadequate. This is clearly the case in Central and Eastern Europe – the world region in which "nation" is most strongly established as a cognitive and evaluative frame independent of and incongruent with the frame of the territorial state.[14]

Weimar homeland nationalism

Origins

Although homeland nationalism in Germany emerged only in the last decades of the nineteenth century and crystallized as a significant

---

[12] Concretely, to be sure, nationalizing and homeland nationalisms may be found together in the same state. This happens when the "core nation" cuts across the state's citizenry such that a substantial fraction of the citizenry does not belong to the core nation, while a substantial fraction of the core nation are not citizens. Serbia is a nationalizing state *vis-à-vis* Albanians in Kosovo and an external national homeland *vis-à-vis* Serbs in Croatia and Bosnia-Hercegovina. Romania is a nationalizing state *vis-à-vis* Hungarians, a homeland *vis-à-vis* Romanians in Moldova. Russia today is a homeland for diaspora Russians, but also (potentially) a nationalizing state *vis-à-vis* non-Russian minorities in Russia. Interwar Germany was of course not only an external national homeland for transborder Germans, but a murderously nationalizing state *vis-à-vis* Jews.

[13] Benedict Anderson, *Imagined Communities: Reflections on the Origin and Spread of Nationalism*, 2nd edn (London: Verso, 1991); on the nation as conceived order, see M. Rainer Lepsius, "The Nation and Nationalism in Germany," *Social Research* 52 (1985).

[14] On cross-cutting conceptions of nationhood in the Soviet and post-Soviet contexts, see chapter 2, pp. 32–40, 45–6.

political force only after the First World War, the incongruence and
tension between the conceived order of the nation and the organizational
reality of the state – a central precondition for the emergence of homeland nationalism – has deep roots in German history.[15] Its matrix was
the distinctive economic, political, and cultural geography of Central
Europe. Two features of that geography are relevant here. First, western
Germany lay in the heart of Europe's "city belt," a legacy of the overland
trade routes of the middle ages, extending from Italy to the North Sea
and the Baltic. In this zone, dubbed "polycephalic" by Stein Rokkan and
Derek Urwin, the density of cities, ecclesiastical principalities, and other
small but autonomous political jurisdictions created obstacles to the
expansion and consolidation of centralized territorial states – obstacles
that were much weaker in the "monocephalic" zones to the west and east
of the city belt, where, in consequence, large centralized states emerged
much earlier.[16] The resultant long-standing fragmentation of political
authority meant that ethnolinguistic and political boundaries did not
even come close to coinciding in Central Europe. A second distinctive
feature of Central European cultural geography has been the broad zone
of ethnoculturally mixed settlement patterns extending eastward from
the area of consolidated German settlement – a legacy of the large-scale
eastward migration of German peasant settlers and colonists that
occurred in several great waves in the high middle ages and again in the
early modern era. Together with the fragmentation of political authority
in western Germany, these extensive mixed zones in its eastern borderlands prevented congruence between ethnolinguistic and political
boundaries.

   Until the second half of the eighteenth century, no cultural or political
significance was attached to the *Volkssprache* (the language of the *Volk*, or
of everyday life, as opposed to the *Staatssprache*, the language of public
affairs). As a result, the lack of even remote congruence between ethnolinguistic and political units had no particular importance.[17] This
changed in the late eighteenth century: the *Volkssprache* was celebrated –

---

[15] I have explored this tension in a different context in *Citizenship and Nationhood in
     France and Germany* (Cambridge, Mass.: Harvard University Press, 1992), Intro-
     duction and chapter 6.
[16] Stein Rokkan and Derek Urwin, *Economy, Territory, Identity: Politics of West European
     Peripheries* (London: Sage, 1983), pp. 7–12, 16–17, 35–9.
[17] This lack of correspondence between linguistically embedded culture and polity, of
     course, was characteristic not only of Germany, but of most of the world before the age
     of nationalism. Its utterly unproblematic quality has been emphasized most vigorously
     by Ernest Gellner in *Nations and Nationalism* (Ithaca: Cornell University Press, 1983).
     For a contrasting view, see Anthony Smith, *The Ethnic Origins of Nations* (Oxford: Basil
     Blackwell, 1986).

most powerfully by Herder – as a matrix of creativity and individuality, and a conception of nation as founded on language and linguistically embedded culture took root among the flourishing German *Bildungs-bürgertum*. From this time on, the imagined community of the ethno-cultural nation was available as a point of orientation, focus of value, source of identity, and locus of allegiance independent of – and potentially conflicting with – the state. Thus was realized one key precondition for homeland nationalism.

Through the end of the eighteenth century, this new ethnolinguistic or ethnocultural understanding of "nation" remained an apolitical, even antipolitical concept, while conceptions of statehood remained uninformed by the national idea. Around the turn of the nineteenth century, however, the two frames of reference – ethnocultural nation and territorial state – came to stand in a relation of dynamic tension to one another. The French Revolution and Napoleonic Wars – especially the crushing and ignominious defeat of Prussia by the French at Jena in 1806 – made a tremendous impression in Germany. That the state must seek to harness the energies of the nation, and the nation to embody itself in a state, became the conventional "progressive" wisdom. How this melding of nation and state might be accomplished was a central question of German political and intellectual life for the first two-thirds of the nineteenth century.

With the founding of the German Reich in 1870–1, representing the triumph of the Prussian-*kleindeutsch* over the Austrian-*grossdeutsch* project for a German nation-state, there was now, for the first time, a state claiming to embody the German nation. Yet the very "incomplete-ness" of this incarnation – the fact that millions of Germans, above all the eight million Austrian Germans, were excluded from the new state – created the possibility for homeland nationalism.[18] Thus in the very act of becoming a nation-state – the long-sought state of and for the ethno-cultural German nation, yet one that failed to incorporate substantial parts of that nation – the new German Reich became at the same time not only a cardinal point of cultural and political reference but also a potential external national homeland – patron, protector, and possible "redeemer" – for the excluded co-nationals.

In the first decade of the Reich, and through most of the second as well, homeland nationalism remained an unactivated potential. After the wars and territorial upheavals involved in the *Reichsgründung*, Bismarck's

---

[18] On the Bismarckian Reich as an "incomplete" (*unvollendet*) nation-state, see Werner Conze, "Nationsbildung durch Trennung," in Otto Pflanze, ed., *Innenpolitische Probleme des Bismarckreiches* (Munich: R. Oldenbourg, 1983).

chief foreign policy priority was to reestablish and maintain a stable European inter-state order so as to make possible the internal consolidation of the state; he repeatedly assured other European powers that the Reich was territorially "saturated." Consistently statist rather than nationalist in orientation, moreover, Bismarck repudiated any suggestion that the Reich had a special responsibility for or concern with ethnic Germans outside its frontiers. Nor was there any significant body of opinion or organized constituency advocating such homeland-nationalist claims during these decades.[19]

The position of Germans outside the Reich, however, was beginning to change. Long-privileged Baltic Germans were increasingly threatened, from the late 1880s on, by Russification, Hungarian Germans by Magyarization. More importantly, German dominance in the Austrian half of the Habsburg Empire was increasingly contested by the growing Slav majority, in particular by vigorous Czech, Polish, and Slovene national movements. In response to this challenge, a clamorous pan-German movement arose among Austrian Germans in the 1880s. Seeking to restore German hegemony in the core Austrian lands through their separation from the overwhelmingly Slav-inhabited outlying territories of Galicia and Dalmatia, the pan-Germans looked to the Reich for support and, covertly, for eventual incorporation of Austro-German lands.[20]

This increasingly beleaguered position of Germans outside the Reich evoked in response an organized movement of support within the Reich. In this way homeland nationalist claims first found organized expression in Germany. The pioneering organization in this respect was the German School Association, which sought to sustain German schools outside the Reich so as to "preserve Germans outside the Reich for Germandom."[21] While this association (renamed Association for Germandom Abroad in 1908) focused on cultural support for co-ethnics abroad, the more radical Pan-German League, founded in the early 1890s, advanced political demands as well, presenting itself as a "national opposition" and

[19] See Theodor Schieder, *Das Deutsche Kaiserreich von 1871 als Nationalstaat* (Cologne and Opladen: Westdeutscher Verlag, 1961), pp. 22ff., 42–3; Hans Rothfels, *Bismarck, der Osten und das Reich* (Stuttgart: W. Kohlhammer, 1960), Part I.

[20] Robert A. Kann, *The Multinational Empire: Nationalism and National Reform in the Habsburg Monarchy, 1848–1918* (New York: Columbia University Press, 1950), vol. I, pp. 97ff; Schieder, *Das Deutsche Kaiserreich als Nationalstaat*, p. 50. Not only pan-Germans but other Habsburg Germans, disappointed by the Monarchy's concessions to non-German nationalities, gradually began to reorient themselves to the Reich. For the case of the Sudeten Germans, see Rudolf Jaworski, *Vorposten oder Minderheit? Der sudetendeutsche Volkstumskampf in den Beziehungen zwischen der Weimarer Republik und der ČSR* (Stuttgart: Deutsche Verlags-Anstalt, 1977), pp. 34–5.

[21] Quoted in Otto Dann, *Nation und Nationalismus in Deutschland 1770–1990* (Munich: C. H. Beck, 1993), p. 191.

advocating the "national consolidation of the entire German *Volkstum* in Central Europe, that is, the eventual establishment of *Grossdeutsch-land*."[22] The League's president, Ernst Hasse, who was also a National Liberal deputy, often demanded in the Reichstag that the Reich actively intervene to support hard-pressed Germans outside the Reich.[23] This initial phase of homeland nationalism reached its peak of intensity in 1897, when violent Austro-German protests against an ordinance establishing Czech alongside German as an official administrative language in Bohemia and Moravia and requiring officials in those lands to know both languages induced a strong protest movement in the Reich as well.[24] In this moment of high enthusiasm for the Austro-German cause, a few influential diplomats and army figures even advocated the incorporation of Austro-German lands into the Reich.[25]

The new homeland nationalism, however, remained politically weak, and proved unable to influence Reich policy. On foreign policy grounds, Bismarck's successors continued to adhere to his strict noninterventionist stance *vis-à-vis Volksdeutsche* outside the Reich, and to exclude any consideration of a possible *Anschluss* of Austro-German lands. Moreover, demands for intervention on behalf of beleaguered *Volksgenossen* had no mass support and only fragmentary elite backing. This reflected not the weakness of nationalism in Imperial Germany but the extent to which nationalist sentiment was focused on and "contained" within the territorial and institutional frame of the Reich. "The nation," for nationalists, no longer necessarily meant the institutionally amorphous *Kulturnation* but rather the *Staatsnation* constituted by the *Reichsgründung* and strengthened in the succeeding decades by the powerfully integrative workings of state-wide institutions, economic dynamism, and geopolitical prestige. This "containment" was far from perfect; nationalism spilled over not only into concern for *Volksdeutsche* outside the Reich but also, and more significantly, into an imperialist *Weltpolitik*. On balance, however, the process of "concentration" of the concept of nation (and of "Deutschland") onto the territory and population of the Reich through the integrative workings of a dynamic, prestigious, "successful"

---

22 Quoted in *ibid.*, p. 192.
23 Schieder, *Das deutsche Kaiserreich als Nationalstaat*, p. 52.
24 A. J. P. Taylor, *The Habsburg Monarchy 1809–1918* (London: Hamish Hamilton, 1948), pp. 181ff.; Robert A. Kann, *A History of the Habsburg Empire, 1526–1918* (Berkeley and Los Angeles: University of California Press, 1974), p. 441. More generally, organizational ties between Reich Germans and Austro-Germans in transborder associations facilitated the development of a homeland-nationalist response in the Reich to the Austro-German predicament. See Dann, *Nation und Nationalismus in Deutschland*, p. 189.
25 Schieder, *Das deutsche Kaiserreich als Nationalstaat*, p. 44.

territorial state at a moment of high geopolitical competition among states did much to weaken support for the transborder appeals of homeland nationalists.[26]

The crystallization of homeland nationalism

This changed dramatically with the First World War and its aftermath. The fate of Germans outside the state – previously a peripheral concern of scattered intellectuals, with no mass support and no bearing on high politics – abruptly became a central preoccupation of nationally minded intellectuals, a focus of vigorous and broad-based associational activity, and an object of continuous and high-level state concern. Weimar Germany "crystallized," in a way that Wilhelmine Germany had not, as an external national homeland for its ethnic co-nationals in other states.[27]

This newly urgent transborder concern with "Germandom" – with what German authors have called *Deutschtumspolitik* or *Volkstumspolitik* – crystallized in response to the drastic and intertwined transformations experienced by the German state and by ethnic Germans living outside its borders in the aftermath of the war. The state suffered not only military defeat, political revolution, and loss of territory, but also – temporarily – loss of standing as a Great Power. The Weimar Republic's territorial boundaries were fixed by a treaty universally denounced, in Germany, as unjust, illegitimate, and humiliating; its constitutional order was under attack from the beginning by the revolutionary Left as well as by the radical Right. With the basic territorial and institutional parameters of statehood thus deeply contested and lacking firm legitimacy, the Weimar Republic proved unable to "embody" the nation or to "contain" nationalism, as the Kaiserreich had done, within the territorial and institutional frame of the state. Because the state had lost much of its binding, integrative power, nationalism was partially de-territorialized and de-institutionalized. Nationhood, which had become firmly, though never exclusively, identified with the prestigious and "successful" state in the Bismarckian and Wilhelmine eras, was now detached from the devalued frame of the defeated state, and

[26] *Ibid.* esp. pp. 40–3, 52, 168–9, n. 75; Jürgen Kocka, "Probleme der politischen Integration der Deutschen, 1867 bis 1945," in Otto Büsch and James Sheehan, eds., *Die Rolle der Nation in der deutschen Geschichte und Gegenwart* (Berlin: Colloquium Verlag, 1985).

[27] For an account of the multiple functional "crystallizations" of the state – each the center of its own "power network," each involving a different set of institutions, tasks, and constituencies – see Michael Mann, *The Sources of Social Power*, vol. II (Cambridge: Cambridge University Press, 1993), pp. 75ff.

again identified primarily with the state-transcending, institutionally amorphous ethnocultural nation or *Volk*.[28]

This *völkisch* reorientation of nationalism reflected not only the weakness and (in the eyes of many nationalists) illegitimacy of the Weimar Republic but also the dramatically embattled position in which ethnic Germans beyond German state frontiers found themselves after the war.[29] Germans outside the Reich – neglecting overseas emigrants, who did not figure centrally in *Volkstumspolitik* – had lived chiefly in the Austro-Hungarian and Russian Empires. Their position, to be sure, had been weakening in the last decades before the war; precisely this had occasioned the initial formulations of homeland-nationalist demands in Wilhelmine Germany. It changed much more drastically, however, with the collapse of the great multinational empires. This was particularly true for the millions of Austro-Germans who were abruptly transformed from the *Staatsvolk* of a Great Power into national minorities in nationalizing Czechoslovakia (roughly 3 million) and in equally nationalist Italy (a quarter of a million). Nearly 2 million Germans from the Hungarian half of the Habsburg Empire became national minorities in rump Hungary, Romania, Yugoslavia, and Czechoslovakia, as did the Baltic Germans in the new states of Estonia, Latvia, and Lithuania. An even sharper and (given German military successes on the Eastern front) entirely unexpected reversal in status was suffered by the million-plus Reich Germans in eastern and predominantly Polish districts of Prussia who suddenly and unexpectedly found themselves beyond the reach of German state authority in the incipient Polish state. All of these new (or newly reconfigured) states understood themselves as nation-states, as the states of and for particular ethnocultural nations; in all of them, Germans faced policies and practices of nationalization resembling in some respects those analyzed in Chapter 4.

It is not enough, however, to focus on the result of this transformation – on the status of ethnic Germans as new minorities in newly nationalizing states. What engaged the attention – and provoked the indignation – of Weimar nationalists were the processes and especially the struggles

---

[28] Martin Broszat, "Die völkische Ideologie und der Nationalsozialismus," *Deutsche Rundschau* 84, no. 1 (1958), 59–60.

[29] The war itself had radically transformed the position of dispersed ethnic German communities in the western parts of the Russian Empire, that is, in the Baltic provinces and Russian Poland. Their fate was connected with the wider German community both by German occupation of these territories and by the tendency of Russia – fighting not only Germany but "German" Austria-Hungary as well – to define Germans, not only Germany, as the enemy. See Werner Conze, *Die Deutsche Nation* (Göttingen: Vandenhoeck and Ruprecht, 1963), p. 104; Dann, *Nation und Nationalismus in Deutschland*, p. 218.

through which the transformation occurred. The reorganization of previously multinational political space along ostensibly national lines in Central and Eastern Europe was a protracted process that spanned several years.[30] It involved not only prolonged negotiations among the victorious Powers but also armed struggles to create "facts on the ground." In some cases the demarcation of boundaries was delayed pending plebiscites; campaigns leading up to these again involved bitter and sometimes violent struggles. While the defeated and disarmed German state was unable to play a major role in this protracted shaping of the postwar settlement, non-state German groups such as the Freikorps captured the imagination of nationalists with their armed struggles on behalf of beleaguered *Deutschtum* in the Baltics, in the mixed German–Polish districts of Poznania and Upper Silesia, and along the German–Slovene frontier in Carinthia.[31] These "heroic" struggles in the ethnic borderlands helped divert nationalists' attention from the "impotent" state to the vigorous, autonomous *Volk*.

Even where the postwar settlement did not transform Germans into minorities, as in the creation of the rump Austrian state, the process of political reconfiguration created fertile ground for homeland nationalism in Germany. As the Austrian half of the Habsburg Empire fractured along national lines in the final stages of the war, Austro-Germans set their sights on union with Germany. Before the war, such a union, although envisioned as an eventuality by some pan-Germans in Austria and Germany, was not a serious possibility: as noted above, Bismarck and his successors consistently repudiated any initiative tending in this direction, since it would have entailed the disintegration of a Great Power that was Germany's chief ally. But with the prewar state system destroyed and the disintegration of the Empire inevitable, these obstacles to *Anschluss* with Germany no longer existed. The principle of national self-determination, moreover, evoked by the Empire's secessionist nationalities and enshrined in President Wilson's Fourteen Points, seemed to provide a powerful warrant for *Anschluss*. On November 12, 1918, the Austrian Provisional National Assembly declared itself a Republic and part of the German Reich; this was endorsed by the

---

[30] Geoff Eley, "Remapping the Nation: War, Revolutionary Upheaval, and State Formation in Eastern Europe, 1914–1923," in Howard Aster and Peter J. Potichnyi, eds., *Ukrainian–Jewish Relations in Historical Perspective*, 2nd edn (Edmonton: Canadian Institute of Ukrainian Studies, University of Alberta, 1990).

[31] Broszat notes that new national legends that arose after the First World War concern not the core state but ethnic Germans in the borderlands and beyond ("Die völkische Ideologie und der Nationalsozialismus," 60). See also Max Hildebert Boehm, "Die Reorganisation der Deutschtumsarbeit nach dem ersten Weltkrieg," *Ostdeutsche Wissenschaft: Jahrbuch des ostdeutschen Kulturrates* 5 (1959), 12–13.

Weimar National Assembly.[32] Support for *Anschluss* in 1918–19 was nearly unanimous, across all party lines, in German Austria and Germany.[33] Yet at the insistence of France, unwilling to create a larger and more populous Germany, the victorious Powers prohibited the union. So while Austria became a German state, the Allies' refusal to allow union with Germany reinforced the conception – basic to homeland nationalism – of Germans as a state-transcending *Volk* to whom the right of national self-determination was denied at the same time that this right was trumpeted in principle as the basis of the postwar settlement.

One further factor nourishing Weimar homeland nationalism was the flow of ethnic German resettlers to Germany.[34] From the territories ceded to Poland after the war there was a mass migration of roughly two-thirds of the ethnic German population.[35] Predominantly urban, and well-schooled in ethnonational struggle from the decades-long efforts before the war to secure the ethnonationally mixed eastern districts of Prussia for "Germandom," these resettlers formed a ready-made constituency and reservoir of leadership for Weimar *Deutschtumspolitik*. The flow of German resettlers from the Baltic states, the Sudetenland, and other formerly Russian and Austro-Hungarian territories, although much smaller, also included many who became actively involved in the "Germandom" cause. Through this latter migration, ethnonational perspectives formed in the great multinational Romanov and Habsburg empires, often without any special reference to Germany, were transposed to and internalized within Germany itself.

Civil society homeland nationalism

Weimar *Deutschtumspolitik* was not confined to the state. It embraced all those, within and outside the state, who articulated, propagated, or tried to inculcate a concern with and sense of responsibility for *Deutschtum* as a whole, and for German minorities in other states in particular.

---

[32] Conze, *Die Deutsche Nation*, p. 109.

[33] Indeed it has been argued that German democrats were even more strongly committed to *Anschluss* than conservatives, partly because they hoped the inclusion of Austria would counter Prussian predominance in the Reich. See Stanley Suval, *The Anschluss Question in the Weimar Era* (Baltimore and London: Johns Hopkins University Press, 1974), pp. 23–4; Michael Laffan, "Weimar and Versailles: German Foreign Policy, 1919–1933," in Laffan, ed., *The Burden of German History 1919–45* (London: Methuen, 1988), p. 84.

[34] Dann, *Nation und Nationalismus in Deutschland*, p. 266; Broszat, "Die völkische Ideologie und der Nationalsozialismus," 61.

[35] Richard Blanke, *Orphans of Versailles: The Germans in Western Poland, 1918–1939* (Lexington: Kentucky University Press, 1993), chapter 2.

Deutschtumspolitik in this broad sense flourished in Weimar civil society. Although some associations and organizations concerned with ethnic Germans outside Germany had been established before the war, scores of new ones sprung up in its aftermath. Many of these, to be sure, were transitory groupings of little significance.[36] Still, Germandom-oriented associational activities did involve considerably wider circles of participants than their prewar analogues. The Association for Germandom Abroad, the only prewar association to retain a central place in Weimar *Volkstumspolitik*, did so by transforming itself into a mass organization with 2 million members and a strong base in the schools.[37] Another major Germandom organization, the German Protective League for Border and Foreign Germandom, united in a loose federation over a hundred Germandom-oriented associations, many émigré-based and focused on particular German minority communities, others based abroad in the minority communities themselves.[38] A third organization, the Organization of German Ethnonational Groups in Europe, linked German minority organizations throughout Europe, and was active primarily in international fora, mainly the League of Nations and the Congress of European Nationalities. Youth and church groups too were involved in Germandom-oriented activities. Trips were arranged for youth groups to familiarize them with ethnic German communities in other states.[39] Church-based associations – the Evangelical Gustav Adolf Association and the Reich Association of Catholic Germans Abroad – provided substantial material as well as moral support for German co-confessionals abroad.[40]

In the associational sphere, then, concern with Germandom across state frontiers was much more vibrant and broad-based than it had been before the war. Public interest in co-nationals abroad was both expressed in and reinforced by what Martin Broszat has described as a "flood of belletristic, polemical-political and half-scientific literature" concerned with Germandom abroad as well as an abundance of newsletters and periodicals on the subject.[41] At its more academic pole, this literature shaded over into *Ostforschung*, research on "the East," which received a

[36] Blanke, *Orphans of Versailles*, p. 151.
[37] Boehm, "Reorganisation," 19; Dann, *Nation und Nationalismus in Deutschland*, p. 267.
[38] Bastiaan Schot, *Nation oder Staat? Deutschland und der Minderheitenschutz* (Marburg/ Lahn: J. G. Herder-Institut, 1988), pp. 106ff.
[39] Conze, *Die Deutsche Nation*, p. 113; Jaworski, *Vorposten oder Minderheit?*, p. 73.
[40] Jaworski, *Vorposten oder Minderheit?*, pp. 71ff.; Karl-Heinz Grundmann, *Deutschtumspolitik zur Zeit der Weimarer Republik: Eine Studie am Beispiel der deutsch-baltischen Minderheit in Estland und Lettland* (Hanover-Döhren: Harro v. Hirschheydt, 1977), p. 124.
[41] Broszat, "Die völkische Ideologie und der Nationalsozialismus," 61

major impetus during and after the war, and much of which focused on the territories ceded to Poland and on other areas of ethnic German settlement in *Ostmitteleuropa*.[42] At its more reportorial pole, it shaded over into "ordinary" journalism, which also (especially the more nationalist oppositional papers) devoted considerable attention to the tribulations of Germans in other states.

The boundary between civil society and the state, in the domain of *Deutschtumspolitik*, was anything but sharp. In 1919–20, the government, prohibited from acting itself, worked through nominally private associations to check the Polish uprising in Poznania in early 1919 and to organize voters in the plebiscite districts in West and East Prussia in 1920.[43] Throughout the Weimar period, the government channeled money to the *Auslandsdeutsche* through ostensibly private but in fact state-controlled intermediary organizations; it also provided funding for the major Weimar Germandom-oriented associations, trying in return, with little success, to promote their coordination and consolidation.[44] Close connections between leading figures in the associations and state agencies concerned with *Auslandsdeutsche* further eroded the boundary.[45]

Yet despite the blurring of this boundary, Germandom-oriented activities in civil society constituted a distinct domain of *Deutschtumspolitik*. These activities created a dense web of relations linking leaders of the various minority German communities with one another and with Germans in the Reich and Austria. And they contributed to the formation of Weimar public opinion, sustaining public interest in and concern with the fate of minority Germans, and supporting the understanding of the German nation as a state-transcending ethnocultural unity.

Discourse and activities in this domain tended to be *Volk*- rather than state-oriented. To be sure, many – probably the overwhelming majority – of those involved in Weimar Germandom-oriented activities, like the Weimar citizenry as a whole, hoped for eventual border revisions that would bring Austria and key portions of territories ceded to Poland into the Reich. Some envisioned a more far-reaching territorial reorganization of Central Europe that would unite all contiguously settled Germans,

---

[42] Michael Burleigh, *Germany Turns Eastward: A Study of Ostforschung in the Third Reich* (Cambridge: Cambridge University Press, 1988); Grundmann, *Deutschtumspolitik*, pp. 125ff.

[43] Schot, *Nation oder Staat?*, pp. 87–8, 111.

[44] Blanke, *Orphans of Versailles*, pp. 150ff. In some instances, government subsidies for *Ostforschung* institutes clearly compromised the integrity of research; see Martin Broszat, *Zweihundert Jahre deutsche Polenpolitik* (Frankfurt: Suhrkamp, 1972), p. 231.

[45] Schot, *Nation oder Staat?*, pp. 93, 99, 109.

including the Sudeten Germans of Czechoslovakia, in a single state. Yet whatever their hopes for territorial revision, these did not directly govern their activities in the sphere of *Deutschtumspolitik*. Border revision was a distant dream, not a concrete goal toward which one could work with any hope of achieving it. From a *Volk*-oriented perspective, moreover, the urgent imperative was not to change state frontiers but to diminish their significance, to strengthen the *Volk* as a self-subsistent, autonomous entity,[46] and to strengthen public awareness of and interest in this state-transcending *Volk*. There were, to be sure, ambiguities and outright contradictions involved in this stance, in this concern to "organize the organic *Volk*," to deploy the financial means of the state to increase the autonomy of the *Volk*.[47] But an underlying *völkisch* orientation did distinguish the homeland nationalism of Weimar civil society from that of the Weimar state.

Official Weimar homeland nationalism

Before the First World War, as I indicated above, the German state had carefully refrained from making commitments to or claims on behalf of ethnic Germans outside the Reich, limiting itself to noncommittal expressions of sympathy for its ethnocultural kin. This changed sharply after the war. The state became continuously implicated in *Deutschtums-politik*.

The core of official *Deutschtumspolitik* involved covert financial support for Germans outside the Reich. Funding was channeled through inter-mediary organizations that were nominally private but in fact financed and controlled by the government; this arrangement permitted the government to avoid public debate and accountability in this domain and thereby to shield this support from the scrutiny both of the minority-harboring states and of the Allies.[48] Through these backdoor channels the Reich provided substantial support for German schools, newspapers, churches, charitable organizations, and social and cultural activities. It provided credit for beleaguered German farming and business interests and sought to help preserve German land ownership.[49] Using its funding

---

[46] The most sophisticated theoretical exposition of this aim can be found in Boehm's *Das eigenständige Volk*.

[47] Broszat, "Die völkische Ideologie und der Nationalsozialismus," 63.

[48] On the most important of these nominally private institutions, the *Deutsche Stiftung*, see especially Norbert Krekler, *Revisionsanspruch und geheime Ostpolitik der Weimarer Republik* (Stuttgart: Deutsche Verlags-Anstalt, 1973), pp. 16ff.; Schot, *Nation oder Staat?*, pp. 132–3.

[49] Krekler, *Revisionsanspruch*, pp. 65ff.

as leverage, moreover, the government sought – albeit with little success – to promote the consolidation of the numerous German organizations abroad and, failing that, to monitor, coordinate and control their activities (again in a discreet, behind-the-scenes manner). The Foreign Affairs Ministry in particular attempted this task of coordination and control, in order to prevent embarrassing incidents or activities (such as openly irredentist activities) that could interfere with Reich foreign policy, to resolve disputes among and promote the unity of minority German organizations, and to promote activities consistent with Reich foreign policy aims.

Rhetorical invocations of the plight of transborder Germans were often highly generalized, referring to *Grenz-* and *Auslandsdeutschtum* as a whole.[50] This generalized rhetoric, however, masked differentiated policies. This is best illustrated by the differing Weimar policies towards transborder Germans in Poland and Czechoslovakia.[51] The situation of Germans in these states – by any reckoning the two most important communities of Germans outside the Reich – was in certain respects quite similar. In both states, Germans were large and (for the most part) territorially concentrated communities.[52] In both states, Germans were borderland minorities, inhabiting regions contiguous to the Reich (and thereby of much greater and more immediate concern to the Reich than, say, the distant Russian Germans). In both states, finally, Germans had been unexpectedly and unwillingly transformed from the *Staatsvolk* of a Great Power into what they perceived as second-class citizens of third-class states.

---

[50] Interwar German public discussion made a standard distinction between the *Grenzdeutsche*, compactly settled in areas adjoining the Reich and part of the contiguously settled German population of Central Europe, and *Auslandsdeutsche* proper, who lived in German enclaves or were dispersed amidst non-German populations.

[51] See Rudolf Jaworski, "The German Minorities in Poland and Czechoslovakia in the Interwar Period," in Smith, ed., *Ethnic Groups in International Relations*; Wolfgang Jacobmeyer, "Die deutschen Minderheiten in Polen und in der Tschechoslowakei in den dreissiger Jahren," *Aus Politik und Zeitgeschichte*, 31 (1986); and Manfred Alexander, "Der Politik der Weimarer Republik gegenüber den deutschen Minderheiten in Ostmitteleuropa, 1918–1926," *Annali dell'Instituto Storico Italo-Germanico in Trento*, vol. IV (Bologna: Mulino, 1978).

[52] German concentration was, however, much greater in Czechoslovakia. Germans comprised nearly a quarter of the total population of the state, and were an absolute majority in 4,000 *Gemeinden* (Jacobmeyer, "Die deutschen Minderheiten," p. 21). In Poland, although there were local German majorities before World War I in some areas ceded after the war to Poland, the great wave of emigration from these regions left "not a single Landkreis or significant town in the area ceded to Poland which still had a German majority" (Richard Blanke, "The German Minority in Inter-war Poland and German Foreign Policy," *Journal of Contemporary History* 25 [1990], 93).

Yet there were also three key differences between Germans in Poland and in Czechoslovakia. First, the borderland Germans of Poland had been citizens of Germany until 1919; some retained their Reich citizenship even after the war. The Sudeten Germans of the Bohemian and Moravian borderlands, by contrast, had been citizens of Austro-Hungary, and had never in modern times been united with the Reich-Germans in a single state. Second, there was a mass exodus of Germans from the newly Polish territories to Germany immediately after the war, and continuing into the 1920s, while there was no comparable large-scale migration of Sudeten Germans to the Reich (or to Austria, for that matter).[53] Third, the Weimar regime had territorial claims against Poland – indeed revision of the Polish border was a fundamental axiom of Weimar foreign policy – but not against Czechoslovakia. These differences were interdependent: all reflected the fact that the borderland territories inhabited by Germans in Poland had long belonged to Germany, while those inhabited by Germans in Czechoslovakia had long been part of a separate state. The Reich and Germans in western Poland were united by longstanding political as well as ethnocultural ties, by ties of common statehood and common citizenship, not merely (as was the case for the relation between the Reich and the Germans of Czechoslovakia) by the ties of common language and culture.

Reflecting these basic differences, Weimar policies and practices concerning co-nationals in Poland and Czechoslovakia differed substantially. Outrage over the territorial settlement in the east, empathy for the large numbers of ethnic Germans – and Reich citizens – who had suddenly come under Polish rule, and apprehensions concerning their large-scale migration to Germany together meant that initial government attention was concentrated almost exclusively on Germans in Poland, specifically on those in the ceded territories. Indeed, far more attention and resources continued throughout the Weimar era to be focused on co-nationals in western Poland than on those elsewhere in the "new abroad."[54] Moreover, attention and resources were concentrated on an immediate and concrete aim in the Polish case: to stop or at least limit the reflux of Germans into the Reich and thereby to secure the continued existence of the German minority in the western borderlands of the new Polish state. To this end, the Reich limited payments of compensation for resettlers (since such payments only encouraged

---

[53] See Chapter 6 for a discussion of post-World War I migrations of ethnic unmixing involving Germans and other formerly dominant nationalities.
[54] Helmut Pieper, *Die Minderheitenfrage und das deutsche Reich 1919–1933/34* (Hamburg: Institut für Internationale Angelegenheiten der Universität Hamburg, 1974), p. 58; Jaworski, "German Minorities," 179.

further resettlement) and developed instead a system of "anticipatory compensation" or "preventive refugee assistance" for Germans still in Poland, involving cash payments to the unemployed, loans to German enterprises, and supplementary cash support for needy German pensioners.[55]

This immediate aim of stopping the influx into Germany, in turn, was inseparably linked to longer-term revisionist aims: as leading Foreign Ministry officials frankly acknowledged in internal documents, it was necessary to preserve a substantial German presence in the ceded territories in order to be able to make ethnodemographically plausible revisionist claims on those territories in the future.[56] Substantial Reich outlays for agricultural credits from 1924 on, intended to preserve German landownership in the ceded territories, were also seen as buttressing future revisionist claims. It would be one-sided, to be sure, to see Weimar support for Germans in Poland solely in terms of Germany's revisionist aspirations.[57] The ties of common citizenship, only recently and (from the German point of view) arbitrarily ruptured, could be seen to require such support, irrespective of possibilities for territorial revision, while limiting the reflux of minority Germans to the Reich was justified by economic as well as ethnopolitical considerations.[58] Moreover, the government discouraged openly irredentist activities by minority organizations; it aimed to preserve the possibility of revision in the long term, not directly to foster an irredentist stance on the part of the minority.[59] Finally, while revisionist hopes focused on parts of the ceded territories (on the "Corridor" that cut off East Prussia from the rest of German territory and on Upper Silesia, not on Poznania), aid was generally distributed to Germans throughout the ceded territories, indeed in many cases to Germans throughout Poland.[60] Yet even when these and other factors are taken into consideration, it remains indisputable that definite revisionist commitments substantially shaped Weimar *Deutschtumspolitik vis-à-vis* Poland.

The same cannot be said for Weimar *Deutschtumspolitik vis-à-vis* Czechoslovakia.[61] In organizational form, to be sure, support for Sudeten Germans looked very much like support for the Germans of

---

55 Krekler, *Revisionsanspruch*, pp. 48–59.
56 Broszat, *Zweihundert Jahre deutsche Polenpolitik*, p. 228.
57 On this point I follow Blanke, *Orphans of Versailles*, esp. pp. 159ff.
58 Blanke, *Orphans of Versailles*, p. 161; Krekler, *Revisionsanspruch*, p. 63.
59 See the 1922 Foreign Ministry circular that is quoted in Krekler, *Revisionsanspruch*, p. 44.
60 Blanke, *Orphans of Versailles*, p. 161.
61 Jaworski, "German Minorities," 179–80.

western Poland: money was channeled through intermediary organizations that were nominally private but in fact closely controlled by the
Reich government. In the cultural and caritative domain, moreover,
the pattern of support was similar, although funding was at a considerably lower level than in Poland. Schools were here too the top priority,
but newspapers, charitable organizations, cultural associations, and
various social and cultural programs and activities were also supported.
Weimar support for Sudeten Germans, however, lacked the urgency, the
immediate practical objectives, and the clear long-run strategic significance of support for the Germans of western Poland. There was no
threat – from harshly nationalizing policies or heavy outmigration – to the
very existence of the German minority in Czechoslovakia, nor was there
any commitment to incorporating Sudeten German lands in the Reich.[62]
The Weimar government encouraged Sudeten Germans to address their
grievances by working within the new state, as loyal Czechoslovak
citizens.[63] Although Sudeten Germans figured centrally in the unfolding
of the Munich crisis and in Hitler's dismemberment of the Czechoslovak
state, they did not – in marked contrast to the Germans of western
Poland – figure centrally in Weimar foreign policy. The Reich did not
object to the postwar incorporation of Sudeten German lands into
Czechoslovakia, but sought rather to establish good relations with the
new state from the outset.[64] And while the status of the Sudeten
Germans was an irritant in German–Czechoslovak relations, those
relations – again in marked contrast to the chronically hostile relations
between Germany and Poland – remained at least "correct" throughout
the Weimar era.

Yet the contrast between Weimar *Deutschtumspolitik* towards Poland
and towards Czechoslovakia, although substantial, should not be
overdrawn. Weimar support for the Sudeten Germans was not purely
cultural, not innocent of political design. Although it had no claims on
Czechoslovak territory, the Reich nonetheless refused to guarantee the
German–Czechoslovak frontier; it preferred to leave the Sudeten
German question – even its territorial aspect – formally open, so as to be

---

[62] It is true that the Reich refused to guarantee Czechoslovak as well as Polish borders,
and some have seen this as an indicator of latent revisionism *vis-à-vis* Czechoslovakia.
But certainly there were no focused, specific revisionist commitments *vis-à-vis*
Czechoslovakia, while such specific revisionist commitments *vis-à-vis* Poland are abundantly documented.

[63] Jaworski, "German Minorities," p. 180. See also F. Gregory Campbell, *Confrontation
in Central Europe: Weimar Germany and Czechoslovakia* (Chicago: University of Chicago
Press, 1975), p. 162.

[64] Peter Krüger, *Die Aussenpolitik der Republik von Weimar* (Darmstadt: Wissenschaftliche
Buchgesellschaft, 1985), pp. 57, 113; Jaworski, *Vorposten oder Minderheit?*, pp. 137–8.

able to extract maximum diplomatic leverage, in pursuit of other foreign policy aims, from its acknowledged status as external national homeland for the Sudeten Germans.[65] Covert government subsidies for radically nationalist Sudeten émigré associations in the Reich, whose radical demands could then be cited, in diplomatic discussions, as evidence of the pressure of public opinion on the government, also suggest the Weimar regime's interest in exploiting the Sudeten German issue as a diplomatic bargaining chip.[66] At the same time, the Reich hoped to work through the Sudeten Germans to influence Czechoslovak foreign policy in a manner favorable to Germany, above all to promote the inter-penetration of the Czechoslovak and German economies as part of a broader, if never precisely defined, aspiration for German economic hegemony in East Central Europe and the Balkans.[67]

In view of this substantial program of covert state support for co-nationals abroad, and the vigor of civil society homeland nationalism, it is surprising that public articulation of homeland nationalist themes by state and government officials remained rather muted and limited. At certain political conjunctures, to be sure, official homeland nationalist rhetoric did become more salient. Thus, for example, Gustav Stresemann, Weimar foreign minister from late 1923 through his death in 1929, used homeland nationalist idioms to counter the nationalist Right's vehement attacks on his *rapprochement* with the Western powers in the 1925 Locarno agreements and his proposal to join the League of Nations. *Rapprochement* with the West, Stresemann argued to his domestic nationalist opponents, would "open up new possibilities" for German revisionism in the East, while League membership would enable Germany more effectively to defend the League-guaranteed rights of its co-nationals,[68] the violation of which had been emphasized above all by the nationalist Right. By comparison with post-Soviet Russia, however, official public pronouncements on the obligation to aid co-ethnics in

[65] Jaworski, *Vorposten oder Minderheit?*, pp. 138–9.
[66] *Ibid.*, p. 141.
[67] See Stresemann's *Denkschrift* of 1925, reprinted in Schot, *Nation oder Staat?*, p. 215; Krüger, *Aussenpolitik*, p. 113; Campbell, *Confrontation*, pp. 77, 266–7; Jaworski, *Vorposten oder Minderheit?*, pp. 187–8; Wolfgang Michalka, "Deutsche Aussenpolitik 1920–1933," in Karl Dietrich Bracher, Manfred Funke, and Hans-Adolf Jacobsen, eds., *Die Weimarer Republik* (Düsseldorf: Droste, 1987), p. 318; Johann Wolfgang Brügel, *Tschechen und Deutsche 1918–1938* (Munich: Nymphenburger, 1967), pp. 221–2.
[68] Annelise Thimme, "Gustav Stresemann: Legende und Wirklichkeit," *Historische Zeitschrift* 181 (1956), 315–16; Carole Fink, "Stresemann's Minority Policies, 1924–29," *Journal of Contemporary History* 14 (1979), 405ff.; Fink, "Defender of Minorities: Germany in the League of Nations, 1926–1933," *Central European History* 4 (1972), 336ff.

other states were neither particularly frequent nor particularly salient in Weimar Germany (a point I return to, and seek to explain, in the final section of this chapter).

In an internal memorandum of 1925, Stresemann made the case for a more energetic and visible official public engagement on behalf of German minorities. After emphasizing the "extraordinarily endangered situation" of German minorities and the "inestimable political, cultural, and economic importance to the Reich" of preserving these communities and their German spirit [*Gesinnung*], Stresemann argued that this end could best be realized by working to influence world public opinion. "*Machtpolitisch*" means – for example, coercive diplomacy or military intervention – were foreclosed by the present European balance of power; and financial help – limited in any event – could help minorities exercise rights, but not compensate for their lack of rights. Thus the "only way open to the German Reich of truly helping its co-nationals [*Volksgenossen*] living under the sovereignty of a foreign state" was to "interest world opinion so strongly in the fate of oppressed German minorities that the majority peoples will be compelled through international pressure to grant them their vital [*lebendsnotwendige*] cultural freedoms" – above all the freedom to establish schools in which children study "not only in the German language, but in the German spirit [*Gesinnung*]." Stresemann conceded that League of Nations supervision of the legal rights granted minorities in the peace treaties had been very weak in practice, indeed "almost illusory." But more important than the working of the League provisions themselves was their importance as a "means of influencing world public opinion." Already, minorities' numerous complaints to the League of Nations had "made the minority problem a question of international interest . . . and a liberal [*grosszügig*] solution of this problem in Europe is seen as a precondition of any lasting peace." Germany should therefore seek to "further strengthen this existing trend of world public opinion." In particular, it should seek to "persuade world public opinion that . . . cultural autonomy is a natural right of every minority." This, after all, was simply "a particular case of the principle – already long recognized by the world in theory – of the self-determination of peoples, and the realization of this principle need not require changes in territorial borders . . . The wish to avoid further violent convulsions in Europe is today . . . so strong, that an idea that promises to reduce the explosiveness of the European situation is bound sooner or later to win over the opinion of the world."[69]

This grand vision remained conspicuously unrealized. Stresemann did

---

[69] Stresemann's *Denkschrift* is printed in full in Schot, *Nation oder Staat?*, pp. 286–92.

give minority protection a somewhat higher profile within the League of Nations; but he did not undertake the wide-ranging campaign envisaged in the 1925 memorandum, and a rather modest German proposal to reform League minority protection procedures was quietly buried. *Auslandsdeutsche* and Weimar nationalists, whose hopes for a forceful German *Minderheitenpolitik* had been aroused by Stresemann's earlier rhetoric, were disappointed.[70] There were several reasons for Stresemann's caution in pressing this agenda in the League. The granting of full cultural autonomy to minorities within Germany – conceived by Stresemann as a key precondition for this campaign – was blocked by Prussian opposition.[71] Moreover, considerable international skepticism regarding German sponsorship of minority protection – in particular the all-too-transparent connection between this sponsorship and Germany's revisionist aspirations – diminished the political attractiveness of such a campaign. Finally, Stresemann was reluctant to expend scarce political capital by pushing too aggressively in the League for minority protection at the expense of other, more immediately pressing foreign policy goals – above all a reduction in German reparations payments and the withdrawal of Allied occupation troops from the Rhineland – to which Stresemann was committed, and for which he required the support of the Western powers.[72]

---

[70] Martin Broszat, "Aussen- und innenpolitische Aspekte der Preussisch-Deutschen Minderheitenpolitik in der Ära Stresemann," in Kurt Klexen and Wolfgang Mommsen, eds., *Politische Ideologien und nationalstaatliche Ordnung* (Munich: R. Oldenbourg, 1968), p. 442; Fink, "Stresemann's Minority Policies," 408ff.; Fink, "Defender of Minorities," 339–40; for more detail, Carole Fink, "The Weimar Republic as the Defender of Minorities, 1919–1933," Ph.D. Dissertation, Yale University, 1968, *passim.*

[71] The best analysis of the interrelation between Germany's internal minority policy and its external concern for the rights of Germans abroad remains Broszat, "Aussen- und innenpolitische Aspekte." While the Foreign Ministry, from 1925 on, pushed for a generous Reich-wide policy of full cultural autonomy for minorities, the proposal foundered on the resistance of state governments – and particularly Prussia, where most minorities were located. In 1928, finally, limited concessions were made regarding minority schooling in Prussia, and Stresemann indeed pushed the minority agenda more vigorously after this time. But this fell far short of the initial demands for full cultural autonomy, which would enable Germany (while avoiding a simple politics of reciprocity and using instead the language of "natural rights") to demand similarly broad cultural autonomy for its own minorities in other states.

[72] Stresemann's one dramatically confrontational League intervention in the sphere of minority protection – a passionate, table-pounding reply to Polish Foreign Minister Zaleski, who had denounced the numerous petitions to the League by the *Deutscher Volksbund*, the major German minority organization in Upper Silesia, as "bordering on treason" – seems to have been a calculated gesture aimed at placating domestic nationalist critics, dismayed at his lack of energetic action on behalf of German minorities (Fink, "Stresemann's Minority Policies," 411; Blanke, *Orphans of Versailles,* pp. 132–3).

After Stresemann's death, Germany did adopt a more aggressive stance in the League in the sphere of *Minderheitenpolitik*, reflecting the generally more confrontational character of foreign policy in Weimar's last years.[73] But this did not occur in the manner foreseen by Stresemann in the 1925 memorandum. Rather than occupy the moral high ground as an advocate of universal minority rights, Germany became embroiled in acrimonious confrontations with Poland over the status of Germans in Poland, indeed precisely in those areas of Poland – the Corridor and Upper Silesia – that were the focus of German revisionist aspirations. Through this and other developments, Germany became increasingly isolated in, and disenchanted with, the League.[74] The League system of minority protection – which never functioned to the satisfaction of minorities, host states, or external national homelands in any event – was on the verge of breaking down. And it did break down soon thereafter: the would-be "defender of minorities" became their greatest persecutor with the Nazi seizure of power; Germany withdrew from the League in October 1933; and Poland renounced its Minority Treaty a year later.

The legacy of Weimar homeland nationalism

Weimar homeland nationalism was a complex – and far from coherent – web of political stances, cultural idioms, organizational networks, and transborder social relations.[75] As a *political* phenomenon, homeland nationalism involved a set of "moves" in both domestic and international political arenas. In the domestic arena, these moves were intertwined with party competition; in the interstate arena, they were bound up with – and generally subordinate to – Germany's efforts to recover sovereignty, revise the Treaty of Versailles, and reestablish its position as a Great Power and regional hegemon. Because of this intertwining, Weimar homeland nationalism cannot be understood solely in terms of its own "internal" logic, cannot be analyzed as an "autonomous" domain of politics. Homeland nationalist stances were often deployed instrumentally, in a more or less consciously calculated fashion, as a means to other ends. At the limit, this could involve a cynical exploitation of homeland nationalist rhetoric for purposes indifferent, indeed hostile, to the specific interests of transborder Germans. In general, however, the

---

[73] Fink, "Defender," 352ff.; Blanke, *Orphans of Versailles*, p. 135.

[74] Fink, "Defender," 354ff.

[75] Political, cultural, organizational, and social-relational aspects of Weimar homeland nationalism were, of course, closely intertwined. I distinguish them here not in order to suggest that these were sharply distinct spheres or forms of homeland nationalism, but rather in order to highlight the complex, multifaceted nature of that nationalism.

resonance and taken-for-granted legitimacy of homeland nationalist discourse in Weimar Germany meant that homeland nationalist stance-taking could be objectively strategic and at the same time subjectively "sincere."

As a *cultural* phenomenon, Weimar homeland nationalism involved the articulation, propagation, and appropriation of a set of idioms of identification with, and responsibility for, transborder Germans. These idioms represented transborder Germans as full members of the German national community, of the German *Volk*. In this discourse, "nation" and "*Volk*" were detached from the frame of the state and implicitly or explicitly redefined in ethnocultural terms. In its more elaborate forms, this expansive outward redefinition of the nation to include transborder Germans was one key component of the broader *völkisch* movement that flourished in Weimar Germany. (The other – more familiar and more fateful – component of *völkisch* thought and discourse was of course the restrictive inward redefinition of the nation to exclude Jews.)[76] This discourse of identification with and responsibility for co-nationals abroad was articulated and propagated by journalists, publicists, scholars in *Ostforschung* institutes, émigrés from transborder German communities, and activists in Germandom-oriented associations and organizations – categories that were often closely overlapping. It was appropriated and used by politicians and state officials as well, but generally in fragmentary fashion and without the anti-statist implications of consistently *Volk*-oriented discourse.

As an *organizational* phenomenon, Weimar homeland nationalism involved a network of state agencies, formally private but more or less state-controlled organizations, and voluntary associations.[77] This network provided a rich variety of organized sites for the development and promotion of interest in, expertise about, and activity on behalf of ethnic Germans beyond the frontiers of the Reich. The leading personnel in these organizations and associations were well connected with one another, partly through overlapping memberships and interlocking directorates, partly through joint participation in a variety of meetings touching on the affairs of *Auslandsdeutsche*. Together, they constituted an organized "public," a structured, differentiated space of communication, discussion, and debate.

---

[76] On the duality of *völkisch* thought, see Broszat, "Die völkische Ideologie und der Nationalsozialismus."

[77] For the official and semi-official organizations, the best sources are Krekler, *Revisionsanspruch*, and Schot, *Nation oder Staat?* For voluntary associations, see especially Jaworski, *Vorposten oder Minderheit?*.

As a *social-relational* phenomenon, finally, Weimar homeland nationalism involved the organized cultivation and maintenance of a dense
network of cross-border relations and the organized provision of a steady
cross-border flow of resources. These relations and resource flows
– funded, for the most part, by a few state agencies but organized in
decentralized fashion through the network of organizations and associations described above – not only linked *Auslandsdeutsche* to Weimar
Germany but, perhaps more importantly, contributed to detaching them
from the states in which they lived. This restructuring of social networks
and relations was most important in the case of the Sudeten Germans.
The networks and relations of Germans in the western borderlands of
Poland had long been framed by the Prussian and German states; in their
case, Weimar homeland nationalism aimed at sustaining or reconstituting social relations that had been disrupted by the change in borders,
not at reorienting those relations in a new direction. The networks and
relations of Sudeten Germans, by contrast, had been framed by the
Habsburg state but were substantially restructured after its collapse. In
part, of course, this involved the reframing of networks and relations by
the new – and administratively comparatively strong – Czechoslovak
state; but it involved at the same time – and in tension with this statist
reframing – a reorientation of external ties (ties outside Bohemia and
Moravia) away from German Austria and toward the German Reich,
reflecting the fact that it was unambiguously Weimar Germany, not the
rump Austrian state, that had assumed the multifaceted role of external
national homeland for Sudeten Germans. The strengthening of Sudeten
German ties with Germany, in turn, encouraged the Sudeten German
elite to look to Germany for solutions to their problems rather than seek
a durable *modus vivendi* within the Czechoslovak state.[78]

The vicissitudes of homeland nationalism after the Nazi seizure of
power lie beyond the scope of this chapter. It is worth noting in passing,
however, that the Nazis appropriated the political, cultural, organizational, and social-relational legacy of Weimar homeland nationalism:

[78] Jaworski, "Die Sudetendeutsche als Minderheit," 35. For a richly detailed account of
this reorientation of social relations, see Jaworski, *Vorposten oder Minderheit?*, pp. 70ff.
Throughout the Weimar period, there was a struggle among Sudeten Germans
between "activists," who favored working within the Czechoslovak state, and who
participated in coalition governments from 1926 through 1938, and "negativists," who
rejected all political engagement in the new state. As Jaworski has shown, however, the
activists were in a weak position, partly because of the strong elite disposition to look
for support to Weimar Germany. Strikingly, even the activist political leaders sought
approval from high officials in Berlin for their decision to enter the Czechoslovak
coalition government (Jaworski, *Vorposten oder Minderheit?*, esp. pp. 179ff.; Campbell,
Confrontation in Central Europe, p. 168).

the calculated deployment of homeland nationalist stances in domestic and international arenas; the *völkisch* idioms of identification with and responsibility for transborder Germans; the network of official, semi-official, and unofficial agencies, organizations, and associations concerned with co-nationals abroad; and the web of cross-border ties and resource flows. In this sense, one can speak of continuity between Weimar and Nazi homeland nationalism.[79] And there was in fact no abrupt break in the early years of the new regime. Indeed, homeland nationalist themes at first receded from public view as the regime focused on internal consolidation, pursued an initially cautious line in foreign policy, and discouraged the press from focusing on the problems of the German minority in Poland in the wake of the German–Polish Non-Aggression Pact of 1934.[80]

Yet the Weimar legacy was radically transformed in the context of the aggressive Nazi foreign policy of the late 1930s (and again in the context of imperialist war and German occupation in the East). The cautious diplomatic use of homeland nationalist themes in Weimar gave way to the blustering fulminations of Hitler in the months preceding the Munich agreement. The *völkisch* discourse of identification with and responsibility for transborder Germans was redefined by the Nazi commitment to establishing a *grossdeutsches Reich* incorporating, minimally, the entire area of consolidated German settlement. The sprawling network of Weimar Germandom-oriented associations was subordinated to the state and party apparatus, and the "traditionalist" homeland nationalist leaders, committed to the integrity and autonomy of German minority communities, were displaced by others who did not scruple to subordinate transborder minorities to the imperatives of Reich foreign policy.[81] The web of cross-border ties, finally, permitted Hitler to use the Sudeten Germans, in 1938, as a fifth column in his plan to destroy the Czechoslovak state.[82]

[79] On the theme of continuity, see Jaworski, *Vorposten oder Minderheit?*, p. 166.

[80] On the German–Polish Non-Aggression Pact and its consequences for the German minority in Poland, see Blanke, *Orphans of Versailles*, pp. 183–206.

[81] Hans-Adolf Jacobsen, *Nationalsozialistische Aussenpolitik 1933–1938* (Frankfurt am Main and Berlin: Alfred Metzner, 1968), pp. 160ff. On "traditionalist" Germandom leaders, see Smelser, *The Sudeten Problem*, pp. 14ff., esp. pp. 17–18. The struggle between traditionalists and radical statists is a major theme of Smelser's book.

[82] For a sophisticated account of the process through which Sudeten Germans, under the leadership of Konrad Henlein's *Sudetendeutsche Heimatfront*, became available as a compliant tool of Hitler's foreign policy, an account emphasizing struggles among Sudeten German factions and among different homeland-nationalist organizations in the Reich, see Smelser, *The Sudeten Problem*. Smelser's account begins in 1933; for the background in Weimar, emphasizing the economic, political, and psychological dependence of Sudeten German elites on Germany, see Jaworski, *Vorposten oder Minderheit?*

Weimar Germany and post-Soviet Russia: homeland nationalisms compared

Like Weimar Germany, post-Soviet Russia offers fertile soil for home-land nationalism. Just as the collapse of the Wilhelmine, Habsburg, and Romanov empires stranded millions of Germans, so the disintegration of the Soviet Union stranded millions of Russians – indeed a far larger number, some 25 million in all[83] – as minorities in an array of successor states. Like the German minorities, the new Russian minorities have been portrayed as threatened by the nationalizing policies and practices of the successor states. Like their interwar counterparts, these states were established as the states of and for particular ethnocultural nations, and have been committed, in varying ways and varying degrees, to diminishing the accumulated economic advantage, cultural influence, and political power the minorities had enjoyed as members of the formerly dominant nations, and to promoting instead the specific interests of the state-"owning" nations. Like Weimar Germany, post-Soviet Russia has suffered a "humiliating" loss not only of territory but of its status as a Great Power, creating an opening for political entrepreneurs with a variety of remedial, compensatory, or restorationist political agendas. As in Weimar Germany, so in post-Soviet Russia bitter stories about separation from beleaguered or endangered ethnic kin have been central to public narratives of humiliation and loss, while commitments to protect those kin have been central to remedial, compensatory, and restorationist projects.

There are many further parallels between Weimar Germany and post-Soviet Russia that bear at least indirectly on homeland nationalism, including deep economic crisis, new and fragile democratic regimes, and geopolitical and economic preponderance *vis-à-vis* the respective "new" and "near" abroads in which their minorities were concentrated.[84] But rather than pursue these similarities, I want to explore in this final section three differences in the forms – and formative contexts – of homeland

---

[83] How many "Russians" were stranded as minorities in Soviet successor states depends, of course, on how "Russian" is defined. The standard figure of 25 million reflects the number of persons living in Soviet republics other than Russia identifying their "nationality" as Russian at the time of the last Soviet census in 1989. Below, I discuss ambiguities in the definition of the "target" of Russian homeland politics.

[84] The expression "new abroad" in interwar Germany, like "near abroad" in post-Soviet Russia, suggested a sphere of influence, a zone that was not quite fully "foreign." Similarly, the prevailing interwar distinction between *Grenzdeutsche* or *Grenzland-deutsche* (borderland Germans) and *Auslandsdeutsche* (foreign Germans) implied that the former, compactly settled in areas adjoining the Reich, were not truly foreign despite being residents and citizens of other states.

nationalism in the two settings. The first concerns the greater visibility of official Russian homeland nationalism, the second the weakness of civil society homeland nationalism in Russia, and the third the ambiguity of the population targeted by Russian homeland nationalism. This is necessarily a limited and highly selective discussion; a full analysis of Russian homeland nationalism would require, minimally, a chapter of its own.

Official Weimar homeland nationalism transpired primarily behind the scenes. Our knowledge of its aims and modalities comes mainly from administrative archives, not from the records of public speech. The homeland nationalism of Weimar civil society – the discourse and activities of Germandom associations, *Ostforschung* institutes, the press and publicistic sphere – was public and visible, but that of the state was largely covert. State and government officials did invoke the obligation of Germany to help ethnic Germans in other states, but such pronouncements were comparatively infrequent, and the theme was not particularly salient in official discourse. Stresemann had envisioned a major public campaign on this issue, using the League of Nations as a platform, but it never occurred. Once Germany joined the League, it proved surprisingly reticent on the issue.

Russia, by contrast, has been anything but reticent; its official homeland nationalism has been conspicuously visible.[85] Public pronouncements on the right, and the obligation, to protect Russians in the near abroad have become a staple of official Russian discourse, figuring prominently in almost all accounts of Russian foreign policy priorities. High state and government officials – up to and including President Yeltsin and Foreign Minister Kozyrev – have issued a steady stream of pronouncements on the issue. These have varied in tone and substance with the audience to which they have been addressed and the domestic and international contexts in which they have been formulated, and it would be a mistake to read too much significance into any particular pronouncement. In general, however, a hardening of position and toughening of rhetoric on transborder Russians can be observed, mirroring the emergence of a generally tougher Russian stance *vis-à-vis* the near abroad, and reflecting the intensifying political challenge from the nationalist Right.[86] Illustrative of this shift was Kozyrev's widely

---

85 I do not mean to suggest that there is not also a crucial covert dimension to Russian homeland nationalism. No doubt there is. My intention here is simply to highlight the public and visible dimension of official Russian homeland nationalism – a dimension largely lacking from official Weimar homeland nationalism.

86 A useful review of the evolution of official Russian policy *vis-à-vis* Russians in the successor states is given by Paul Kolstoe, *Russians in the Former Soviet Republics* (London: Hurst, 1995), chapter 10.

reported assertion in April 1995 that armed force might be needed in certain cases to protect the rights of compatriots.[87]

This demonstrative stance-taking by officials has been complemented by an official codification of the "fundamental guidelines" of Russian policy vis-à-vis "compatriots" in the near abroad.[88] Drafted on presidential initiative, and formally approved by the government on August 31, 1994, this document is worth dwelling on for a moment. Compared with other pronouncements of state and government officials on the issue, the document is quite moderate in tone and substance, repeatedly stressing conformity with international law and norms and commitment to realizing its aims through bilateral agreements with the successor states. Yet it forthrightly outlines a series of thirty-nine governmental measures in support of compatriots abroad, grouping them under four headings as "political-legal and informational," "diplomatic," "economic," and "social and cultural."

"Political-legal and informational" measures include establishing Russian-language radio and television programming in the near abroad and ensuring its unimpeded functioning; working together with the Russian (russkii) and Slavic communities in the successor states, and providing information enabling the Russian Federation media to "report objectively" on the near abroad, "paying special attention to the situation of compatriots and the protection of their rights." Diplomatic measures include raising the issue of the rights of compatriots in international fora, especially the United Nations and the Organization (formerly Conference) for Security and Cooperation in Europe; concluding agreements on citizenship (read: dual citizenship) with the countries of the near abroad; and working through Russian and world public opinion to pressure near abroad governments to modify their domestic legislation. Economic measures include cultivating ties between enterprises in Russia and enterprises employing compatriots in the near abroad; directly purchasing such enterprises (partly in exchange for cancellation of debts owed to Russia); establishing cross-border joint enterprises specifically aimed at aiding compatriots; and threatening a variety of economic sanctions including the curtailment of trade and a change in

---

[87] *Nezavisimaia gazeta*, April 19, 1995; *Rossiiskie vesti*, April 19, 1995; *Izvestiia*, April 20, 1995.
[88] Osnovnye napravleniia gosudarstvennoi politiki Rossiiskoi Federatsii v otnoshenii sootechestvennikov, prozhivaiushchikh za rubezhom (Utverzhdeny postanovleniem Pravitel'stva Rossiiskoi Federatsii ot 31 Avgusta 1994, No. 1064) [Fundamental Guidelines of the State Policy of the Russian Federation Concerning Compatriots Living Abroad (Ratified by Resolution of the Government of the Russian Federation of August 31, 1994, No. 1064)].

the customs regime in the case of "gross violations of the rights of compatriots." Social and cultural measures, finally, include providing "technical, informational, and financial help" to the Russian-language press in the near abroad; supporting a variety of Russian (*russkii*) cultural institutions and activities; founding Russian (*rossiiskii*) universities, institutes, faculties, and gymnasia in the near abroad; admitting compatriots to secondary and higher educational institutions in Russia; and providing textbooks and training teachers for Russian-language education in the near abroad.

Although the Weimar government in fact adopted a number of similar measures, it did not and – given the then prevailing strength of norms of nonintervention – could not admit to maintaining direct contacts with transborder ethnic Germans, funding their organizations, supporting (and thereby controlling) their economic life, or supporting the German-language press and German-language educational institutions in its "new abroad." The Russian government's forthright acknowledgment of these measures, together with the salience and frequency of official pronouncements on this issue, reflects two key differences in the international context of homeland nationalism between the interwar period and the present. The first difference is normative and institutional. The principle of territorial sovereignty was far more robust in the interwar period than it is today. The League of Nations Minority Treaties imposed certain obligations on the post-World War I successor states; but these were bitterly resented and denounced as unacceptable intrusions in internal affairs, less because of their content (the provisions of the Minority Treaties were actually rather weak) than because of the then unacceptable symbolism of violated sovereignty.[89] This sort of denunciatory language, to be sure, still circulates today, but it has an antiquated flavor. By comparison with the interwar period, the exclusive claims of the nation-state to internal sovereignty have weakened through the growth of a complex web of cross-border jurisdictions in various policy domains, while transborder concern about the rights of minorities – like transborder concern for human rights – has acquired new levels of institutionalized international legitimacy.[90]

[89] Contributing to the resentment was the fact that the minority protection obligations were not universal, but were imposed only on the new (or newly enlarged) states.

[90] On international institutionalized legitimacy in the context of an emergent "world polity," see John W. Meyer, "The World Polity and the Authority of the Nation-State," in George M. Thomas, John W. Meyer, Francisco O. Ramirez, and John Boli, *Institutional Structure: Constituting State, Society, and the Individual* (Newbury Park, Calif.: Sage, 1987). On the institutionalized international legitimacy of human rights discourse, see Yasemin Soysal, *Limits of Citizenship: Migrants and Postnational Membership in Europe* (Chicago: University of Chicago Press, 1994).

The second salient difference is geopolitical. Russian military, political, and economic preponderance *vis-à-vis* the Soviet successor states is much greater than that of Weimar Germany *vis-à-vis* East Central Europe. This certainly holds for the initial decade of Weimar, and one could argue that it holds even for the first few years of the Nazi regime. A convincing argument has been made, to be sure, that Germany's long-term geopolitical position in Europe had actually improved as a result of the territorial settlement following World War I,[91] while no one would make a parallel claim about post-Soviet Russia. In the short and medium term, however, Weimar Germany was in a much weaker position *vis-à-vis* its "new abroad" than is post-Soviet Russia today. Defeated and disarmed, it was (temporarily) militarily weaker even than Poland and Czechoslovakia; its freedom of action in foreign policy – even with respect to its structurally weak eastern neighbors – was reduced to a minimum. Russia, by contrast, enjoys vastly greater freedom of action, and far greater power, *vis-à-vis* its near abroad. This unambiguous and unchallenged regional geopolitical and economic preponderance enables Russia to adopt an assertive stance on Russian minorities abroad, while at the same time the normative erosion of strong claims to sovereignty and the new international legitimacy of transborder concerns with minorities enable it to frame its tough talk in the idioms of human and minority rights.

This suggests a further contextual difference between Weimar and contemporary Russian homeland nationalism. Weimar foreign policy was consistently focused on revising the Treaty of Versailles; and this revisionism always included a commitment to eventual, albeit (at least under Stresemann) peaceful changes in territorial borders. Russia, on the other hand, although – or perhaps precisely because – it is overwhelmingly dominant geopolitically, is not necessarily committed to territorial revision. The present borders of the Russian Federation are universally seen as arbitrary, as lacking any historical sanction or normative dignity; yet they are not universally regarded as in urgent need of revision. Territorial revision is indeed pushed by certain political entrepreneurs, who claim to find intolerable the existence of Ukraine or Belarus as a separate state or the fact that 6 million Russians live under

[91] The core of the argument is that the new states of East Central Europe, lacking substantial protection from the Western powers, and likely to be forced eventually (given the inevitably growing strength of Germany and the Soviet Union) to choose between Berlin and Moscow, were (given their fundamental anti-Soviet disposition) structurally inclined to align themselves with Germany. See Andreas Hillgruber, "'Revisionismus' – Kontinuität und Wandel in der Aussenpolitik der Weimarer Republik," *Historische Zeitschrift* 237 (1983), 600ff.

Kazakh rule. But it lacks the axiomatic, fundamental, unquestioned status it possessed in Weimar Germany.[92] There is a rough elite consensus on the need to restore Russia's status as a world or at least continental Power; but there is no consensus that this necessarily requires border adjustments, let alone the wholesale reincorporation of the newly independent states. This has nothing to do with the "moderation" of the Russian leadership, or with the initial "Atlanticist," pro-Western orientation of Russian foreign policy (which did not last long in any event). It has to do with a secular decline in the "material" significance of territory – with the partial "de-territorialization" and "economization" of power, at least in the more economically "advanced" world regions – and at the same time, in seeming opposition to this, with the institutional reification and "sacralization" of existing territorial frontiers in international discourse and international organizations.[93] The former makes border changes less necessary; the latter makes them more difficult. By comparison with the interwar period, borders have become more "inviolable," but they have also become more insignificant. This dual development makes territorial revisionism a costly, "inefficient," and, it could be argued, ultimately unnecessary way to augment state power, even for many of those whose agendas are commonly labeled "neo-imperialist."[94]

The public rhetoric of homeland nationalism was well suited to Russian moves to consolidate a position of hegemony without territorial incorporation in the near abroad. Homeland nationalism, by definition, cuts across territorial boundaries; it asserts a form of nonterritorial jurisdiction over citizens of another state. It can therefore help establish and legitimize extraterritorial influence and control, as Russia has sought to do in the near abroad. The fit between homeland nationalist

---

[92] One reason for this is that territorial revision was clearly focused, in Weimar Germany, on the Polish Corridor, Danzig, and Upper Silesia; although maximal positions varied, these were universal minimum demands. In the Russian case, revisionism is not clearly focused. The present boundaries of the Russian Federation are indeed felt to be arbitrary, but there is no consensual sense of what – or more precisely where – a minimally "adequate" Russia would be.

[93] On the declining significance of territory, see Richard Rosecrance, *The Rise of the Trading State: Commerce and Conquest in the Modern World* (New York: Basic Books, 1986).

[94] Drawing on Michael Doyle's definition of empire, Ronald Suny argues against conflating an "imperial project" proper, involving the establishment (or reestablishment) of full sovereignty by a center over a distinct and subordinate periphery, with "Great Power hegemony," involving a relation of domination between separate states, and suggests that the latter is more likely in the case of post-Soviet Russia. See his "Ambiguous Categories: States, Empires and Nations," *Post-Soviet Affairs* 11, no. 2 (1995), 193–4.

idioms and Weimar foreign policy priorities was less close. Homeland nationalist rhetoric was generalized, referring to all transborder Germans. Yet, as argued above, Weimar foreign policy *vis-à-vis* the two neighboring states with the largest German communities – Poland and Czechoslovakia – was sharply distinct, governed in the former case by deep antagonism and fundamental territorial claims, in the latter by "correct" relations and an effort to increase German economic influence in *Mitteleuropa*. Partly for this reason, and partly because of the more limited international legitimacy of transborder concern with minority rights in the interwar period, homeland nationalist idioms were less well suited to the public articulation and justification of Weimar foreign policy.

If the official homeland nationalism of post-Soviet Russia has been more public and visible than that of Weimar Germany, civil society homeland nationalism has been much less visible in the Russian case. Reportage and commentary on Russians outside Russia has figured prominently in the Russian press, and there is an emergent counterpart to Weimar *Ostforschung* in various research institutes conducting research on the near abroad. Given the degree of state control over the broadcast media, however, as well as state support for – and sometimes direct commissioning of – research, these belong only partially and ambiguously to the sphere of civil society. Oppositional political parties and factions, as well as individual political entrepreneurs, have made ample use of homeland nationalist rhetoric to castigate the government for failing to take bolder measures in defense of Russians in the near abroad;[95] but they too can scarcely be conceptualized as part of civil society, since their homeland nationalism, although defined in opposition to government policy and practice, arises directly from the struggle for political power. The core of civil society homeland nationalism in Weimar Germany – the dense and vigorous network of associations concerned with co-ethnics abroad – has no counterpart in post-Soviet Russia. This reflects of course the general weakness of civil society in Soviet successor states. In Weimar Germany, moreover, civil society homeland nationalism could build, ideologically and organizationally, on an established prewar tradition of concern for Germandom abroad. Needless to say, there was no comparable tradition of concern for Russians outside Russia in the Soviet era.

The population targeted by Weimar homeland nationalism was relatively clearly defined. In practice, to be sure, it was not always evident

---

[95] The stances of Russian political parties on the issue of Russians in the near abroad are reviewed by Kolstoe, *Russians*, pp. 276ff.

precisely who belonged to this population, especially in regions (such as Upper Silesia or parts of East Prussia) of fluid ethnocultural identity. In principle, however, everyone agreed that German claims as external national homeland concerned the *Grenz- und Auslandsdeutsche* of Central and Eastern Europe, and that these borderland and foreign Germans were defined by their ethnocultural nationality.

In Russia, by contrast, there is no agreement even in principle about the circle of persons addressed by Russian homeland claims.[96] Five terms have been widely used to identify the relevant population. Most clearly paralleling Weimar homeland nationalism are claims to protect *russkie*, that is Russians by ethnocultural nationality. The second term, *rossiiane*, also ordinarily translated as "Russians," construes Russianness not with reference to ethnocultural nationality – or rather not with reference to *Russian* ethnocultural nationality – but with reference to *Rossiia*, that is, to the Russian state, or to Russia understood in a territorial sense. This formulation, in turn, can be interpreted in a subjective-political sense, in terms of identification with the Russian state or with Russia as *rodina* (homeland, native land, mother country), or, more commonly, in an objective-ethnocultural sense, in terms of membership of one of the many ethnocultural groups considered indigenous to Russia. This latter meaning is sometimes designated by the expression *etnicheskie rossiiane*, seemingly oxymoronic in its juxtaposition of the adjective "ethnic" and a derivative of the expressly nonethnic noun *Rossia*. In practice, *rossiiane* serves more as a "politically correct" substitute for *russkie*, one that acknowledges the multinational population of Russia, than as an alternative way of construing the population for whom Russia is a homeland.[97]

The third widely used term is *russkoiazychnye*, or Russian-speakers. Although almost all Soviet citizens spoke Russian to some extent,

---

[96] See Kolstoe, *Russians*, pp. 260ff.; Mark Beissinger, "The Persisting Ambiguity of Empire," *Post-Soviet Affairs* 11, no. 2 (1995), 169–70.

[97] As of 1989, the largest groups of *rossiiane* (other than ethnic Russians) outside Russia were Tatars, Jews (considered to be *rossiiane* under the Soviet nationality regime because they had, in principle, "their own" national territory within the RSFSR, although fewer than 5% of the inhabitants of this remote patch of land on the Chinese border identified their nationality as Jewish in 1989), Lezgins, Ossetians, Bashkir, Mordvinians, Chuvash, and Chechens (calculated from Gosudarstvennyi komitet SSSR po statistike, *Natsional'nyi sostav naseleniia SSSR*, pp. 5–11). In so far as members of these national groups, outside "their own" ethnonational territories, have tended to assimilate to Russians, they could indeed plausibly be construed as part of the population Russia could claim to protect. In this case, however, Russia would be claiming to protect them in their quality as "Russian-speakers," not in their national quality as Tatars, Jews, etc. On the avoidance of the term *russkie*, see Kolstoe, *Russians*, pp. 260–1.

russkoiazychnye does not designate Russian-speakers in this purely linguistic sense. It points rather to two analytically distinct categories of persons (in addition to Russians by ethnocultural nationality) who might identify with Russians in the non-Russian successor states and with Russia as an external national homeland. The first category includes people living for long periods outside "their own" national state and tending to identify with and assimilate to the Russians in that state (especially Ukrainians and Belarusians but also members of other dispersed national groups such as Armenians and Jews).[98] The second category includes people who live in "their own" national state ("their own" in the sense that it corresponds to their official Soviet-era passport nationality or their self-identified ethnocultural nationality) but whose primary language (and sometimes even mother tongue) is Russian and who consequently may identify politically with Russians in that state and coalesce with them in resisting programs of linguistic nationalization.[99]

The fourth term, *sootechestvenniki*, means compatriots, that is people who share a common fatherland (*otechestvo*). In the post-Soviet context, however, this original, clearly political meaning has been overlaid by a *mélange* of criteria based on some combination of descent, ethnicity, past citizenship, and spiritual-cultural orientation. Thus *sootechestvenniki* have been defined by one expert as "former subjects of the Russian Empire or citizens of the USSR and their direct descendants, not presently possessing Russian citizenship but belonging to one of the ethnic groups of Russia and considering themselves spiritually and culturally-ethnically tied to Russia."[100] This incongruous blend of legal, ethnographic, and identitarian notions has become the term of choice in official documents.

[98] David Laitin has suggested that Russian-speakers in this sense, together with the ethnic Russians in non-Russian successor states, may be in the course of forming a new "Russian-speaking" nationality, distinct from the Russian nationality. See "Identity in Formation: The Russian-Speaking Nationality in the Post-Soviet Diaspora," paper presented at the Annual Meeting of the American Political Science Association, 1994.

[99] Dominique Arel has suggested that this latter category may be particularly significant in Ukraine. See "Language and Group Boundaries in the Two Ukraines," paper presented at conference on "National Minorities, Nationalizing States, and External National Homelands in the New Europe," Bellagio Study and Conference Center, Italy, August 1994.

[100] This definition was formulated by a working group headed by Professor Igor Blishchenko, Director of the Independent Institute of International Law, as reported in "Rossiia vnov' prinimaet sootechestvennikov iz zarubezh'ia," *Izvestiia*, September 8, 1992. I am grateful to Pål Kolstø for calling this to my attention. Similar definitions were given to me in interviews with officials of the Russian Ministry of Nationalities and Regional Policy in June 1994 and July 1995. The *Izvestiia* article refers to "relatives in direct ascending line" rather than to descendants, but it is clear from the context and from other documents (including an article by Blishchenko himself) that this is simply

The final term is *grazhdane* (citizens). The protection of one's own citizens residing in other states, it would seem, is completely distinct from homeland nationalism, the defining feature of which is the claim to protect non-citizen co-nationals. Yet the distinction is not so clear-cut in the post-Soviet context. *Grazhdane* is often used (in political speech if not in official documents) metaphorically, as a rough synonym of *sootechestvenniki*;[101] it is also used, again metaphorically, in connection with the claim that Russia has responsibility for all former Soviet citizens. Moreover, Russia has sought to convert co-nationals into fellow citizens.[102] It has sought to conclude agreements on dual citizenship with other successor states.[103] More recently, Russian officials have suggested that, even in the absence of such agreements, Russia might accord citizenship on application to individual petitioners from the near abroad, even to those who possess the citizenship of another successor state.[104] Doing so on a large scale would strengthen Russia's jurisdictional claims in the near abroad, and provide a convenient pretext for intervention.[105]

a reportorial error. See for example I. P. Blishchenko, A. Kh. Abasidze, and E. V. Martynenko, "Problemy gosudarstvennoi politiki Rossiiskoi Federatsii v otnoshenii sootechestvennikov," *Gosudarstvo i pravo* 2 (1994), 10, which offers a similar definition but omits the reference to membership in one of the ethnic groups of Russia.

101   Kolstoe, *Russians*, p. 261.
102   Beissinger, "The Persisting Ambiguity of Empire," 171.
103   An agreement has been signed with Turkmenistan, and similar ones are being negotiated with Kyrgyzstan, Tajikistan, and Belarus. See "Na chto setuet seto," *Rossiiskie vesti*, July 6, 1995.
104   The legal basis for such a practice was established in 1993, when a key provision of the original 1991 Russian citizenship law, barring the acquisition of Russian citizenship by persons possessing other citizenships except where dual citizenship was permitted by international agreement, was repealed.
105   From the standpoint of international law, Russia's claim to protect its citizens in the near abroad, if they also held the citizenship of the state in which they were residing, would be problematic at best. Traditionally, the protection of citizens abroad, known in the legal literature as diplomatic protection, has been permitted when the person in question was a citizen *only* of the state claiming to protect him or her, and not also of the state in which he or she was residing. In recent decades, however, the incidence of dual (and multiple) citizenship has increased sharply, and in a variety of situations courts have had to determine which of two or more formal citizenships should be treated as a person's "effective" citizenship, reflecting the more "real" and substantial ties between a person and a state. Partly as a result of the development of this notion of "effective" citizenship, the traditional bar on the diplomatic protection of dual citizens (when one of the citizenships is that of the state in which the person to be protected is residing) has been eroded; states' claims to protect such persons, although controversial, have received some measure of international judicial approval in cases where the "effective" citizenship of the person in question (ordinarily reflecting habitual residence as well as a preponderance of social, economic, political, and cultural ties) is that of the state claiming to protect him or her. Note, however, that this is a relatively narrow exception; it would provide no legal warrant, for example, for a Russian claim to protect a person holding both Russian and Kazakhstani citizenship and residing

The shifting and ambiguous vocabulary of homeland claims enables Russia to play in multiple registers, and to advance multiple and only partly overlapping jurisdictional claims in the near abroad. Through a kind of division of semantic labor, *russkie* provides cultural resonance and emotional power (and is therefore most useful in the context of domestic political competition), while *rossiiane, russkoiazychnye,* and *sootechestvenniki* (terms entirely foreign to everyday speech, and lacking – with the partial exception of the last – any kind of cultural resonance and emotional power) designate a broader target population and can therefore be used in international contexts and in official documents to expand Russia's jurisdictional claims in the near abroad (and to represent those claims as transcending a narrow ethnic interest in protecting ethnic Russians). An expansive politics of citizenship, finally, enables Russia to combine the traditional (and from the point of view of international law more legitimate) rhetoric of protecting citizens in other states with homeland nationalist claims to protect noncitizen co-nationals. This opportunistic use of multiple idioms is further evinced in the somewhat incongruous marriage of a vocabulary of human rights to that of homeland nationalism, as in the frequent claim that Russia must protect the human rights of (ethnic) Russians in the near abroad.

Conclusion

Weimar homeland nationalism, I suggested above, was a complex web of political stances, cultural idioms, organizational networks, and transborder social relations. Russian homeland nationalism can also be regarded in this way. As a political phenomenon, homeland nationalism has been more salient, in both domestic and interstate contexts, in post-Soviet Russia than in Weimar Germany. Pronouncements on homeland nationalist themes have been more central to both governmental and oppositional political discourse, and to domestic political competition, than was the case in Weimar Germany. Like Weimar homeland nationalism, Russian homeland nationalism is doubly "intertwined" – with domestic political competition on the one hand, and with efforts to

habitually in Kazakhstan. Since the vast majority of Russians in the near abroad are long-term residents of the states in which they live, it is hard to see how their "effective" citizenship could be construed as that of the Russian Federation. The proliferation of dual citizenship among Russians of the near abroad, therefore, would not (from the standpoint of international law) provide Russia with a blanket *legal* justification for intervention in the near abroad, although it would undoubtedly strengthen the domestic *political* rationale for such intervention. On diplomatic protection and dual citizenship, see Loïc Darras, "La double nationalité," Thesis in Law, Paris, 1986, pp. 631ff.

consolidate Russian hegemony in the near abroad on the other. In both domestic and interstate contexts, homeland nationalist stances have been deployed instrumentally, as a calculated means to other ends. But again as in Weimar, this instrumental exploitation of homeland nationalist stances has occurred – and has indeed only been possible – against the background of taken-for-granted shared understandings concerning the plight of Russians in the near abroad and the obligation of the Russian state to do something on their behalf.

The dual embeddedness of homeland nationalism, as a political phenomenon, in wider domestic and interstate political contexts, means that it lacks its own autonomous logic and dynamic. As a political phenomenon, homeland nationalism is a set of moves, a set of stances, a family of related discursive claims – but the "game" in which these moves are activated, in which they pay off, or fail to pay off, is not the game of homeland politics, but the wider domestic and interstate "games." The "value" or appropriateness of a homeland stance or move depends on the state of the game at a particular moment – on the rules of the game and the resources possessed by competing players.[106] In general, the greater international legitimacy and institutionalization of cross-border concern with minorities makes homeland nationalist "moves" more appropriate and more useful than they were in the interwar period. The domestic political arena in post-Soviet Russia also induces homeland nationalist moves, if only because there are so few politically profitable competing idioms today. Given the background of the widely shared, taken-for-granted sense that *something* ought to be done for successor state Russians,[107] homeland nationalist idioms have been adopted in the competition for domestic political power almost by default, *faute de mieux*.

As a cultural idiom, Russian homeland nationalism has been much more uncertain, ambiguous, and fluctuating than its Weimar counterpart. Weimar homeland nationalist discourse could build on the *grossdeutsch* tradition of the mid-nineteenth century and on the tradition of concern for Germans in the Habsburg and Romanov territories that developed in the late Bismarckian and Wilhelmine eras. Because of the lack of a comparable tradition in Russia, homeland nationalist discourse has had to be assembled by "bricolage" from various available and

---

[106] For an extended discussion of rules and resources as constitutive of "structure," critically engaging and reformulating Giddens' notion of the "duality of structure" and Bourdieu's notion of habitus, see William H. Sewell, Jr., "A Theory of Structure – Duality, Agency, and Transformation," *American Journal of Sociology* 98, no. 1 (1992).

[107] This shared understanding, to be sure, is itself shaped and sustained by the media and is therefore, in part, a product as well as a condition of homeland nationalism.

legitimate cultural "scraps." Lacking indigenous roots, it has had to be cobbled together from a variety of discursive traditions: from "classical" homeland nationalism, from the legal rhetoric of diplomatic protection of citizens in other states, from human rights discourse, from the vocabulary of Great Power politics. As a result, the discourse has been multivocal and opportunistic, playing, as argued above, on multiple registers, and lacking consistency. The ambiguous and partly incongruous vocabulary for identifying the targets of homeland nationalist claims is but one indicator of this.

As an organizational phenomenon, Russian homeland nationalism lacks the strong associational base in civil society that characterized Weimar homeland nationalism; the network of organizations concerned with Russians in the near abroad is therefore much more state-centered. As a social-relational phenomenon, finally, Russian homeland nationalism, like its Weimar counterpart, involves the cultivation and maintenance of cross-border relations and the provision of a flow of cross-border resources. The process of organizing resource flows and reconstituting networks and relations disrupted by the breakup of the Soviet Union is still incipient; and too little is known at present to make substantive claims about it. In the long run, however, the political disposition of Russian and Russophone minorities in the successor states – in particular, the degree to which and manner in which they look to Russia for solutions to their problems, rather than work them out within the frame of the successor states – will be significantly shaped by these relations and resource flows, and on the degrees and forms of integration with Russia (and of detachment from successor state contexts) that they generate.

6   Aftermaths of empire and the unmixing of peoples

Migration has always been central to the making, unmaking, and remaking of states. From the polychromatic political landscapes of the ancient world, with their luxuriant variety of forms of rule, to the more uniform terrain of the present, dominated by the bureaucratic territorial state, massive movements of people have regularly accompanied – as consequence and sometimes also as cause – the expansion, contraction, and reconfiguration of political space.[1]

This centrality of migration to political expansion, contraction, and reconfiguration is amply illustrated in the history of the Russo-Soviet state. "The history of Russia," wrote Vasilii Kliuchevskii, dean of nineteenth-century Russian historians, "is the history of a country which colonizes itself."[2] That colonization began in the mid-sixteenth century, when conquest of the Kazan and Astrakhan khanates permitted Russian peasant settlement to expand into the fertile black earth zone heretofore controlled by hostile Turkic nomads. It did not end until the postwar decades of the twentieth century, when industrial and agricultural development strategies drew large numbers of Russians to peripheral regions, most dramatically, in terms of ethnodemographic consequences, to Kazakhstan, Estonia, and Latvia. Throughout these four centuries, the eastward, southward, and (more recently) westward dispersion of

---

[1] See for example Aristide R. Zolberg, "Contemporary Transnational Migrations in Historical Perspective: Patterns and Dilemmas," in Mary M. Kritz, ed., *U.S. Immigration and Refugee Policy* (Lexington, Mass.: D. C. Heath, 1983); Aristide R. Zolberg, Astri Suhrke, and Sergio Aguayo, *Escape from Violence: Conflict and the Refugee Crisis in the Developing World* (New York: Oxford University Press, 1989); Michael R. Marrus, *The Unwanted: European Refugees in the Twentieth Century* (New York: Oxford University Press, 1985); Myron Weiner, "Security, Stability and International Migration" and "Rejected Peoples and Unwanted Migrants in South Asia," both in Weiner, ed., *International Migration and Security* (Boulder, Colo.: Westview, 1993).

[2] Quoted in Richard Pipes, *Russia Under the Old Regime* (New York: Scribner's, 1974), p. 14.

Russians from their initially small region of core settlement has been intimately linked to the expansion and consolidation of the Russian state and its Soviet successor. It has comprised one of the greatest episodes of colonization in human history.[3]

State-sponsored migrations linked to the expansion and consolidation of Romanov and Soviet rule embraced of course many others besides Russians. A few scattered examples will have to suffice here. Russian conquests were often effected, or facilitated, by inducing the non-Russian military or economic elites of the territories in question to move to new lands.[4] As the state, and peasant settlement, expanded southward toward the vast Kazakh steppe, Cossacks, recruited with extensive land grants, were settled along its northern perimeter as military frontier guards.[5] German colonists, attracted by the lands, subsidies, religious autonomy, fiscal privileges, and service exemptions promised by Catherine II, began to settle the lower Volga frontier region in the 1760s.[6] The Russian government encouraged the mass emigration of Crimean Tatars to the Ottoman Empire after the Crimean War; and it induced, and partly compelled, the mass emigration of Caucasian Muslims, most of them Circassians, in the same period.[7] Most notorious, of course, are the vast deportations ordered by Stalin during and after the Second World War, including the mass deportations of elites from the newly annexed Western territories, the allegedly preventative deportation of Germans and Koreans, and the punitive deportation of entire nationalities for the collaboration of some of their

---

[3] See now the excellent overview of this process in Paul Kolstoe, *Russians in the Former Soviet Republics* (London: Hurst, 1995), chapters 2 and 3. See also Marc Raeff, "Patterns of Russian Imperial Policy Toward the Nationalities," in Edward Allworth, ed., *Soviet Nationality Problems* (New York: Columbia University Press, 1971); Pipes, *Russia Under the Old Regime*, pp. 13–16; Alexandre Bennigsen and S. Enders Wimbush, "Migration and Political Control: Soviet Europeans in Soviet Central Asia," in William H. McNeill and Ruth S. Adams, eds., *Human Migration: Patterns and Policies* (Bloomington: Indiana University Press, 1978), pp. 36–43; Frederick S. Starr, "Tsarist Government: The Imperial Dimension," in Jeremy Azrael, ed., *Soviet Nationality Policies and Practices* (New York: Praeger, 1978), p. 11; Walker Connor, *The National Question in Marxist-Leninist Theory and Strategy* (Princeton: Princeton University Press, 1984), pp. 304ff.

[4] Raeff, "Patterns of Russian Imperial Policy," 27.

[5] George J. Demko, *The Russian Colonization of Kazakhstan 1896–1916* (Bloomington: Indiana University Press, 1969), pp. 36–43.

[6] Fred Koch, *The Volga Germans* (University Park: Pennsylvania State University Press, 1977), pp. 6ff.

[7] Alan Fisher, *The Crimean Tatars* (Stanford, Calif.: Hoover Institution Press, 1978), pp. 88–9; Kemal Karpat, *Ottoman Population 1830–1914* (Madison: University of Wisconsin Press, 1985), pp. 66–70.

members: Karachai, Kalmyks, Chechen, Ingush, Balkars, and Crimean Tatars.[8]

If politically governed migrations were central, for four centuries, to the construction and consolidation of the Russian and Soviet states, they are already proving central to the reconfiguration of political authority in post-Soviet Eurasia. Substantial migrations within and from Transcaucasia and Central Asia have already occurred in connection with the progressive erosion and eventual collapse of Soviet authority and the incipient reorganization of rule along national lines.[9] But it is the potential for much vaster migrations, rather than the scale of existing flows, that has focused attention and concern on migration in the last few years.

That potential has been viewed with special alarm in Northwestern and Central European capitals and in Moscow, the former envisioning a mass westward exodus of millions, perhaps tens of millions of ex-Soviet citizens, the latter fearing a vast, chaotic, and brutal "unmixing of peoples" entailing, in particular, an uncontrollable influx into Russia of the Russian and Russophone population from the non-Russian successor states. Articulated in crude and undifferentiated fashion, these fearful visions, jointly propagated by Western, Soviet, and post-Soviet journalists and politicians, have done more to obscure than to enhance our understanding of the actual and prospective dynamics of post-Soviet migrations. The former vision, to be sure, seems recently to have lost its hold on European public opinion. The alarmist rhetoric, sensationalist headlines, and cataclysmic imagery of 1990 and 1991, warning of the imminent inundation of Western Europe, have all but disappeared – no doubt because the expected onslaught failed to materialize. The vision of mass ethnic unmixing, however, remains powerful. Its plausibility is

---

8 Robert Conquest, *The Nation Killers: The Soviet Deportation of Nationalities* (New York: Macmillan, 1970); A. M. Nekrich, *The Punished Peoples* (New York: Norton, 1978); Gerhard Simon, *Nationalism and Policy Toward the Nationalities in the Soviet Union* (Boulder, Colo.: Westview Press, 1991), pp. 173–218.

9 For overviews of post-Soviet migrations, see Zhanna Zaionchkovskaia, ed., *Byvshii SSSR: vnutrenniaia migratsiia i emigratsiia* [The Former USSR: Internal Migration and Emigration] (Moscow: Institut problem zaniatosti, Rossiiskaia Akademiia Nauk, 1992); G. C. Vitkovskaia, *Vynuzhdennaia migratsiia: problemy i perspektivy* [Forced Migration: Problems and Perspectives] (Moscow: Institut narodnokhoziaistvennogo prognozirovaniia, Rossiiskaia Akademiia Nauk, 1993); Zhanna Zaionchkovskaia, ed., *Migratsionnaia situatsiia v Rossii; sotsial'no-politicheskie aspekty* [The Migration Situation in Russia: Social-Political Aspects] (Moscow: Institut narodnokhoziaistvennogo prognozirovaniia, Rossiiskaia Akademiia Nauk, 1994); and Zhanna Zaionchkovskaia, ed., *Migratsionnye protsessy posle raspada SSSR* [Migration Processes After the Breakup of the USSR] (Moscow: Institut narodnokhoziaistvennogo prognozirovaniia, Rossiiskaia Akademiia Nauk, 1994).

enhanced by the Yugoslav refugee crisis, which resulted directly from the dissolution of a multinational state and the incipient reconfiguration of political authority along national lines.[10] It is thus understandable that the specter of an analogous "unmixing of peoples" in post-Soviet Eurasia – the specter of "ethnic cleansing" on a vaster canvas – haunts discussions of post-Soviet migration.

Without belittling the potential dangers of a chaotic and brutal unmixing of peoples in certain parts of the former Soviet Union, I seek in this chapter to provide a more nuanced and differentiated analysis of the relation between political reconfiguration and migrations of ethnic unmixing in post-Soviet Eurasia. Although such migrations are likely to be highly variegated, potentially involving scores of ethnonational groups and migration trajectories, I focus here on a single set of flows – on the actual and potential migration to Russia of ethnic Russians and other Russophone residents of the non-Russian successor states.[11] I restrict the scope of the discussion in this manner for both analytical and substantive reasons. Analytically, this will permit a more sustained and differentiated discussion of the migratory dynamics of this group. Substantively, not only do the 25-million-odd Russians represent by far the largest pool of potential ethnomigrants,[12] but the manner in which and extent to which they become involved in migrations of ethnic unmixing will be fraught with consequences for Russian domestic politics and for relations between Russia and the non-Russian successor states.

I analyze the reflux of Russians from the ex-Soviet periphery in broad historical and comparative perspective, considering them alongside earlier post-imperial migrations that ensued when a ruling ethnic or national group in a multinational empire was abruptly transformed, by

---

10 Robert M. Hayden, "Constitutional Nationalism in the Formerly Yugoslav Republics," *Slavic Review* 51, no. 4 (1992).

11 In what follows, I use the term "Russians" for convenience, on the understanding that it includes not only the 25 million residents of non-Russian republics who identified themselves as Russian in the 1989 census but also certain other Russophone residents of the non-Russian successor states whose migration behavior is likely to be similar – above all, the roughly 1.4 million Ukrainian and Belarusian residents of non-Slavic successor states who, in 1989, identified their native language as Russian (calculated from Gosudarstvennyi komitet SSSR po statistike, [USSR State Committee for Statistics], *Natsional'nyi sostav naseleniia SSSR* [National Composition of the Population of the USSR] (Moscow: Finansy i statiska, 1991).

12 To these one might add the more than 5 million Russians living in autonomous formations of the Russian Federation in which Russians comprised less than 50% of the population in 1989 (calculated from *ibid.*, pp. 34–48). But the problem of unmixing within the Russian Federation, while deserving analysis in its own right, lies beyond the scope of this chapter.

the shrinkage of political space and the reconfiguration of political authority along national lines, into a national minority in a set of new nation-states. Three such cases are examined: Balkan Muslims during and after the disintegration of the Ottoman Empire, Hungarians after the collapse of the Habsburg Empire, and Germans after the collapse of the Habsburg Empire and the German Kaiserreich.[13] From this excursus into comparative history I extract four general analytical points, and bring them to bear on the post-Soviet migration of Russians to Russia. I adopt this historical and comparative approach not because the past offers precise analogs of the present – it does not – but because consideration of a variety of partially analogous cases can enrich and improve our understanding of the intertwined dynamics of migration and political reconfiguration.

Muslim/Turkish migration from the Balkans

Consider first the Ottoman case. The protracted disintegration of the Ottoman Empire spanned well over a century, from the late eighteenth century to the aftermath of the First World War. Throughout this period, and even earlier, the shrinkage of Ottoman political space was accompanied by centripetal migration of Muslims from the lost territories to remaining Ottoman territories.[14] But it was the last half-century of Ottoman disintegration, and the formation of national states in its wake, that produced mass displacements. It was this unprecedented wholesale restructuring of populations, linked to the transformation of multinational empires into nation-states, that led Lord Curzon to speak of the "unmixing of peoples."[15]

While the details of these migrations are far too complex – and too contested[16] – to analyze here, a few general points should be emphasized. The first concerns the magnitude of the unmixing. Several million people were uprooted from Bulgaria, Macedonia, Thrace, and western

---

[13] Migrations of ethnic unmixing in the aftermath of empire, of course, do not involve only, or even most importantly, the former ruling groups. One need think only of the murderous deportation of Armenians from northeastern Turkey, to say nothing of the centrality of deportation to the genocidal policies and practices of the Nazi regime. This chapter focuses on migrations of formerly dominant nationalities because these are most closely analogous to post-Soviet migrations of Russians to Russia – a phenomenon that, because of its potential magnitude and the dangers associated with it, deserves investigation in its own right.

[14] Kemal Karpat, *An Inquiry into the Social Foundations of Nationalism in the Ottoman State* (Princeton, NJ: Center of International Studies, 1973), p. 106.

[15] Marrus, *Unwanted*, p. 41.

[16] Karpat, *Ottoman Population*.

Anatolia alone in the last quarter of the nineteenth and first quarter of the twentieth century. The migrations radically simplified the ethnic demography of these regions, constructing relatively homogeneous populations where great heterogeneity had been the norm. In 1870, for example, Muslims (Turks, Bulgarian-speaking Pomaks, and Circassian and Crimean resettlers from Russia) were at least as numerous as Orthodox Christian Bulgarians in most of what would later become Bulgaria. By 1888, however, the Muslim share of the population of Bulgaria (including Eastern Rumelia) had fallen to roughly a quarter, and by 1920 Muslims comprised only 14 percent of the population.[17] Similarly, between 1912 and 1924 the intricately intermixed population of Macedonia and Thrace – comprised mainly of Turkish-speaking Muslims, Greeks, and Slavs identifying themselves mainly as Bulgarians, with none of these constituting a majority – was sifted, sorted, and recomposed into relatively homogeneous blocks corresponding to state frontiers: northern Macedonia became solidly Slavic, southern and western Macedonia predominantly Greek, and eastern Thrace (along with western Anatolia) purely Turkish.[18]

The unmixing of peoples initially followed ethnoreligious rather than ethnolinguistic lines, with Muslims moving south and east and Christians moving north and west.[19] It was thus not only ethnic Turks who retreated toward core Ottoman domains, but also other Muslims, notably Bulgarian-speaking Pomaks and Serbo-Croat-speaking Bosnians as well as Circassians and Crimean Tatars who had earlier fled from Russia to the Ottoman Balkans.[20] Language became more important over time as the Ottoman rump state increasingly assumed an ethnically Turkish identity and as the Orthodox Christian Balkan successor states came into increasing conflict with one another. As a result, there was secondary intra-Christian ethnic unmixing, primarily between Greeks and Bulgarians, superimposed on the primary Muslim–Christian unmixing. But even as late as 1923, the Lausanne Convention providing for a massive and compulsory Greco-Turkish population exchange defined the population to be exchanged in religious rather than ethnolinguistic terms.[21]

---

[17] Joseph Rothschild, *East Central Europe Between the Two World Wars* (Seattle: University of Washington Press, 1974), p. 327; Karpat, *Ottoman Population*, pp. 50–1.
[18] A. A. Pallis, "Racial Migrations in the Balkans during the Years 1912–1924," *Geographical Journal* 66, no. 4 (1925), 316.
[19] Marrus, *Unwanted*, p. 41.
[20] Karpat, *Inquiry*, pp. 1–2; Karpat, *Ottoman Population*, pp. 65ff.
[21] Stephen P. Ladas, *The Exchange of Minorities: Bulgaria, Greece and Turkey* (New York: Macmillan, 1932), pp. 377ff.

War was central to the mass unmixing of Balkan peoples.[22] Beginning
with the Russo-Turkish War of 1877, intensifying in the Balkan Wars of
1912–13, and culminating in the aftermath of the First World War,
almost all of the large-scale migrations occurred in direct or indirect
connection with military campaigns. This is true, most obviously and
directly, of spontaneous flight before advancing armies, in the wake
of retreating ones, or as a result of attacks on civilian populations –
depressingly prevalent in all the military campaigns of this period, and
often intended precisely to provoke mass migration.[23] But other
migrations, too, were indirectly caused by war. This is true, for example,
of the Muslim migration to Turkey under the terms of the Greco-
Turkish population exchange mandated by the Lausanne Convention.
Its counterpart – the million-strong Orthodox Christian migration from
Turkey to Greece in 1922, which had already been virtually completed
by the time the Lausanne Convention was signed – was directly
engendered by war: Greeks fled in panic amidst the violence and terror
accompanying the Turkish counteroffensive of 1922, which drove the
Greek armies in a rout from the regions of western Anatolia and eastern
Thrace that they had occupied since the Greek invasion of 1919. Because
Turkey did not wish to allow these refugees to return *en masse* to Turkey,
fearing that this would only help perpetuate Greek irredentist ambitions,
it agreed to accept in return the compulsory resettlement in Turkey of the
(mostly ethnic Turkish) Muslim citizens of Greece.[24] Thus although
the latter were not directly uprooted by war, their migration was
nonetheless an indirect product of the Greek invasion of Turkey and the
Turkish counteroffensive; it would not have occurred in the absence of
the Greco-Turkish war.

To underscore the centrality of war to mass migrations of ethnic
unmixing in the Balkans between 1875 and 1924 is not to suggest that it
was war as such that was responsible for these migrations. It was rather
a particular kind of war. It was war at the high noon of mass ethnic
nationalism, undertaken by states bent on shaping their territories in
accordance with maximalist – and often fantastically exaggerated –
claims of ethnic demography and committed to molding their heterogeneous populations into relatively homogeneous national wholes. Not
all wars entail the massive uprooting of civilian populations. Wars fought
in the name of national self-determination, however, where the national

22 Marrus, *Unwanted*, pp. 42ff., 96ff.
23 Karpat, *Ottoman Population*, pp. 71ff.; Marrus, *Unwanted*, pp. 45, 98ff.
24 Marrus, *Unwanted*, p. 102. The question of who was responsible for the compulsory
     rather than voluntary character of the Greco-Turkish population exchange is much
     disputed. For a balanced account, see Ladas, *Exchange of Minorities*, pp. 335ff., 725.

"self" in question is conceived in ethnic rather than civic terms, but where the population is intricately intermixed, *are* likely to engender ethnic unmixing through migration, murder, or some combination of both. Migrations of ethnic unmixing were thus engendered not by war as such, but by war in conjunction with the formation of new nation-states and the ethnic "nationalization" of existing states in a region of intermixed population and at a time of supercharged mass ethnic nationalism.

Despite their paroxysmal intensity and "finality" at particular places and times, Balkan migrations of ethnic unmixing have been protracted. This holds particularly of the outmigration of Muslim Turks from the Balkan successor states. The major phase of unmixing lasted fifty years, from 1875 to 1924, coinciding with the progressive disintegration of the Ottoman state and its final demise in the Kemalist uprising in the aftermath of the First World War. But the outmigration of Turks (though no longer of large numbers of non-Turkish Muslims) continued thereafter, albeit more intermittently and on a smaller scale. Bulgaria, in particular – the Balkan state with the largest ethnically Turkish minority – has experienced, in fits and starts, a substantial ongoing "repatriation" of ethnic Turks to Turkey. Nearly 100,000 left under administrative pressure from the Bulgarian side in 1934–39;[25] another 155,000 were pressured to leave in 1950–51.[26] The most recent, and most massive, exodus occurred in 1989, a few years after the extremely harsh assimilation campaign of 1984–85, in which public use of the Turkish language was banned and Turks were forced to adopt Bulgarian names; when the borders were suddenly opened in 1989, 370,000 Bulgarian Turks fled to Turkey, more than 40 percent of the total Bulgarian Turkish population (although 155,000 returned to Bulgaria within a year).[27]

Finally, the fluctuating but generally favorable policies of the Ottoman government toward the immigration of Balkan Muslims, and of the Turkish government toward the immigration of Balkan Turks, have significantly shaped the incidence, volume, and timing of the migrations. The openness to immigration had economic-demographic roots: both the Ottoman state and the Turkish Republic through the interwar period viewed their territories, and Anatolia in particular, as underpopulated, and sought to encourage immigration in order to promote demographic

---

[25] Joseph B. Schechtman, *European Population Transfers 1939–1945* (New York: Oxford University Press, 1946), pp. 493–4.
[26] Alexandre Popovic, *L'Islam balkanique: les musulmans du sud-est européen dans la période post-ottomane* (Berlin: Osteuropa-Institut, 1986), p. 100.
[27] Darina Vasileva, "Bulgarian Turkish Emigration and Return," *International Migration Review* 26 (1992), 348.

growth and economic development.[28] But there was also an ideological
and cultural dimension to late Ottoman and Turkish immigration policy.
In the mid-nineteenth century, the Ottoman government was still largely
indifferent to the cultural characteristics of potential immigrants,
welcoming, and even seeking specifically to induce, the immigration of
non-Muslims.[29] But as the late Ottoman Empire came to view itself as
a specifically Muslim state (and in its last few years as an incipient
Turkish national state), and as the Turkish successor state, defining itself
as a nation-state, sought to weld its population into a homogeneous
nation, the general openness to immigration was succeeded by a selective
openness to Muslims (especially, though not exclusively, those from
former Ottoman domains) and, in the Turkish Republic, by a still more
selective openness to ethnic Turks from Balkan successor states, who, as
Interior Minister Sukru Kaya Bey put it in 1934, could scarcely be
expected to "live as slave where the Turk previously was the master."[30]

Magyar migration from Hungarian successor states

Our second case is that of ethnic Hungarians after the collapse of the
Habsburg Empire in the First World War. That sudden collapse differed
sharply from the protracted decay of the Ottoman Empire. Hungarian
rule in the Hungarian half of the Empire, far from decaying, had become
increasingly consolidated in the half-century preceding the outbreak
of war. Unlike the decentralized Austrian half of the Empire, the
Hungarian half, although ethnically heterogeneous (Magyars comprised
only about half the population), was politically unitary, ruled by a
centralized, fiercely nationalistic, and almost exclusively Magyar
bureaucracy.[31] This internally autonomous quasi-nation-state was
dismembered by the postwar settlement. The shrinkage of political space
was dramatic. The 1920 Treaty of Trianon stripped Hungary of two-
thirds of its land and three-fifths of its prewar population (though in
so doing it largely confirmed a *de facto* state of affairs, the territories
in question having been occupied and controlled, with tacit Allied
backing, by Romanian, Czech, and Serbian forces since the winter of

---

[28] Schechtman, *European Population Transfers*, pp. 488ff.; Karpat, *Ottoman Population*,
pp. 61ff.
[29] Karpat, *Ottoman Population*, pp. 62ff.
[30] Quoted in Schechtman, *European Population Transfers*, p. 490.
[31] C. A. Macartney, *Hungary and Her Successors: The Treaty of Trianon and its
Consequences, 1919–1937* (London: Oxford University Press, 1937), pp. 20–6; A. J. P.
Taylor, *The Habsburg Monarchy 1809–1918* (London: Hamish Hamilton, 1948),
pp. 185–6.

1918–19).[32] Although about 70 percent of the lost population was non-Magyar, over 3 million Magyars suddenly became national minorities in neighboring nation-states, including most importantly 1.7 million Magyars in Transylvania, which was awarded to Romania; a million in Slovakia and Ruthenia, which went to Czechoslovakia; and 450,000 in Vojvodina, which became part of Yugoslavia.[33]

These new minorities emigrated in substantial numbers in the years immediately following the First World War. But the post-Habsburg migration of Hungarians was quite different from the late- and post-Ottoman migrations of Turks. In the first place, a far smaller share of the Hungarian population migrated. In the six years immediately following the First World War, when most of the migration occurred, about 424,000 Hungarians migrated to Hungary from territories ceded to Romania, Czechoslovakia, and Yugoslavia, representing 13.4 percent, 13.7 percent, and 9.5 percent respectively of the ethnic Hungarian population of the lost territories.[34] Thereafter, apart from a renewed surge in the aftermath of the Second World War – including an organized Hungarian–Slovak population exchange at the insistence of Czechoslovakia, bent on ridding the country of its troublesome minorities[35] – there was little Magyar migration to Hungary from neighboring states until the late 1980s.[36] Although we lack directly comparable figures, Balkan Turkish/Muslim migrations to remaining Ottoman domains and Turkey were undoubtedly much larger, both in absolute numbers and in proportion to the Balkan Turkish/Muslim population.

Ethnic Hungarian migration from the lost territories remained comparatively limited in scope because it was primarily an elite migration, confined for the most part to the upper and middle classes. The migration had three analytically distinct phases.[37] First to flee were

---

[32] Macartney, *Hungary and Her Successors*, p. 1; Istvan Mocsy, "Radicalization and Counterrevolution: Magyar Refugees from the Successor States and Their Role in Hungary, 1918–1921," Ph.D. Dissertation, University of California, Los Angeles, 1973, chapter 2; Rothschild, *East Central Europe*, p. 155.

[33] Rothschild, *East Central Europe*, p. 155.

[34] Mocsy, "Radicalization and Counterrevolution," 8–9.

[35] Kalman Janics, *Czechoslovak Policy and the Hungarian Minority, 1945–48* (New York: Columbia University Press, 1982); Dariusz Stola, "Forced Migrations in European History," *International Migration Review* 26 (1992), 337; László Szöke, "Hungarian Perspectives on Emigration and Immigration in the New European Architecture," *International Migration Review* 26 (1992), 306.

[36] I do not include wartime Hungarian–Romanian population exchanges within Transylvania, for this territory reverted to Romanian control at the end of the war (on these exchanges see Schechtman, *European Population Transfers*, pp. 425ff.).

[37] Mocsy, "Radicalization and Counterrevolution."

those most closely identified with the repressive and exploitative aspects of Hungarian rule – and therefore those with the most to fear from a new regime. This group, many of whom fled before the consolidation of Romanian, Czechoslovak, and Serbian/Yugoslav rule, included great landowners, military men, and state and county officials connected with the courts and the police. Second, de-Magyarization of public administration, state employment, and education deprived many middle-class Hungarians of their positions as officials, teachers, railroad and postal employees, etc. and engendered a second group of refugees, who fled less in fear than out of economic displacement and loss of social status. Third, agrarian reform, by breaking up the great Hungarian-owned estates, displaced and pushed toward emigration not only the landowners themselves but the larger category of managers and employees whose livelihood depended on the estates. The peasant masses, however, who made up the large majority of the ethnically Hungarian population in the lost territories, did not migrate in significant numbers. Neither their interests nor their identities were immediately threatened by the change in sovereignty; indeed Hungarian peasants in areas ceded to Romania and Czechoslovakia actually benefited modestly from land distributions attendant on agrarian reform.[38]

About 85 percent of the 1918–24 migrants arrived in rump Hungary between late 1918 and the end of 1920.[39] The steep tapering off of the influx thereafter no doubt reflected a declining demand for resettlement on the part of those remaining in the ceded territories. But it also reflected efforts by the Hungarian government, beginning in 1921, to stem the influx by granting entry permits only in exceptional cases. This restrictive policy reflected the economic cost of supporting the refugees, a very large number of whom remained on the bloated state payroll. But it also reflected ideological concerns: the government did not want its revisionist case to be weakened by the mass emigration of Magyars from the lost territories.[40]

The Magyar exodus from the lost territories to rump Hungary, then, was numerically limited by the fact that it remained an essentially middle- and upper-class phenomenon. But it amounted nonetheless to a substantial influx into Hungary, increasing the size of the post-Trianon Hungarian population by about 5 percent in a few years. And the refugees' impact on interwar Hungarian politics – magnified by the predominance of *déclassé* gentry among them and by their concentration in cities, especially Budapest – was much greater than these numbers

[38] *Ibid.*, pp. 96ff.
[39] *Ibid.*, p. 9.   [40] *Ibid.*, chapter 10.

would suggest. Radicalized by their traumatic territorial and social displacement, the refugees played a key role in counter-revolutionary movements of 1919–20 and the White Terror of 1920. Throughout the interwar period, they buttressed right-wing forces, exercising an influence disproportionate to their numbers in parliament and public life. Above all, their zealous, uncompromising, and integral revisionism, demanding the full restoration of the lost territories, powerfully constrained interwar Hungary's foreign policy, preventing any reconciliation with neighboring states and making more likely the fateful alignment with Fascist Italy and Nazi Germany.[41]

Just as the great 1989 exodus of Bulgarian Turks to Turkey marked the continuation of an intermittent process of unmixing spanning more than a century, so too the centripetal migration of ethnic Hungarians resumed, forty years after the last significant episode, in the late 1980s.[42] The flow began well before the fall of the Ceauşescu regime; some 36,000 Romanian citizens – three-quarters of them ethnic Hungarians – who fled to Hungary during the late 1980s were residing in Hungary by the end of 1989.[43] Since the fall of Ceauşescu, definitive resettlement has been overshadowed by informal labor migration, made possible by the much greater freedom of movement between the two countries (and by the lax enforcement of work permit requirements). If the literature on labor migration in other settings is any guide, however, this migration is likely to lead to substantial permanent resettlement, especially on the part of ethnic Hungarians. Romanians, too, have been drawn to Hungary by its relatively attractive labor market. Yet this is by no means a purely economic migration. For Hungarians from Romania – but not for their Romanian neighbors and fellow citizens – ethnic nationality functions as a form of social capital, generating superior migration opportunities. Their language skills and extended family ties give them access to richer networks of information about migration and employment opportunities; and their ethnic nationality may secure them preferential treatment in encounters with border guards and customs officials, with interior ministry bureaucrats having discretionary authority to grant permanent residence permits and citizenship, with labor inspectors checking workers' documents at workplaces, or with policemen checking documents on the street.

---

[41] *Ibid.*
[42] My account of the most recent phase of ethnic unmixing involving Hungarians is based on interviews with officials of the Office for Transborder Hungarians in summer 1994 and 1995 and on discussions with ethnic Hungarians in Cluj, Romania (the largest city in Transylvania) in August 1995.
[43] See Szöke, "Hungarian Perspectives on Emigration and Immigration," 308.

Since 1991, when war broke out in Yugoslavia, Hungarians from Romania have been joined by migrants (again mostly ethnic Hungarians) from Serbian Vojvodina (home, before the war, to some 340,000 Hungarians) and from the Croatian region of Eastern Slavonia, fleeing war, conscription, and economic crisis. In some cases, Voivodina Hungarians have been pressured to leave their homes by Serb refugees who had been resettled in their midst. From the Transcarpathian region of southwestern Ukraine, where there are about 170,000 Hungarians, there has been little resettlement (and that mainly on the part of intellectuals); migration has instead taken the form of cross-border petty commerce, exploiting the huge economic disparities between the two states. In Slovakia, the southern part of which is home to some 600,000 Hungarians, nationalizing policies have heightened ethnic tensions; but these have to date been played out much more strongly at the elite level than in everyday life. In the absence of significant economic incentives, there has been little migration to Hungary.

German migration from Habsburg and Hohenzollern successor states

Our final comparative case is that of ethnic Germans. We have encountered them twice before, as targets of Polish nationalizing nationalism on the one hand (Chapter 4) and of Weimar homeland nationalism on the other (Chapter 5); we have seen that the former encouraged, while the latter sought to forestall, large-scale ethnic unmixing. Here I consider the problem in more detail.

After World War I, some 4.5 to 5 million Germans were suddenly transformed from ruling nationality or *Staatsvolk* in the Austrian half of the Habsburg Empire and in some eastern, predominantly Polish districts of the German Kaiserreich into beleaguered national minorities in the new and highly nationalist nation-states of Czechoslovakia and Poland as well as in equally nationalist Italy. Another 2 million Germans from the Hungarian half of the Habsburg Empire, while not, in the last decades of the Empire, a ruling nationality in the same sense, had nonetheless enjoyed a secure status; apart from the 220,000 Germans of the western Hungarian Burgenland, ceded to Austria after the war,[44] they too suddenly became national minorities – albeit initially less embattled and beleaguered ones – in Hungary, Romania, Yugoslavia, and Czechoslovakia. Altogether, some 6.5 million Germans became national

---

[44] Alfred Bohman, *Bevölkerung und Nationalitäten in Südosteuropa* (Cologne: Verlag Wissenschaft und Politik, 1969), p. 36.

minorities including well over 3 million Sudeten Germans in Czechoslovakia, over 1.25 million Germans in the territories ceded by Germany and Austria-Hungary to Poland, half a million in territory ceded by Hungary to Romania, half a million in territory ceded by Austria and Hungary to Yugoslavia, half a million in rump Hungary, and a quarter million in the newly Italian South Tyrol.[45]

In response to this great status transformation, there appears to have been negligible migration of Germans from the Hungarian half of the former Habsburg Empire, and relatively little migration from the non-German parts of the Austrian half of the Empire, yet very heavy migration to Germany from the territories ceded by Germany to Poland. The lack of migration of Germans from former Hungarian territories is understandable. Their status changed least in the aftermath of empire. Ever since the Compromise of 1867 gave Hungarians a free hand in their half of the Empire, they, not Germans, had been the ruling nationality. It was Hungarians, not Germans, who were the large landowners, judges, prosecutors, bureaucrats, teachers, and postal and railway employees in the non-Magyar areas, and who fled in fear or emigrated after losing their livelihoods when these areas passed to the non-Hungarian successor states. Germans, by contrast, suffered no such dramatic status reversal with the dismemberment of Hungary, and had no special impetus to flee. In rump Hungary, relatively homogeneous ethnically and preoccupied with territorial revisionism and with the fate of fellow Magyars in the neighboring states, German–Hungarian relations were not particularly tense. Nor were Germans (unlike Hungarians) centrally implicated, in the early interwar years, in the national conflicts of Romania or Yugoslavia. It is therefore not surprising that the Germans of the Hungarian part of the Habsburg Empire remained in place after its dissolution.

For Germans from Hohenzollern Germany and the Austrian half of the Habsburg Empire, the abrupt transformation from ruling nationality to beleaguered national minority was much more drastic, and these new minorities were immediately plunged into harsh national conflicts in the successor states. At first glance, one might have expected similar post-imperial migration patterns on the part of these ex-Hohenzollern and

[45] Robert A. Kann, *The Multinational Empire: Nationalism and National Reform in the Habsburg Monarchy, 1848–1918* (New York: Columbia University Press, 1950), vol. II, pp. 301ff.; Walter Kuhn, "Das Deutschtum in Polen und sein Schicksal in Kriegs- und Nachkriegszeit," in Werner Markert, ed., *Polen* (Cologne and Graz: Bohlau, 1959); Werner Nellner, "Grundlagen und Hauptergebnisse der Statistik," in Eugen Lemberg and Friedrich Edding, eds., *Die Vertriebene in Westdeutschland* (Kiel: Ferdinand Hart, 1959), vol. I, p. 67.

ex-Habsburg Germans. Yet there were sharp differences. Adequate Austrian statistics are lacking for the crucial first few years after the breakup of the Empire.[46] Yet while there appears to have been considerable migration of former Imperial civil servants and military personnel from the successor states to Vienna,[47] there was certainly no mass influx. And while Austrians were unhappy with the peace settlement – with the exclusion of the Sudeten and South Tyrolean Germans from the Austrian successor state, and even more with the prohibition of *Anschluss* onto Germany – the migrants that did arrive in Vienna, quite unlike their politically powerful and radically irredentist Hungarian counterparts in Budapest, do not seem to have been strongly committed to recovering lost territories or to have had any impact on interwar Austrian politics.[48]

From the territories ceded to Poland by Germany, on the other hand, there was a mass exodus of ethnic Germans – some 600,000 to 800,000 in the immediately postwar years.[49] The large majority of these came from Posen and Polish Pomerania and resettled in the immediate aftermath, and even in anticipation, of the transfer of sovereignty.[50] Another substantial group arrived somewhat later from the portion of Upper Silesia that was awarded, after the 1921 plebiscite, and accompanying violent struggles, to Poland. More than half of the ethnic German population of the formerly German territories that were incorporated into interwar Poland had migrated to Germany within ten years.[51] The exodus was even heavier from urban areas in the lost territories. Ethnic German "public officials, schoolteachers, members of the liberal professions, and [unskilled and semiskilled] workmen [but not artisans] disappeared almost entirely from the towns of the western Polish

---

[46] Alfred Bohman, *Bevölkerung und Nationalitäten in der Tschechoslowakei* (Cologne: Verlag Wissenschaft und Politik, 1975), p. 146.

[47] Marrus, *Unwanted*, p. 74.

[48] Some Sudeten German nationalists, to be sure, did move to Germany, where they became part of the Weimar homeland nationalist scene described in Chapter 5 and, at the radical end of the spectrum, conducted an irredentist campaign urging the incorporation of Sudeten German lands into the Reich. Their numbers were small, however, and they had no appreciable influence on Weimar politics. Radical émigré nationalists were more significant players in the homeland nationalist field in the Nazi period; see Ronald M. Smelser, *The Sudeten Problem, 1933–1938: Volkstumspolitik and the Formulation of Nazi Foreign Policy* (Folkestone, UK: Dawson, 1975), esp. pp. 29ff.

[49] Eugene M. Kulischer, *Europe on the Move: War and Population Changes, 1917–47* (New York: Columbia University Press, 1948), p. 175; Richard Blanke, *Orphans of Versailles: The Germans in Western Poland 1918–1939* (Lexington: University Press of Kentucky, 1993), pp. 32ff.

[50] Martin Broszat, *Zweihundert Jahre deutsche Polenpolitik* (Frankfurt: Suhrkamp, 1972), p. 212.

[51] Schechtman, *European Population Transfers*, pp. 259ff.; somewhat higher estimates are given in Broszat, *Zweihundert Jahre deutsche Polenpolitik*, p. 212.

provinces."[52] By 1926 the German urban population of Posen and Polish Pomerania had declined by 85 percent.[53]

Why was ethnic German outmigration in the aftermath of empire so much heavier from the formerly German territories of Poland than from Habsburg successor states? Why, in particular, was there mass emigration from western Poland but no substantial emigration from interwar Czechoslovakia? The 3 million Sudeten Germans of Bohemia, Moravia, and Czech Silesia, after all, were among the most politically alienated of successor state Germans. Highly nationalistic, and looking down on Czechs, over whom they felt historically destined to rule, they were initially unwilling to live as minorities in a Czechoslovak state. Clearly desiring, and formally proclaiming, unification with Austria, and assuming that the Paris peacemakers would recognize their asserted right to self-determination, they were bitterly disappointed when it became clear that the historic frontiers of the Habsburg provinces would be maintained, and the Sudeten territories incorporated into Czechoslovakia.[54] Yet no substantial emigration ensued; nor did large-scale migration occur later in response to what Sudeten Germans interpreted as a government policy systematically favoring Czechs in economic and cultural matters and aimed at weakening the ethnodemographic position of Germans.

The mass ethnic German emigration from western Poland but not from the Sudeten lands shows that the sudden transformation from ruling nationality to beleaguered and politically alienated national minority does not in and of itself generate migrations of ethnic unmixing. Two other factors shaped these strikingly different patterns of post-imperial migration. First, migration to Germany was less of a displacement for the ethnic Germans of the new Polish state than migration to Austria would have been for their Sudeten counterparts. Germany had been defeated in war, diminished in territory, and transformed into a republic; but it was still "the same" state, one to which ethnic Germans who found themselves under unwelcome Polish jurisdiction could plausibly return. The state of the Sudeten Germans, however, had vanished; there was no state for them to return to. Rump Austria was not "their" state; it was not a diminished and transformed Habsburg Empire but rather a completely different state.[55]

---

[52] Schechtman, *European Population Transfers*, p. 261.

[53] Blanke, *Orphans of Versailles*, p. 34.

[54] Bohman, *Bevölkerung und Nationalitäten in der Tschechoslowakei*, pp. 39ff.; Rothschild, *East Central Europe*, pp. 78–81; Smelser, *The Sudeten Problem*, pp. 8–9.

[55] Interwar Hungary, on the other hand, *was* essentially a (much) diminished and transformed version of prewar Hungary; it was in an important sense "the same" state.

Second, Sudeten Germans were much more deeply rooted and compactly settled than the Germans of western Poland. Germans comprised – and had for hundreds of years – the overwhelming majority (over 95 percent of the population) throughout most of the Sudeten lands on the northern, western, and southern perimeter of Bohemia and Moravia.[56] Ethnic Germans were in the minority, however, in the territories ceded by Germany to Poland after the First World War. More important, they had been an embattled, demographically eroding, and artificially sustained minority even before the war, when the territories still belonged to Germany. The Prussian and German governments had made strenuous efforts to assimilate the ethnic Poles and to induce ethnic Germans to settle and remain in these frontier districts, but to little avail. The harsh efforts to Germanize the Polish population were counterproductive, alienating the Poles and reinforcing their Polish national identity.[57] The region's ethnic Germans, moreover, participated disproportionately in the heavy east–west internal migration from the agrarian east to the industrial west in the late nineteenth and early twentieth century, thereby weakening the ethnically German element in the east in spite of massive state efforts to sustain it. Having thus had a precarious and embattled existence even before the war, under German sovereignty, the ethnic German population of these territories lacked the rootedness and firm attachment to the region of their counterparts in the Sudeten region. And they had every reason to expect the new Polish government to attempt just as vigorously and heavy-handedly to Polonize its western borderlands as the German government had sought to Germanize the same territories before the war. That expectation was not disappointed: the policy of the Polish government toward the ethnic German minority was considerably harsher than that of the Czechoslovak government.[58] They were therefore much more likely to emigrate once sovereignty passed to Poland, and even, in substantial numbers, in anticipation of the transfer of sovereignty.

The migration of ethnic Germans from the western provinces of the new Polish state was heavier, both in absolute numbers and in proportion to the size of the new minorities, than any migration from

---

For this reason, among others, migration to rump Hungary on the part of ethnic Hungarians from the successor states was no doubt more plausible than migration to rump Austria on the part of ethnic Germans.

[56] Bohman, *Bevölkerung und Nationalitäten in der Tschechoslowakei*, p. 117.

[57] Broszat, *Zweihundert Jahre deutsche Polenpolitik*; Hans-Ulrich Wehler, "Polenpolitik im Deutschen Kaiserreich," in Wehler, ed., *Krisenherde des Kaiserreichs*, 2nd edn (Göttingen: Vandenhoeck and Ruprecht, 1979); Richard Blanke, *Prussian Poland in the German Empire (1871–1900)* (Boulder, Colo.: East European Monographs, 1981).

[58] Blanke, *Orphans of Versailles*.

ex-Habsburg lands, including the migration of ethnic Hungarians to rump Hungary. German migration to Germany involved at least half of the German population of the ceded territories, the Hungarian migration to Hungary only about 13 percent of the ethnic Hungarian population of the ceded territories. Yet although nationalist publicists accused Poland of deliberately driving out Germans from the border areas,[59] and although the resettlers (including small but vigorous nationalist groups from Czechoslovakia, the Baltics, and other areas of German settlement) did become active participants in various homeland nationalist associations, German migration does not seem to have had the political impact of its Hungarian counterpart. This was partly because German losses – of territory and of ethnic brethren – were much less extensive than Hungary's, and resettlers from lost territories comprised a much smaller fraction of the population of interwar Germany than of interwar Hungary. The German resettlers, moreover, more closely approximated a cross-section of the German population of the lost territories than did their Hungarian counterparts, whose predominantly elite composition amplified their voice in interwar politics.

For Germans, then, little ethnic unmixing occurred in the aftermath of the collapse of the Habsburg Empire. The overwhelming majority of the more than 5 million Germans who became national minorities in the successor states remained in those states throughout the interwar period. Yet mass ethnic unmixing in this region was only postponed, not forestalled. Today there are scarcely any Germans in Czechoslovakia or the former Yugoslavia, and there are only small residual communities of Germans in Hungary and Romania. Of ex-Habsburg Germans in successor states other than Austria, only those of the Italian South Tyrol survive today as a relatively intact community (despite a harsh Italian-ization campaign in the interwar period and a 1939 German–Italian agreement, at Mussolini's request, to resettle them in Germany).[60] Most of the ex-Habsburg Germans – including virtually all of the Sudeten Germans – were expelled, with Allied acquiescence, in the final stages and immediate aftermath of the Second World War (along with an even larger group of Germans from the eastern provinces of interwar Germany, who fled the advancing Red Army or were driven out in the aftermath of the war). By 1950 there were in the Federal Republic and German Democratic Republic some 12 million ethnic German *Vertriebene* or expellees. Of these about 7 million were German citizens

[59] Schechtman, *European Population Transfers*, pp. 259–60.
[60] *Ibid.*, pp. 48–65.

from the eastern territories of interwar Germany, now annexed by
Poland and (in the case of the area around Königsberg/Kaliningrad) the
Soviet Union. The remaining 5 million were citizens of other states –
mainly Habsburg successor states.[61] Between 1950 and 1987, another
1.5 million ethnic Germans from Eastern Europe and the Soviet Union
were resettled in the Federal Republic, over half of them from Poland.[62]
Since then, with the liberalization of travel and emigration, nearly
2 million *Spätaussiedler*[63] have settled in the Federal Republic, lured by
its fabled prosperity, and taking advantage of the automatic immigration
and citizenship rights that continue to be offered to ethnic Germans from
the so-called *Vertreibungsgebiete*, i.e. the territories from which Germans
were driven out after the war.[64] As a result, the once-vast German
diaspora of Eastern Europe and Russia is today undergoing a rapid, and
probably final, dissolution.

Ethnic unmixing in the aftermath of empire: some general characteristics

From this excursus into comparative history four general analytical
points emerge. The first concerns the great variation in the degree,
timing, and modalities of ethnic unmixing in the aftermath of empire –
variation between the three cases we have considered, but also, and
equally important, variation within each case over time, across regions,
and among social classes. Consider just a few of the more striking dimensions of variation. In some regions (for example the Sudeten German
lands of Bohemia and Moravia) unmixing has been virtually complete; in
others (notably the Hungarian successor states) only a relatively small
minority of the former dominant group has migrated. In some cases (for
example that of Germans in provinces ceded after World War I to
Poland) large-scale migration occurred in the immediate aftermath of
political reconfiguration or (in much of the Balkans) in the course of
wars that produced the reconfiguration; in other cases (the ex-Habsburg

---

[61] Nellner, "Grundlagen und Hauptergebnisse der Statistik," pp. 122ff.
[62] Jürgen Pusskepeleit, "Zugangsentwicklung, Ungleichverteilung und ihre Auswirkungen
auf die Kommunen," in Karl Otto, ed., *Westwärts-Heimwärts? Aussiedlerpolitik zwischen
"Deutschtümelei" und "Verfassungsauftrag"* (Bielefeld: AJZ, 1990), p. 165.
[63] In German usage, *Aussiedler* (ethnic German resettlers from Eastern Europe and the
former Soviet Union) were distinguished from *Übersiedler* (Germans who moved from
East to West Germany). *Spätaussiedler* ("late resettlers") are those who have come
recently from Eastern Europe and the former Soviet Union, decades after the postwar
expulsion of Germans from these territories.
[64] See my *Citizenship and Nationhood in France and Germany* (Cambridge, Mass.: Harvard
University Press, 1992), pp. 168ff.

Germans) mass migration occurred only much later. In many cases migrants fled actual or immediately feared violence (for example Muslims and others in the Russo-Turkish and Balkan Wars, and millions of Germans in the final stages of the Second World War) or were compelled to move by the state (Turks from Greece in 1923–24, Germans in the aftermath of the Second World War); in other cases (German *Spätaussiedler* and the recent Hungarian migrants to Hungary) migrations occurred in more deliberate fashion, as the aggregate result of innumerable individual calculations of well-being.

A corollary of the first point is that there was nothing foreordained about postimperial migrations of ethnic unmixing. The reconfiguration of political space along national lines did not automatically entail a corresponding redistribution of population. Neither migration nor even the propensity to migrate was inexorably engendered by the status transformation from dominant, state-bearing nationality in a multinational state to national minority in a successor state. Much depended on the manner in which political reconfiguration occurred (notably the extent to which it was effected through or accompanied by war or other types of organized or disorganized violence); on the ethnodemographic characteristics, especially the rootedness, of the new minority; on the anticipated and actual policies of the successor states toward the minority; on the availability and quality of the resettlement opportunities in an external national "homeland"; on the plausibility and attractiveness of mobilization as an alternative to migration, of "voice" as an alternative to "exit"; and so on.

Second, postimperial ethnic unmixing has been a protracted, if intermittent, process,[65] spanning three-quarters of a century for Hungarians and Germans, and more than a century for Turks. And it continues today: it is striking that all three ethnonational groups have experienced dramatic new waves of migratory unmixing in the last five years. One should think about ethnic unmixing in the aftermath of empire not as a short-term process that exhausts itself in the immediate aftermath of political reconfiguration, but rather as a long-term process in which, according to political and economic conjuncture in origin and destination states, migratory streams may dry up altogether for a time, persist in a steady trickle, or swell suddenly to a furious torrent.

Third, in the protracted course of postimperial migratory unmixings, the phases of greatest intensity have for the most part been closely linked to actual or threatened violence, especially during or immediately after

---

[65] Aristide Zolberg, "The Formation of New States as a Refugee-Generating Process," *Annals of the American Academy of Political and Social Science* 467 (1983), 37.

wars. I emphasized above the importance of war as a direct and indirect cause of the Balkan migrations. And the bulk of the ethnic German migration occurred in the final stages of World War II and in the mass expulsions immediately following the war. Yet the centrality of war and, more generally, violence does not mean that postimperial ethnic unmixing can be neatly subsumed under the rubric of "forced migration." That rubric is in fact too narrow and misleading. Some such migrations were, of course, directly compelled or forced in the most literal sense, and others, while not quite so literally coerced, were nonetheless powerfully induced by credible threats or well-grounded fears of imminent force or violence. But other cases do not satisfy even this expanded, looser definition of forced or coerced migration. This is the case for the great majority of Germans leaving the western provinces of Poland after the First World War, although Nazi propaganda claimed otherwise, and for Germans leaving Eastern Europe and the Soviet Union after 1950; it is also the case for most of the Hungarian migration in the aftermath of the Habsburg collapse and for almost all of the Hungarian migration from Romania in the last decade. Even the mass Turkish exodus from Bulgaria in 1989, while certainly provoked by the communist government of Bulgaria during its last months in power, is not adequately characterized as a forced migration.[66] More generally, even where fear is a central motive of the migrants, it is not always appropriate to speak of forced migrations. Many German migrants from territories ceded to Poland after the First World War, and many Hungarian migrants from Habsburg successor states, were no doubt moved in part by diffuse fears and anxieties about their future well-being in the new states; but they were not thereby forced migrants. Fear is a capacious concept: there is a great distance between migration arising from a sharply focused fear of imminent violence and migration engendered by a diffuse fear, concern, or anxiety about one's opportunities, or the opportunities of one's children, in the future. The conception of forced migration is simply not very useful as an umbrella concept here; it is insufficiently differentiated, and it obscures the fact that there is almost always, even in the case of flight from immediately threatening violence, a more or less significant element of will or choice involved in the act of migration. To question the usefulness of an insufficiently differentiated, overextended concept of forced migration, needless to say, is not to deny the importance of intimidation and violence as means deliberately employed to provoke migration.

[66] Vasileva, "Bulgarian Turkish Emigration and Return."

Fourth, except where whole communities were indiscriminately targeted for removal (as in the Greco-Turkish transfers of 1922–24 or in the expulsion of Sudeten Germans), there was a pronounced social selectivity to postimperial migrations of ethnic unmixing (as there is to many other migrations). Most vulnerable to displacement were groups dependent, directly or indirectly, on the state. This included military, police, and judicial personnel; bureaucrats and teachers; postal and railway employees; and workers in enterprises owned by the state or dependent on state subsidies or contracts. This selectivity of ethnic unmixing was apparent in all the migrations we considered but was demonstrated most dramatically in the post-World War I Hungarian migrations, where the peasant majority remained entirely in place, while the Magyar state-dependent stratum virtually disappeared from the successor states. The reasons for this differential susceptibility to emigration are obvious. The new nation-states were all nationalizing states, committed, in one way or another, to reversing historic patterns of discrimination by the former imperial rulers and to promoting the language, culture, demographic position, economic flourishing, and political hegemony of the new state-bearing nation. Short of enacting overtly discriminatory legislation, one of the main instruments available to the new states in pursuit of these goals was control over recruitment to state employment.

Russian migration from Soviet successor states in comparative and historical perspective

In the light of the foregoing, how best can we think about the actual and potential migration to Russia of the 25 million successor state Russians? To begin with (and following the same four points), we should not think of it as a unitary process, evincing the same patterns and following the same stages and rhythms throughout the former Soviet Union. Instead we should think of it as a congeries of related but distinct migrations (or non-migrations, as may be the case from some successor states), exhibiting distinct patterns and rhythms. We should expect, that is, great variation in patterns of post-Soviet Russian migration – variation both among and within successor states.

It follows that we should not think of the reflux of Russians to the Russian Federation as an automatic process, inexorably accompanying the breakup of the Soviet Union. We must avoid conceiving the causes of migration in overgeneralized terms. It is not adequate, for instance, to conceive of Russians leaving the successor states simply because they have been transformed from dominant nationality throughout the Soviet

Union to national minorities in the non-Russian successor states. The forces, processes, and conditions engendering Russian migration need to be conceived in much more specific and differentiated terms. It then becomes apparent that what is in general terms a uniform process – the transformation of Russians from dominant state-bearing nationality into national minorities in successor states – is in fact highly variegated and uneven, and that the specific migration-engendering forces, processes, and conditions are unevenly and contingently rather than uniformly and automatically associated with the reconfiguration of political authority along national lines in post-Soviet Eurasia.

Earlier postimperial migrations of ethnic unmixing, we have seen, were protracted; indeed they continue to this day. A broad time horizon seems advisable in thinking about post-Soviet migrations as well. This means looking back as well as forward. For the present Russian reflux toward Russia is not new and unprecedented. Selective ethnic unmixing began long before the explosion of nationalist protest under Gorbachev. The centuries-old current of Russian migratory expansion into non-Russian areas slowed and, in some cases, reversed itself during the last three decades. There was a substantial net Russian outflow from Georgia and Azerbaijan during each of the last three Soviet intercensal periods (1959–70, 1970–79, and 1979–89), and from Armenia in 1979–89. During the last intercensal period there was also a net outflow of Russians, for the first time, from Moldova, Kazakhstan, and each of the Central Asian republics. And even though net Russian immigration continued, during the last intercensal period, to the Baltics and the Slavic west (Ukraine and Belarus), the rates of such Russian in-migration declined over the last three intercensal periods in each of these republics except Lithuania.[67] The current and future phases of the Russian reflux toward Russia should therefore be understood not as initiating but as continuing and reinforcing a reversal of historic Russian migration patterns – a reversal the origins of which long antedate the breakup of the

---

[67] Barbara Anderson and Brian Silver, "Demographic Sources of the Changing Ethnic Composition of the Soviet Union," *Population and Development Review* 15 (1989), 640–2. Migratory unmixing also involved other nationalities. For three decades, for example, there has been substantial net migration of Armenians from Georgia and Azerbaijan to Armenia, and a modest net migration of Azeris from Georgia and Armenia to Azerbaijan. For these nationalities, the refugee flows of the last few years, following the outbreak of Armenian–Azeri ethnic violence in 1988, have only reinforced a long-term trend toward ethnic unmixing in Transcaucasia (*ibid.*, 638–40; Brian Silver, "Population Redistribution and the Ethnic Balance in Transcaucasia," in Ronald Grigor Suny, ed., *Transcaucasia: Nationalism and Social Change* [Ann Arbor: Michigan Slavic Publications, 1983], p. 377).

Soviet Union.[68] A broad time horizon also requires that we try to look beyond the immediately visible problems, crises, and migration currents to think, in an admittedly speculative mode, about the longer-term dynamics of political reconfiguration and ethnic unmixing in post-Soviet Eurasia.

The historically crucial role of war and, more broadly, violence in engendering postimperial migrations of ethnic unmixing, especially the most intense phases of such migrations, holds out the possibility that ethnic Russians might avoid being swept up by the kind of cataclysmic mass migrations that are almost invariably driven by war or at least by actual or threatened violence. Even in the absence of war or significant violence *directed against Russians*, to be sure, many Russians from Transcaucasia and Central Asia have been moving, and will no doubt continue to move, to Russia. But these migrations have not been, and need not be, cataclysmic, even if – to take a hypothetical limiting case – the entire Russian population of Central Asia (excluding Kazakhstan) and Transcaucasia were to migrate to Russia over, say, a ten-year period. Nor can recent and current migrations of Russians from these and some other regions be conceived as forced *(vynuzhdennyi)* migrations, although they are often referred to as such in Russian discussions. The fact that such migrations have been *induced* by political reconfiguration and changes in the political, economic, and cultural status of Russians does not mean that they have been *forced*. Even so, as I argue below, substantial Russian resettlement from these regions would significantly strain the Russian Federation. Yet it is important to distinguish between this mode of non-forced, non-cataclysmic unmixing and the vastly more disruptive and dangerous migrations that could ensue should ethno-political conflict in Kazakhstan or Ukraine become militarized or otherwise linked to large-scale violence.

One specific migration-engendering process central to earlier after-maths of empire was that of "ethnic succession" among officials and other state employees. It was this that accounted for the pronounced social selectivity of those earlier migrations of ethnic unmixing, with the state-dependent stratum of the former *Staatsvolk* heavily overrepresented among emigrants. Here the implications for post-Soviet migration are mixed. On the one hand, almost everyone is dependent, directly or indirectly, on the state, increasing the scope for ethnonational conflict. Although privatization may eventually reduce this dependence, it is itself

---

[68] Zhanna Zaionchkovskaia, "Effects of Internal Migration on the Emigration from the USSR," paper presented at conference on "Prospective Migration and Emigration from the Former Soviet Union," RAND, Santa Monica, Calif., November 1991.

a state-dependent process, affording ample occasion for ethnonational conflict over modes of appropriation of public assets and enterprises. But while the scope for ethnic conflict over jobs and resources is greater in the post-Soviet than, say, the post-Habsburg case, given the near-universal dependence on the state, the opportunities for ethnic succession *in its classic sphere*, namely public administration, are smaller. The Soviet Union was unlike earlier multinational empires in its deliberate culti- vation and institutional empowerment, in the peripheral republics, of numerous non-Russian national intelligentsias – coupled, of course, with harsh repression of deviant political behavior.[69] As a result, the adminis- trative apparatus of the periphery – monopolized by members of the imperial *Staatsvolk* in the old multinational empires, and consequently a prime target for ethnic succession in their aftermath – was already staffed largely by members of the titular nationalities. Public administration therefore does not provide the successor states with comparable oppor- tunities for the wholesale promotion of the new state-bearing nation at the expense of the former ruling nationality.[70] Nonetheless, competition for jobs in all sectors of the economy is bound to intensify as economic restructuring generates higher levels of unemployment, especially in regions where the labor force of the titular nationality is growing extremely rapidly.[71] Given the persisting centrality of the state in economic life, as well as the institutionalized expectations of "owner- ship" of "their own" polities held by titular elites (discussed in Chapter 2), such competition is sure to be politicized along ethnonational lines, albeit to differing degrees in different successor states. Intensifying labor market competition in the Soviet southern tier already contributed to gradual Russian outmigration during the last decade,[72] and it will no doubt continue to do so, although specifically political factors will probably become increasingly important in generating out-migration from those regions. The extent to which conflict over jobs and resources will generate out-migration of Russians from other regions, however,

[69] On the early Soviet policy of *korenizatsiia* and subsequent modes of preferential treat- ment, in higher education and state employment, for members of titular nationalities, see Simon, *Nationalism*; Philip G. Roeder, "Soviet Federalism and Ethnic Mobiliz- ation," *World Politics* 43 (1991).

[70] Indeed in comparative perspective, it is misleading to speak of Russians as the "ruling nationality" in the Soviet Union. They were a favored nationality in certain respects, and they were clearly the *Staatsvolk*, the state-bearing nationality, of the Soviet Union, but they were not a ruling nationality in the same sense as were Muslim Turks in the Ottoman Balkans, Hungarians in their half of the Habsburg Empire in its last half- century, or Germans in the heavily Polish Prussian east before the First World War.

[71] Zaionchkovskaia, "Effects of Internal Migration on Emigration."

[72] *Ibid.*

rather than ethnopolitical mobilization on their part, remains to be seen, and will depend on a variety of other factors, some of them sketched below.

A selective and uneven unmixing[73]

To understand the dynamics of the current and future Russian reflux toward Russia, it is not enough to point to the transformation of Russians from confident *Staatsvolk* into beleaguered minority. Nor can one appeal in sweeping terms – as do Russian nationalists – to the persecution of and discrimination against Russians in the successor states. The most salient fact about Russian migration from the successor states is its unevenness; and we need an analytical framework that can help explain this unevenness.

The response of the Russian diaspora to political, cultural, and economic reconfiguration in the aftermath of Soviet disintegration has been strikingly varied.[74] Emigration from non-Russian territories is only one of an array of possible responses. Other responses include individual assimilation, or at least acculturation, to the dominant local population, and collective mobilization for equal civil rights, for special cultural or linguistic rights, for territorial political autonomy, for secession, or even for the restoration of central control. The extent of Russian out-migration thus depends in part on the plausibility, feasibility, and attractiveness of alternative responses.

Ethnodemographic variables such as the size, concentration, and rootedness of the Russian populations in the territories in question, as well as the trajectory of these variables over time, comprise a first set of factors governing the relative attractiveness of migration. Where the Russian population is small, scattered, or weakly rooted, and especially when it has already been shrinking, the prevailing response to local nationalisms is likely to be emigration, together with a certain amount of apolitical individual acculturation or assimilation. A large, concentrated, and deeply rooted Russian population, on the other hand, is more likely to remain in place and engage in collective political action. Duration of residence obviously contributes to rootedness – not only how long a given individual or family has resided in the territory, but also how long the community has existed. Past and present ties to the land also

---

73 This section draws on part of my "Political Dimensions of Migration From and Among Soviet Successor States," in Myron Weiner, ed., *International Migration and Security*, (Boulder, Colo.: Westview Press, 1993).
74 For an overview, see Kolstoe, *Russians*.

contribute to rootedness: peasant communities, and to a lesser extent even the urban descendants of such peasant settlers, are ordinarily more deeply rooted than historically purely urban settlements. Among Russian diaspora communities, rootedness may be greatest in northern and eastern Kazakhstan[75] and in eastern and southern Ukraine;[76] it is probably weakest in the historically purely urban settlements of Central Asia. In wider historical and comparative perspective, however, it should be noted that none of the successor state Russian communities is as deeply rooted as peasant communities have tended to be.

A second set of factors includes the terms of membership and the texture of everyday life for Russians in the new nation-states. By terms of membership I mean the extent to which the rewritten rules of the political game in the new nation-states – especially those bearing on the language of education, the language of public life, the criteria of citizenship and the rights of permanent residents who are not granted, or do not seek, citizenship in the new states – impose cultural, economic, or political costs on the local Russian populations. More important than formal legislation, however, will be the everyday experience of successor state Russians. Actual or feared violence, in particular, will stimulate out-migration from weakly rooted Russian communities, and it will stimulate demands for restoration of central control, or for territorial autonomy, in deeply rooted Russian communities. Informal hostility toward Russians, even without the threat of violence, may have the same effects. Anti-Russian attitudes and practices are particularly important in Central Asia, given the high degree of segregation between Russians and indigenous nationalities and the more classically colonial character of Russian domination there. The great question mark is northern and eastern Kazakhstan, where the same segregation and quasi-colonial situation has existed, yet where the Russian settler population is more deeply rooted, dating from massive rural colonization in the late nineteenth century. Russians in Kazakhstan might be compared in this

---

[75] Already in 1911, 40% of the population of an area roughly approximating the northern two-thirds of present-day Kazakhstan were peasant colonists from European Russia. By contrast, only 6% of the population of the remaining parts of Russian Central Asia (today's southern Kazakhstan, plus the four republics of Central Asia proper) were Russians. See Richard Pierce, *Russian Central Asia 1867–1917* (Berkeley: University of California Press, 1960), p. 137.

[76] In 1897, ethnic Russians comprised 12% of the population of the nine Ukrainian provinces of the Russian Empire, and a much higher fraction of the population in the industrialized Donbass region and elsewhere in southern Ukraine; see Paul Robert Magocsi, *Ukraine: A Historical Atlas* (Toronto: University of Toronto Press, 1985), commentary to Map 18.

respect with French settler colonists in Algeria,[77] while Russians in the cities of Central Asia might be more aptly compared with urban Europeans in colonies without deeply rooted European rural settlements.

A further set of factors likely to shape the Russian response to political reconfiguration concerns the prospective economic or political advantages that might induce Russians to remain in a successor state despite anti-Russian sentiment and nationalistic language and citizenship legislation.[78] Such advantages are likely to be especially relevant in the Baltic states, which may be seen as having more favorable prospects than other successor states for economic integration into Europe and for maintaining public order and establishing liberal institutions.

A final set of factors concerns the orientation and policies of the Russian state toward the various communities of diaspora Russians. These include not only "domestic" policies toward immigrants and refugees from the successor states in matters of citizenship, immigration, and relocation or integration assistance (housing, employment, etc.), but also Russian "foreign policy" initiatives *vis-à-vis* the successor states, seeking either to forestall repatriation to Russia or, if repatriation cannot be forestalled, to regulate it. Russia might seek to prevent a potentially destabilizing massive influx of Russians by negotiating favorable conditions for the diaspora communities, for example, in matters of citizenship and cultural facilities. In a harsher mode, it might engage in coercive diplomacy or even intervene with military force to reassert control over all or part of a refugee-producing successor state, say a hypothetically radically nationalist Kazakhstan.[79] In general, differential policies of the Russian state toward the various diaspora communities may differentially affect the propensity of diaspora Russians to emigrate.

On the basis of these considerations, we can expect sharply differing rates of migration to Russia on the part of different diaspora groups.[80] Migration will probably be the dominant Russian response to non-Russian nationalisms in Central Asia (excluding Kazakhstan) and

---

[77] On settler colonialism, see Ian Lustick, *State-Building Failure in British Ireland and French Algeria* (Berkeley: Institute of International Studies, University of California, 1985).

[78] By political advantages I understand here greater security or stability.

[79] On coercive diplomacy, see Weiner, "Security, Stability, and International Migration," 23–4.

[80] Besides the contextual variables sketched here, characterizing successor states, their Russian communities, and Russian state policy, a set of individual-level variables will be important determinants of Russian out-migration. These include age, professional or occupational qualifications, language knowledge, family connections in Russia, and so on.

Transcaucasia. The Russian population of Central Asia, although large, is exclusively urban and not deeply rooted; and it faces the greatest informal hostility from the indigenous nationalities. The Russian population of Transcaucasia is small and rapidly shrinking. Already during the 1980s, as I noted above, there was substantial Russian emigration from Central Asia and Transcaucasia, and the rate of emigration has increased since the collapse of Soviet authority. Russian out-migration rates are likely to remain much lower from areas with territorially concentrated and historically rooted Russian populations such as eastern and southern Ukraine, northern and eastern Kazakhstan, Moldova east of the Dniester, and northeastern Estonia. There, we are more likely to see – and in some cases, of course, already are seeing – collective political responses on the part of Russians to non-Russian nationalisms. Elsewhere in the Baltic states, comparatively bright medium- and long-term economic prospects can be expected to limit the scale of out-migration.

This means that of the 25 million Russians in the non-Russian successor states, only a small fraction – if nonetheless a large group in absolute numbers – is at high risk of being induced or forced to flee to Russia in the next few years. The Russians most likely to resettle in Russia are those in Central Asia (3.3 million in 1989) and Transcaucasia (785,000). Many of these – though we do not have a very precise idea how many – have already moved, with the heaviest proportional outflow from violence-torn Tajikistan.[81] This pool of actual and potential migrants amounts to less than 3 percent of the total population of Russia. In principle, the resettlement of even a substantial fraction of this migrant pool might benefit Russia. For decades, Soviet demographers and economic planners have been concerned about rural depopulation in central Russia and about labor deficits in areas of Russia that were targeted for development projects. In practice, however, it will be difficult for the state to steer resettlement in accordance with

---

[81] Statistics on migration flows in recent years are derived from bureaucratic procedures (registering with local authorities or applying for special status as a refugee or forced migrant). With the withering away of the state, many migrants avoid such procedures. Statistics thus capture only a part of the flow, by most estimates only a relatively small part (Vitkovskaia, *Vynuzhdennaia migratsiia*, p. 3.) Drawing on these official statistics, Sergei Shakhrai, Russian minister of nationalities, remarked in March 1994 that 356,000 *rossiiane* – a category that includes other ethnic groups indigenous to Russia in addition to ethnic Russians – had migrated to Russia from Central Asia "in recent years" (quoted in John Dunlop, "Will the Russians Return from the Near Abroad?," *Post-Soviet Geography* 35 [1994], 206). The actual number is no doubt considerably higher. For estimates of the post-Soviet outflows from individual Central Asian states, see *ibid.*, 207ff.

demographic and economic needs. Far from benefiting Russia, the migration to Russia in the next few years of a substantial fraction of Central Asian and Transcaucasian Russians would probably place a significant strain on the Russian state, which, in the throes of economic crisis, and having no experience with immigration or refugee flows, is largely unprepared to handle a substantial influx of resettlers or refugees.

Such migration would pose a greater strain on the Central Asian societies, given the Russian or European monopoly or quasi-monopoly of many technical occupations in these countries. The outflow of skilled specialists in the last few years has already disrupted enterprises. Fearing further, more serious disruptions, ruling elites of the Central Asian successor states have urged, and sought to induce, Russians and other Europeans to remain. How successful they will be remains to be seen. Retaining Russians and other Slavs will certainly be easier than retaining those with more attractive resettlement opportunities (especially Germans and Jews, whose Central Asian settlements have been rapidly shrinking). Much will depend on successor state governments' ability to maintain public order and on the overall social and political atmosphere in these states.

Much more serious than even a near-complete Russian exodus from Central Asia would be a massive Russian exodus from the core areas of Russian settlement in the non-Russian successor states, Ukraine and Kazakhstan, with some 11.4 and 6.2 million Russians, respectively, in 1989, accounting for 70 percent of the total Russian diaspora.[82] With large, territorially concentrated, and historically rooted communities in these states, I have suggested, Russians are unlikely to leave in large numbers unless (1) government policies and popular practices in

---

[82] In the case of Ukraine, the precision suggested by census figures, even when rounded to the nearest hundred thousand, is entirely spurious. For while the boundary between Russians and other Slavs on the one hand and Kazakhs on the other is sharp in Kazakhstan, the boundary between Russians and Ukrainians in Ukraine is anything but. The very categories "Russian" and "Ukrainian" as designators of ethnic nationality rather than legal citizenship are, from a sociological point of view, deeply problematic in the Ukrainian context, where rates of intermarriage are extremely high, and where nearly 2 million of those designating their ethnic nationality as Ukrainian in the 1989 census admitted to not speaking Ukrainian as their native language *or* as a second language they could "freely command" – a figure many consider to be greatly underestimated. (For the data on language, see Gosudarstvennyi komitet SSSR po statistike, *Natsional'nyi sostav naseleniia SSSR*, pp. 78–9.) A self-conscious ethnically Russian minority *as distinct from the Russophone population* may emerge in Ukraine, but it cannot be taken as given. For an argument that political cleavages in Ukraine will follow linguistic rather than ethnic lines, see Dominique Arel, "Language and Group Boundaries in the Two Ukraines," paper presented at conference on "National Minorities, Nationalizing States, and External National Homelands in the New Europe," Bellagio Study and Conference Center, Italy, August 1994.

Ukraine and Kazakhstan take on a much more sharply anti-Russian orientation than they have at present and (2) intensifying ethnonational conflict is militarized or otherwise linked with actual or threatened violence. Although there is no immediate prospect of this occurring, it must be reckoned a real possibility over the longer term, especially in Kazakhstan, given the potent historical memories that can be mobilized around the tremendous suffering inflicted by the Soviet state, with whose projects Russian settlers – at least in the case of Kazakhstan – can be all too easily identified.

Besides the tremendous economic problems it would entail, large-scale resettlement of Russians from Ukraine or Kazakhstan to Russia could also be politically destabilizing. The still-modest reflux of Russians to Russia – represented as forced migration – already provides abundant grist for the mills of Russian nationalists. A much larger Russian exodus from these core areas of Russian settlement in the near abroad, especially one occurring in response to sharply anti-Russian state policies or instances or threats of violence, would further strengthen the national-ists, and the refugees could form key constituencies for radical nationalists committed to recovering control of what they claim are "historically Russian" territories. In other instances, including, as we saw above, interwar Hungary, displaced and dispossessed refugees have provided constituencies for extreme nationalist parties and programs.

Conclusion

Post-Soviet Eurasia has entered what is likely to be a protracted period of political reconfiguration, involving simultaneously the reconstitution of political authority, the redrawing of territorial boundaries, and the restructuring of populations. These multiple reconfigurations, together with massive economic transformations, have already entailed consider-able migration, and will no doubt entail considerably more, possibly on a scale unseen since the aftermath of the Second World War. The largest of these migrations – and one particularly fraught with political impli-cations – has been and will continue to be that of successor state Russians to Russia. Surveying earlier instances of ethnic unmixing in the aftermath of empire, this chapter has sought to come to grips analytically with the patterns and dynamics that are likely to characterize that migration. Arguing against overgeneralized explanations or prognostications of ethnic unmixing, it points to the need for a more nuanced, differentiated approach that would take systematic account of the varied and multiform conditions facing successor state Russians and their varied and multi-form responses, including migration, to those conditions.

Bibliography

Abbott, Andrew. "From Causes to Events: Notes on Narrative Positivism." *Sociological Methods and Research* 20 (1992), 428–55.

Akzin, Benjamin. *States and Nations*. Garden City, NY: Doubleday, 1966.

Alexander, Manfred. "Die Politik der Weimarer Republik gegenüber den deutschen Minderheiten in Ostmitteleuropa, 1918–1926." Pp. 341–67 in *Annali dell'Instituto Storico Italo-Germanico in Trento*, vol. IV. Bologna: Mulino, 1978.

Amende, Ewald, ed. *Die Nationalitäten in den Staaten Europas: Sammlung von Lageberichten*. Vienna: Wilhelm Braumüller, 1931.

Anderson, Barbara, and Brian Silver. "Demographic Sources of the Changing Ethnic Composition of the Soviet Union." *Population and Development Review* 15 (1989), 609–56.

Anderson, Benedict. *Imagined Communities: Reflections on the Origin and Spread of Nationalism*. Revised edn. London: Verso, 1991.

Arel, Dominique. "Language and Group Boundaries in the Two Ukraines." Paper presented at conference on "National Minorities, Nationalizing States, and External National Homelands in the New Europe," Bellagio Study and Conference Center, Italy, August 1994.

Armstrong, John. "The Autonomy of Ethnic Identity: Historic Cleavages and Nationality Relations in the USSR." Pp. 23–43 in Alexander Motyl, ed., *Thinking Theoretically About Soviet Nationalities*. New York: Columbia University Press, 1992.

Azrael, Jeremy, ed. *Soviet Nationality Policies and Practices*. New York: Praeger, 1978.

Bauer, Otto. *Die Nationalitätenfrage und die Sozialdemokratie*. Vienna: I. Brand, 1907.

Beetham, David. "The Future of the Nation-State." Pp. 208–22 in Gregor McLennan, David Held, and Stuart Hall, eds., *The Idea of the Modern State*. Milton Keynes, UK and Philadelphia: Open University Press, 1984.

Beissinger, Mark. "Elites and Ethnic Identities in Soviet and Post-Soviet Politics." Pp. 141–69 in Alexander J. Motyl, ed., *The Post-Soviet Nations: Perspectives on the Demise of the USSR*. New York: Columbia University Press, 1992.

"The Persisting Ambiguity of Empire." *Post-Soviet Affairs* 11, no. 2 (1995), 149–84.

Bennigsen, Alexandre, and S. Enders Wimbush. "Migration and Political Control: Soviet Europeans in Soviet Central Asia." Pp. 173–87 in William H. McNeill and Ruth S. Adams, eds., *Human Migration: Patterns and Policies*. Bloomington: Indiana University Press, 1978.

Bilinsky, Yaroslav. "The Concept of the Soviet People and Its Implications for Soviet Nationality Policy." *Annals of the Ukrainian Academy of Arts and Sciences in the United States* 14 (1978–80), 87–133.

Birch, Julian. "Border Disputes and Disputed Borders in the Soviet Federal System." *Nationalities Papers* 15, no. 1 (1987), 43–70.

Blanke, Richard. "The German Minority in Inter-War Poland and German Foreign Policy." *Journal of Contemporary History* 25 (1990), 87–102.

Orphans of Versailles: The Germans in Western Poland, 1918–1939. Lexington: University Press of Kentucky, 1993.

Prussian Poland in the German Empire (1871–1900). Boulder, Colo.: East European Monographs, 1981.

Blishchenko, I. P., A. Kh. Abasidze, and E. V. Martynenko. "Problemy Gosudarstvennoi politiki Rossiiskoi Federatsii v otnoshenii sootechestvennikov" [Problems of the State Policy of the Russian Federation in Relation to Compatriots]. *Gosudarstvo i pravo* [State and Law] 2 (1994), 3–14.

Boehm, Max Hildebert. *Das eigenständige Volk*. Göttingen: Vandenhoeck and Ruprecht, 1932.

"Die Reorganisation der Deutschtumsarbeit nach dem ersten Weltkrieg." *Ostdeutsche Wissenschaft: Jahrbuch des ostdeutschen Kulturrates* 5 (1959), 9–34.

Bohman, Alfred. *Bevölkerung und Nationalitäten in der Tschechoslowakei*. Cologne: Verlag Wissenschaft und Politik, 1975.

Bevölkerung und Nationalitäten in Südosteuropa. Cologne : Verlag Wissenschaft und Politik, 1969.

Borneman, John. *Belonging in the Two Berlins*. New York: Cambridge University Press, 1992.

Bourdieu, Pierre. "Codification." Pp. 76–86 in Bourdieu, *In Other Words*.

"L'identité et la représentation: éléments pour une réflexion critique sur l'idée de région." *Actes de la recherche en sciences sociales* 35 (1980), 63–72.

In Other Words: Essays Towards a Reflexive Sociology. Stanford: Stanford University Press, 1990.

Language and Symbolic Power. Cambridge, Mass.: Harvard University Press, 1991.

"Social Space and Symbolic Power." Pp. 123–40 in Bourdieu, *In Other Words*.

"Social Space and the Genesis of Groups." *Theory and Society* 14 (1985), 723–44.

Bourdieu, Pierre, and Loïc Waquant. *An Invitation to Reflexive Sociology*. Chicago: University of Chicago Press, 1992.

Bremmer, Ian. "Nazarbaev and the North: State-Building and Ethnic Relations in Kazakhstan." *Ethnic and Racial Studies* 17, no. 4 (1994), 619–35.

"Post-Soviet Nationalities Theory: Past, Present, and Future." In Bremmer and Taras, eds., *New States, New Politics*.

"Russians as Ethnic Minorities in Ukraine and Kazakhstan." Paper presented at conference on "National Minorities, Nationalizing States, and External Homelands," Bellagio Study and Conference Center, Italy, 1994.

Bremmer, Ian and Ray Taras, eds. *New States, New Politics: Building the Post-Soviet Nations*. Cambridge: Cambridge University Press, forthcoming 1996.

Breuilly, John. *Nationalism and the State*. Chicago: University of Chicago Press, 1985.

Brock, Peter. "Polish Nationalism." Pp. 310–72 in Sugar and Lederer, eds., *Nationalism in Eastern Europe*.

Broszat, Martin. "Aussen- und innenpolitische Aspekte der Preussisch-Deutschen Minderheitenpolitik in der Ära Stresemann." Pp. 393–445 in Kurt Klexen and Wolfgang Mommsen, eds., *Politische Ideologien und nationalstaatliche Ordnung*. Munich: R. Oldenbourg, 1968.

"Die völkische Ideologie und der Nationalsozialismus." *Deutsche Rundschau* 84, no. 1 (1958), 53–68.

Zweihundert Jahre deutsche Polenpolitik. Frankfurt: Suhrkamp, 1972.

Brubaker, Rogers. *Citizenship and Nationhood in France and Germany*. Cambridge, Mass.: Harvard University Press, 1992.

"Citizenship Struggles in Soviet Successor States." *International Migration Review* 26 (1992), 269–91.

"East European, Soviet, and Post-Soviet Nationalisms: A Framework for Analysis." Pp. 353–78 in Frederick D. Weil, ed., *Research on Democracy and Society*, vol. 1. Greenwich, Conn.: JAI Press, 1993.

"Political Dimensions of Migration From and Among Soviet Successor States." Pp. 39–64 in Weiner, ed., *International Migration and Security*.

Brügel, Johann Wolfgang. *Tschechen und Deutsche 1918–1938*. Munich: Nymphenburger, 1967.

Burleigh, Michael. *Germany Turns Eastward: A Study of Ostforschung in the Third Reich*. Cambridge: Cambridge University Press, 1988.

Calhoun, Craig. "Nationalism and Ethnicity." *Annual Review of Sociology* 19 (1993), 211–39.

"The Problem of Identity in Collective Action." Pp. 51–75 in Joan Huber, ed., *Macro-Micro Linkages in Sociology*. Newbury Park, Calif.: Sage, 1991.

Campbell, F. Gregory. *Confrontation in Central Europe: Weimar Germany and Czechoslovakia*. Chicago: University of Chicago Press, 1975.

Carr, E. H. *The Bolshevik Revolution*. London: Macmillan, 1950.

Chazan, Naomi, ed. *Irredentism and International Politics*. Boulder, Colo., and London: Lynne Rienner and Adamantine Press, 1991.

Chinn, Jeff, and Steven D. Roper. "Ethnic Mobilization and Reactive Nationalism: The Case of Moldova." Manuscript, 1994.

Cohen, Leonard. *Broken Bonds: The Disintegration of Yugoslavia*. Boulder, Colo.: Westview Press, 1993.

Comaroff, John. "Humanity, Ethnicity, Nationality: Conceptual and Comparative Perspectives on the U.S.S.R." *Theory and Society* 20 (1991), 661–89.

Connor, Walker. "The Impact of Homelands Upon Diasporas." Pp. 16–46 in Sheffer, ed., *Modern Diasporas in International Politics*.

"Nation-Building or Nation-Destroying?" *World Politics* 24 (1972), 319–55.

The National Question in Marxist-Leninist Theory and Strategy. Princeton, NJ: Princeton University Press, 1984.

Conquest, Robert. *The Nation Killers: The Soviet Deportation of Nationalities*. New York: Macmillan, 1970.

Conze, Werner. *Die Deutsche Nation*. Göttingen: Vandenhoeck and Ruprecht, 1963.

"Nationsbildung durch Trennung." Pp. 95–119 in Otto Pflanze, ed., *Innenpolitische Probleme des Bismarckreiches*. Munich: R. Oldenbourg, 1983.

Cooper, Robert, and Mats Berdal. "Outside Intervention in Ethnic Conflicts." Pp. 181–205 in Michael Brown, ed., *Ethnic Conflict and International Security*. Princeton, NJ: Princeton University Press, 1993.

Dann, Otto. *Nation und Nationalismus in Deutschland 1770–1990*. Munich: C. H. Beck, 1993.

Darras, Loïc. "La double nationalité." Thesis in Law, Paris, 1986.

Demko, George J. *The Russian Colonization of Kazakhstan 1896–1916*. Bloomington: Indiana University Press, 1969.

d'Encausse, Hélène Carrère. *The End of the Soviet Empire: The Triumph of the Nations*. New York: Basic Books, 1993.

Le grand défi: Bolcheviks et nations 1917–1930. Paris: Flammarion, 1987.

Denich, Bette. "Dismembering Yugoslavia: Nationalist Ideologies and the Symbolic Revival of Genocide." *American Ethnologist* 21, no. 2 (1994), 367–90.

"Unmaking Multi-Ethnicity in Yugoslavia: Metamorphosis Observed." *Anthropology of East Europe Review* 11, nos. 1–2 (1993), 43–53.

Denitch, Bogdan. *Ethnic Nationalism: The Tragic Death of Yugoslavia*. Minneapolis: University of Minnesota Press, 1994.

Deutsch, Karl. *Nationalism and Social Communication*. Cambridge, Mass. and New York: The Technology Press of the Massachusetts Institute of Technology and John Wiley, 1953.

DiMaggio, Paul, and Walter Powell. "Introduction." Pp. 1–38 in Powell and DiMaggio, eds., *The New Institutionalism in Organizational Analysis*. Chicago: University of Chicago Press, 1991.

Drakulic, Slavenka. *The Balkan Express: Fragments From the Other Side of War*. New York: W. W. Norton, 1993.

Dreifelds, Juris. "Immigration and Ethnicity in Latvia." *Journal of Soviet Nationalities* 1, no. 4 (1990–91), 43–81.

Dunlop, John. "Will the Russians Return from the Near Abroad?" *Post-Soviet Geography* 35 (1994), 204–15.

Eley, Geoff. "German Politics and Polish Nationality: The Dialectic of Nation-Forming in the East of Prussia." *East European Quarterly* 18 (1984), 335–64.

"Remapping the Nation: War, Revolutionary Upheaval, and State Formation in Eastern Europe, 1914–1923." Pp. 205–46 in Howard Aster and Peter J. Potichnyi, eds., *Ukrainian–Jewish Relations in Historical Perspective*. 2nd edn. Edmonton: Canadian Institute of Ukrainian Studies, University of Alberta, 1990.

Esman, Milton. "The Chinese Diaspora in Southeast Asia." Pp. 130–63 in Sheffer, ed., *Modern Diasporas in International Politics*.

Fink, Carole. "Defender of Minorities: Germany in the League of Nations, 1926–1933." *Central European History* 4 (1972), 330–57.

"Stresemann's Minority Policies, 1924–29." *Journal of Contemporary History* 14 (1979), 403–22.

"The Weimar Republic As the Defender of Minorities, 1919–1933." Ph.D. dissertation, Yale University, 1968.

Fisher, Alan. *The Crimean Tatars.* Stanford, Calif.: Hoover Institution Press, 1978.

Foye, Stephen. "The Soviet Armed Forces: Things Fall Apart." *RFE/RL Research Report* 1, no. 1 (1992), 15–19.

Furet, François, and Denis Richet. *La Révolution française.* Paris: Hachette, 1965.

Gellner, Ernest. *Nations and Nationalism.* Ithaca, NY: Cornell University Press, 1983.

Gleason, Gregory. *Federalism and Nationalism: The Struggle for Republican Rights in the USSR.* Boulder, Colo.: Westview Press, 1990.

Glenny, Misha. *The Fall of Yugoslavia: The Third Balkan War.* London: Penguin, 1992.

Goldstone, Jack. "Predicting Revolutions: Why We Could (and Should) Have Foreseen the Revolutions of 1989–1991 in the U.S.S.R. and Eastern Europe." *Contention* 2, no. 2 (1993), 127–52.

Gosudarstvennyi komitet SSSR po statistike [USSR State Committee for Statistics]. *Natsional'nyi sostav naseleniia SSSR* [National Composition of the Population of the USSR]. Moscow: Finansy i Statistika, 1991.

Grillo, Ralph, ed. *"Nation" and "State" in Europe: Anthropological Perspectives.* London: Academic Press, 1980.

Grmek, Mirko *et al.*, eds., *Le Nettoyage ethnique: documents historiques sur une idéologie serbe.* Paris: Fayard, 1993.

Grundmann, Karl-Heinz. *Deutschtumspolitik zur Zeit der Weimarer Republik: eine Studie am Beispiel der deutsch-baltischen Minderheit in Estland und Lettland.* Hanover-Döhren: Harro v. Hirschheydt, 1977.

Hammel, Eugene A. "The Yugoslav Labyrinth." Pp. 1–33 in Eugene A. Hammel, Irwin Wall, and Benjamin Ward, eds., *Crisis in the Balkans.* Berkeley: Institute of International Studies, University of California, 1993.

Handler, Richard. "Is 'Identity' a Useful Cross-Cultural Concept?" Pp. 27–40 in John Gillis, ed., *Commemorations: The Politics of National Identity.* Princeton, NJ: Princeton University Press, 1994.

Hayden, Robert. "Constitutional Nationalism in the Formerly Yugoslav Republics." *Slavic Review* 51, no. 4 (1992), 654–73.

Hechter, Michael. *Principles of Group Solidarity.* Berkeley: University of California Press, 1987.

Heraclides, Alexis. "Secessionist Minorities and External Involvement." *International Organization* 44, no. 3 (1990), 341–78.

Hillgruber, Andreas. "'Revisionismus' – Kontinuität und Wandel in der Aussenpolitik der Weimarer Republik." *Historische Zeitschrift* 237 (1983), 597–621.

Hobsbawm, Eric. *The Age of Extremes: The Short Twentieth Century, 1914–1991.* London: Michael Joseph, 1994.

Nations and Nationalism Since 1780. Cambridge: Cambridge University Press, 1990.

Hodnett, Grey. "The Debate Over Soviet Federalism." *Soviet Studies* 18, no. 4 (1967), 458–82.

Horowitz, Donald. *Ethnic Groups in Conflict*. Berkeley: University of California Press, 1985.

"Irredentas and Secessions: Adjacent Phenomena, Neglected Considerations." Pp. 9–22 in Chazan, ed., *Irredentism and International Politics*.

Huttenbach, Henry R., ed. *Soviet Nationality Policies*. London and New York: Mansell, 1990.

"Implementing Language Laws: Perestroika and its Legacy in Five Republics." Special issue of *Nationalities Papers* 23, no. 3 (1995).

Jacobmeyer, Wolfgang. "Die deutschen Minderheiten in Polen und in der Tschechoslowakei in den dreissiger Jahren." *Aus Politik und Zeitgeschichte*, no. 31 (1986), 17–25.

Jacobsen, Hans-Adolf. *Nationalsozialistische Aussenpolitik 1933–1938*. Frankfurt am Main and Berlin: Alfred Metzner, 1968.

Janics, Kalman. *Czechoslovak Policy and the Hungarian Minority, 1945–48*. New York: Columbia University Press, 1982.

Jaszi, Oscar. *The Dissolution of the Habsburg Monarchy*. Chicago: University of Chicago Press, 1929.

Jaworski, Rudolf. "Die Sudetendeutsche als Minderheit in der Tschechoslowakei 1918–1938." Pp. 29–38 in Wolfgang Benz, ed., *Die Vertreibung der Deutschen aus dem Osten*. Frankfurt am Main: Fischer Taschenbuch, 1985.

"The German Minorities in Poland and Czechoslovakia in the Interwar Period." Pp. 169–85 in Paul Smith, ed., *Ethnic Groups in International Relations*.

Vorposten oder Minderheit? Der sudetendeutsche Volkstumskampf in den Beziehungen zwischen der Weimarer Republik und der ČSR. Stuttgart: Deutsche Verlags-Anstalt, 1977.

Kagedan, Allan. "Territorial Units as Nationality Policy." Pp. 163–76 in Huttenbach, ed., *Soviet Nationality Policies*.

Kaiser, Robert, and Jeff Chinn. "Russian–Kazakh Relations in Kazakhstan." *Post-Soviet Geography* 36 (1995), 257–73.

Kann, Robert A. *A History of the Habsburg Empire, 1526–1918*. Berkeley and Los Angeles: University of California Press, 1974.

The Multinational Empire: Nationalism and National Reform in the Habsburg Monarchy, 1848–1918. 2 vols. New York: Columbia University Press, 1950.

Karklins, Rasma. *Ethnic Relations in the USSR: The Perspective From Below*. Boston: Allen and Unwin, 1986.

Karpat, Kemal. *An Inquiry into the Social Foundations of Nationalism in the Ottoman State*. Princeton, NJ: Center of International Studies, 1973.

Ottoman Population, 1830–1914. Madison: University of Wisconsin Press, 1985.

Keddie, Nikki. "Can Revolutions Be Predicted? Can Their Causes Be Understood?" *Contention* 1, no. 2 (1992), 159–82.

Khazanov, Anatoly. *After the USSR: Ethnicity, Nationalism, and Politics in the Commonwealth of Independent States*. Madison, Wisconsin: University of Wisconsin Press, 1995.

Kionka, Riina. "Russia Recognizes Estonia's Independence." *Report on the USSR* 3, no. 5 (1991), 3–6.

Koch, Fred. *The Volga Germans*. University Park, Pa: Pennsylvania University Press, 1977.

Kocka, Jürgen. "Probleme der politischen Integration der Deutschen, 1867 bis

1945." Pp. 119–36 in Otto Büsch and James Sheehan, eds., *Die Rolle der Nation in der deutschen Geschichte und Gegenwart*. Berlin: Colloquium Verlag, 1985.

Kohn, Hans. *The Idea of Nationalism*. New York: Collier Books, 1944.

Kolstoe, Paul. "Nation-Building in Eurasia." Forthcoming in *Journal of Democracy* (January 1996).

Russians in the Former Soviet Republics. London: Hurst, 1995.

Kolstoe, Paul, and Andrei Edemsky. "The Dniester Conflict: Between Irredentism and Separatism." *Europe-Asia Studies* 45, no. 6 (1993), 973–1000.

Koroteyeva, Victoria. "The Old Imperial Power or an Emerging Nation: Russian Responses to Ethnic Separatism." Paper presented at conference on "Nations, States and Ethnic Identity," European University Institute, Florence, May 1992.

Korzec, Pawel. "The Minority Problem of Poland, 1918–1939." Pp. 199–219 in S. Vilfan, ed., *Ethnic Groups and Language Rights*. Aldershot, Hants (UK) and New York: Dartmouth Publishing Company and New York University Press, 1993.

"The Ukrainian Problem in Interwar Poland." Pp. 187–209 in Paul Smith, ed., *Ethnic Groups in International Relations*.

Koszel, Bogdan. "Nationality Problems in Upper Silesia." Pp. 211–33 in Paul Smith, ed., *Ethnic Groups in International Relations*.

Krekler, Norbert. *Revisionsanspruch und geheime Ostpolitik der Weimarer Republik*. Stuttgart: Deutsche Verlags-Anstalt, 1973.

Krüger, Peter. *Die Aussenpolitik der Republik von Weimar*. Darmstadt: Wissenschaftliche Buchgesellschaft, 1985.

Kuhn, Walter. "Das Deutschtum in Polen und sein Schicksal in Kriegs- und Nachkriegszeit." Pp. 138–64 in Markert, ed., *Polen*.

Kulischer, Eugene M. *Europe on the Move: War and Population Changes, 1917–47*. New York: Columbia University Press, 1948.

Kymlicka, Will. *Multicultural Citizenship: A Liberal Theory of Minority Rights*. Oxford: Oxford University Press, 1995.

Ladas, Stephen P. *The Exchange of Minorities: Bulgaria, Greece and Turkey*. New York: Macmillan, 1932.

Laffan, Michael. "Weimar and Versailles: German Foreign Policy, 1919–1933." Pp. 81–102 in Laffan, ed., *The Burden of German History 1919–45*. London: Methuen, 1988.

Laitin, David. "The Four Nationality Games and Soviet Politics." *Journal of Soviet Nationalities* 2, no. 1 (1991), 1–28.

"Identity in Formation: The Russian-Speaking Nationality in the Post-Soviet Diaspora." Paper presented at the Annual Meeting of the American Political Science Association, 1994.

"The National Uprisings in the Soviet Union." *World Politics* 44 (1991), 139–77.

Laitin, David, and Ian Lustick. "Hegemony and the State." *States and Social Structures Newsletter* 9 (1989), 1–4.

Lapidus, Gail. "Ethnonationalism and Political Stability: The Soviet Case." *World Politics* 36 (1984), 555–80.

"From Democratization to Disintegration: The Impact of Perestroika on the National Question." Pp. 45–70 in Gail Lapidus and Victor Zaslavsky, eds.,

From Union to Commonwealth: Nationalism and Separatism in the Soviet Republics. Cambridge: Cambridge University Press, 1992.

Lederer, Ivo. "Nationalism and the Yugoslavs." Pp. 396–438 in Sugar and Lederer, eds., *Nationalism in Eastern Europe.*

Lee, Marshall M., and Wolfgang Michalka. *German Foreign Policy 1917–1933.* Leamington Spa, UK: Berg, 1987.

Lepsius, M. Rainer. "The Nation and Nationalism in Germany." *Social Research* 52 (1985), 43–64.

Lewis, E. Glyn. "Migration and Language in the U.S.S.R." Pp. 310–41 in Joshua Fishman, ed., *Advances in the Sociology of Language,* vol I. The Hague: Mouton, 1972.

Lewis, Robert A. "The Migration of Russians Outside Their Homeland." *Nationalities Papers* 20, no. 2 (1992), 35–40.

Linz, Juan J., and Alfred Stepan. *Problems of Democratic Transition and Consolidation: Southern Europe, South America, and Post-Communist Europe.* Baltimore and London: Johns Hopkins University Press, 1996.

Livezeanu, Irina. *Cultural Politics in Greater Romania: Regionalism, Nation Building, and Ethnic Struggle, 1918–1930.* Ithaca, NY and London: Cornell University Press, 1995.

Lustick, Ian. "Becoming Problematic: Breakdown of a Hegemonic Conception of Ireland in Nineteenth-Century Britain." *Politics and Society* 18 (1990), 39–73.

"Israeli State-Building in the West Bank and the Gaza Strip: Theory and Practice." *International Organization* 41 (1987), 151–71.

State-Building Failure in British Ireland and French Algeria. Berkeley: Institute of International Studies, University of California, 1985.

Macartney, C. A. *Hungary and Her Successors: The Treaty of Trianon and Its Consequences, 1919–1937.* London: Oxford University Press, 1937.

National States and National Minorities. London: Oxford University Press, 1934.

Magaš, Branka. *The Destruction of Yugoslavia.* London: Verso, 1993.

Magocsi, Paul Robert. *Historical Atlas of East Central Europe.* Seattle: University of Washington Press, 1993.

Ukraine: A Historical Atlas. Toronto: University of Toronto Press, 1985.

Mann, Michael. *The Sources of Social Power,* vol. II: *The Rise of Classes and Nation-States, 1760–1914.* Cambridge: Cambridge University Press, 1993.

Marcus, Joseph. *Social and Political History of Jews in Poland, 1919–1939.* Berlin: Mouton, 1983.

Markert, Werner, ed. *Polen.* Cologne and Graz: Bohlau, 1959.

Markus, Ustina. "Lukashenko's Victory." *Transition* 1, no. 14 (1995), 75–8.

Marrus, Michael R. *The Unwanted: European Refugees in the Twentieth Century.* New York: Oxford University Press, 1985.

Massell, Gregory J. "Modernization and National Policy in Soviet Central Asia: Problems and Prospects." Pp. 265–91 in Paul Cocks, ed., *The Dynamics of Soviet Politics.* Cambridge, Mass.: Harvard University Press, 1976.

Mendelsohn, Ezra. *The Jews of East Central Europe Between the Two World Wars.* Bloomington: Indiana University Press, 1983.

"A Note on Jewish Assimilation in the Polish Lands." Pp. 141–9 in Bela Vago, ed., *Jewish Assimilation in Modern Times*. Boulder, Colo.: Westview, 1981.

Menon, Rajan. "In the Shadow of the Bear: Security in Post-Soviet Central Asia." *International Security* 20, no. 1 (1995), 149–81.

Meyer, John W. "The World Polity and the Authority of the Nation-State." Pp. 41–71 in George M. Thomas, John W. Meyer, Francisco O. Ramirez, and John Boli, *Institutional Structure: Constituting State, Society, and the Individual*. Newbury Park, Calif.: Sage, 1987.

Michalka, Wolfgang. "Deutsche Aussenpolitik 1920–1933." Pp. 303–26 in Karl Dietrich Bracher, Manfred Funke, and Hans-Adolf Jacobsen, eds., *Die Weimarer Republik*. Düsseldorf: Droste, 1987.

Misiunas, Romuald J., and Rein Taagepera. *The Baltic States: Years of Dependence, 1940–1980*. Berkeley: University of California Press, 1983.

Mocsy, Istvan. "Radicalization and Counterrevolution: Magyar Refugees From the Successor States and Their Role in Hungary, 1918–1921." Ph.D. dissertation, University of California, Los Angeles, 1973.

Motyl, Alexander J. *Sovietology, Rationality, Nationality*. New York : Columbia University Press, 1990.

Will the Non-Russians Rebel? Ithaca and London: Cornell University Press, 1987.

Nahaylo, Bohdan, and Victor Swoboda. *Soviet Disunion: A History of the Nationalities Problem in the USSR*. New York: Free Press, 1990.

Nekrich, Aleksandr. *The Punished Peoples*. New York: W. W. Norton, 1978.

Nellner, Werner. "Grundlagen und Hauptergebnisse der Statistik." Pp. 61–144 in Eugen Lemberg and Friedrich Edding, eds., *Die Vertriebene in Westdeutschland*, vol. I. Kiel: Ferdinand Hart, 1959.

Neményi, László. "The Dynamics of Homeland Politics: The Hungarian Case." Paper presented at conference on "National Minorities, Nationalizing States, and External National Homelands in the New Europe," Bellagio Study and Conference Center, Italy, August 1994.

Nettl, J. P. "The State As a Conceptual Variable." *World Politics* 20 (1968), 559–92.

O' Donnell, Guillermo, and Philippe Schmitter. *Transitions From Authoritarian Rule: Tentative Conclusions About Uncertain Democracies*. Baltimore, Md.: Johns Hopkins University Press, 1986.

Offe, Claus. "Capitalism by Democratic Design – Democratic Theory Facing the Triple Transition in East Central Europe." *Social Research* 58, no. 4 (1991), 865–92.

"Das Dilemma der Gleichzeitigkeit: Demokratisierung, Marktwirtschaft und Territorialpolitik in Osteuropa." Pp. 57–80 in Offe, *Der Tunnel am Ende des Lichts: Erkundungen der politischen Transformation im neuen Osten* (Frankfurt: Campus Verlag, 1994.

Olson, Mancur. *The Logic of Collective Action: Public Goods and the Theory of Groups*. Cambridge, Mass.: Harvard University Press, 1971.

Pallis, A. A. "Racial Migrations in the Balkans during the Years 1912–1924." *Geographical Journal* 66, no. 4 (1925), 315–31.

Peukert, Detlev J. K. *The Weimar Republic*. New York: Hill and Wang, 1993.

Pieper, Helmut. *Die Minderheitenfrage und das Deutsche Reich 1919–1933/34.* Hamburg: Institut für Internationale Angelegenheiten der Universität Hamburg, 1974.

Pierce, Richard. *Russian Central Asia 1867–1917.* Berkeley: University of California Press, 1960.

Pinto, Louis. "Une fiction politique: la nation." *Actes de la recherche en sciences sociales* 64 (1986), 45–50.

Pipes, Richard. *The Formation of the Soviet Union.* Cambridge, Mass.: Harvard University Press, 1964.

  Russia Under the Old Regime. New York: Scribner's, 1974.

Polonsky, Antony. *Politics in Independent Poland.* Oxford: Oxford University Press, 1972.

Pool, Jonathan. "Soviet Language Planning: Goals, Results, Options." Pp. 223–49 in Azrael, ed., *Soviet Nationality Policies and Practices.*

Popovic, Alexandre. *L'Islam balkanique: les musulmans du sud-est européen dans la période post-ottomane.* Berlin: Osteuropa-Institut, 1986.

Pusskepeleit, Jürgen. "Zugangsentwicklung, Ungleichverteilung und ihre Auswirkungen auf die Kommunen." Pp. 161–75 in Karl Otto, ed., *Westwarts-Heimwarts? Aussiedlerpolitik zwischen "Deutschtumelei" und "Verfassungsauftrag".* Bielefeld: AJZ, 1990.

Raeff, Marc. "Patterns of Russian Imperial Policy Toward the Nationalities." Pp. 22–42 in Edward Allworth, ed., *Soviet Nationality Problems.* New York: Columbia University Press, 1971.

Rahr, Alexander. "Are El'tsin and Gorbachev Now Allies?" *Report on the USSR* 3, no. 27 (1991), 6–9.

Rauschning, Hermann. *Die Entdeutschung Westpreussens und Posens.* Berlin: Reimar Hobbing, 1930.

Roeder, Philip G. "Soviet Federalism and Ethnic Mobilization." *World Politics* 43 (1991), 196–232.

Rokkan, Stein. "Dimensions of State Formation." Pp. 562–600 in Tilly, ed., *The Formation of National States in Western Europe.*

Rokkan, Stein, and Derek Urwin. *Economy, Territory, Identity: Politics of West European Peripheries.* London: Sage, 1983.

Roos, Hans. "Polen zwischen den Weltkriegen." Pp. 19–68 in Markert, ed., *Polen.*

Rosecrance, Richard. *The Rise of the Trading State: Commerce and Conquest in the Modern World.* New York: Basic Books, 1986.

Rothfels, Hans. *Bismarck, der Osten und das Reich.* Stuttgart: W. Kohlhammer, 1960.

Rothschild, Joseph. *East Central Europe Between the Two World Wars.* Seattle: University of Washington Press, 1974.

  Ethnopolitics: A Conceptual Framework. New York: Columbia University Press, 1981.

Rudensky, Nikolai. "Russian Minorities in the Newly Independent States." Pp. 58–77 in Roman Szporluk, ed., *National Identity and Ethnicity in Russia and the New States of Eurasia.* Armonk, NY and London: M. E. Sharpe, 1994.

Rusinow, Dennison. "Nationalities Policy and the 'National Question.'" Pp. 131–65 in Pedro Ramet, ed., *Yugoslavia in the 1980s.* Boulder, Colo.: Westview Press, 1985.

Sahlins, Marshall. "The Return of the Event, Again: With Reflections on the Beginnings of the Great Fijian War of 1843 to 1855 Between the Kingdoms of Bau and Rewa." Pp. 37–99 in Aletta Biersack, ed., *Clio in Oceania: Toward a Historical Anthropology.* Washington and London: Smithsonian Institution Press, 1991.

Savoskul, Sergei. "Russkie novogo zarubezh'ia" [Russians of the Near Abroad]. *Obshchestvennye nauki i sovremennost'* [Social Sciences and the Present] 5 (1994), 90–101.

Schechtman, Joseph B. *European Population Transfers 1939–1945.* New York: Oxford University Press, 1946.

Schieder, Theodor. *Das Deutsche Kaiserreich von 1871 als Nationalstaat.* Cologne and Opladen: Westdeutscher Verlag, 1961.

"Typologie und Erscheinungsformen des Nationalstaats in Europa." Pp. 65–86 in Schieder, *Nationalismus und Nationalstaat.* Göttingen: Vandenhoeck and Ruprecht, 1991.

Schot, Bastiaan. *Nation oder Staat? Deutschland und der Minderheitenschutz.* Marburg/Lahn: J. G. Herder-Institut, 1988.

Schwartz, Lee. "Regional Population Redistribution and National Homelands in the USSR." Pp. 121–61 in Huttenbach, ed., *Soviet Nationality Policies.*

Seraphim, Hans Jürgen. "Wirtschaftliche Nationalitätenkämpfe in Ostmitteleuropa." *Leipziger Vierteljahrsschrift für Südosteuropa* 1, no. 4 (1937–38), 42–58.

Seton-Watson, Hugh. *Nations and States.* Boulder, Colo.: Westview, 1977.

The Russian Empire 1801–1917. Oxford: Oxford University Press, 1967.

Sewell, William H., Jr. "A Theory of Structure – Duality, Agency, and Transformation." *American Journal of Sociology* 98, no. 1 (1992), 1–29.

"Three Temporalities: Toward an Eventful Sociology." In Terrence J. McDonald, ed., *The Historic Turn in the Human Sciences.* Ann Arbor: University of Michigan Press, forthcoming.

Sheffer, Gabriel, ed. *Modern Diasporas in International Politics.* London and Sydney: Croom Helm, 1986.

"A New Field of Study: Modern Diasporas in International Politics." Pp. 1–15 in Sheffer, ed., *Modern Diasporas in International Politics.*

Shlapentokh, Vladimir, Munir Sendich, and Emil Payin, eds. *The New Russian Diaspora.* Armonk, NY and London: M. E. Sharpe, 1994.

Silver, Brian. "Population Redistribution and the Ethnic Balance in Transcaucasia." Pp. 373–95 in Ronald Grigor Suny, ed., *Transcaucasia: Nationalism and Social Change.* Ann Arbor: Michigan Slavic Publications, 1983.

Simon, Gerhard. *Nationalism and Policy Toward the Nationalities in the Soviet Union.* Boulder, Colo.: Westview Press, 1991.

Slezkine, Yuri. "The USSR As a Communal Apartment, or How a Socialist State Promoted Ethnic Particularism." *Slavic Review* 53, no. 2 (1994), 414–52.

Smelser, Ronald M. *The Sudeten Problem, 1933–1938: Volkstumspolitik and the Formulation of Nazi Foreign Policy.* Folkestone, UK: Dawson, 1975.

Smith, Anthony. *The Ethnic Origins of Nations.* Oxford: Basil Blackwell, 1986.

National Identity. London: Penguin, 1991.

State and Nation in the Third World. New York: St. Martin's, 1983.

"State-Making and Nation-Building." Pp. 228–63 in John A. Hall, ed., *States in History.* Oxford: Basil Blackwell, 1986.

Smith, G. E. "Ethnic Nationalism in the Soviet Union: Territory, Cleavage, and Control." *Environment and Planning C: Government and Policy* 3 (1985), 49–73.

Smith, Paul. "Introduction." Pp. 1–11 in Smith, ed., *Ethnic Groups in International Relations.*

Smith, Paul, ed. *Ethnic Groups in International Relations.* Aldershot, Hants (UK) and New York: Dartmouth Publishing Company and New York University Press, 1991.

Snyder, Jack. "Nationalism and the Crisis of the Post-Soviet State." *Survival* 35, no. 1 (1993), 5–26.

Soboul, Albert. "De l'Ancien Régime à l'Empire: problème national et réalités sociales." *L'Information historique* (1960), 58–64, 96–104.

Somers, Margaret R. "Narrativity, Narrative Identity, and Social Action: Rethinking English Working-Class Formation." *Social Science History* 16 (1992), 591–630.

Soysal, Yasemin. *Limits of Citizenship: Migrants and Postnational Membership in Europe.* Chicago: University of Chicago Press, 1994.

Stadler, Karl R. *Austria.* London: Ernest Benn, 1971.

Starr, Frederick S. "Tsarist Government: The Imperial Dimension." Pp. 3–38 in Azrael, ed., *Soviet Nationality Policies and Practices.*

Stola, Dariusz. "Forced Migrations in European History." *International Migration Review* 26 (1992), 324–41.

Sugar, Peter, and Ivo Lederer, eds. *Nationalism in Eastern Europe.* Seattle: University of Washington Press, 1994 [1969].

Suhrke, Astri, and Lela Gardner Noble, eds. *Ethnic Conflict in International Relations.* New York: Praeger, 1977.

Suny, Ronald Grigor. "Ambiguous Categories: States, Empires and Nations." *Post-Soviet Affairs* 11, no. 2 (1995), 185–96.

"Nationalist and Ethnic Unrest in the Soviet Union." *World Policy Journal* 6, no. 3 (1989), 503–29.

The Revenge of the Past: Nationalism, Revolution, and the Collapse of the Soviet Union. Stanford: Stanford University Press, 1993.

Suval, Stanley. *The Anschluss Question in the Weimar Era.* Baltimore and London: Johns Hopkins University Press, 1974.

Szöke, László. "Hungarian Perspectives on Emigration and Immigration in the New European Architecture." *International Migration Review* 26 (1992), 305–23.

Szporluk, Roman. "History and Russian Nationalism." *Survey* 24, no. 3 (1979), 1–17.

"Reflections on Ukraine After 1994: The Dilemmas of Nationhood." *The Harriman Review* 7, nos. 7–9 (1994): 1–10.

Szücs, Jenő. *Nation und Geschichte.* Budapest: Corvina, 1974.

Táncos, Vilmos. "Kettős hatalmi szerkezet a Székelyföldön" [Dual Power Structure in the Szekler Lands]. Manuscript (1994).

Taylor, A. J. P. *The Habsburg Monarchy 1809–1918.* London: Hamish Hamilton, 1948.

The Origins of the Second World War. New York: Atheneum, 1961.

Thimme, Annelise. "Gustav Stresemann: Legende und Wirklichkeit." *Historische Zeitschrift* 181 (1956), 287–338.

Thompson, E. P. *The Making of the English Working Class.* New York: Vintage, 1963.

Tilly, Charles. *Coercion, Capital, and European States.* Cambridge, Mass. and Oxford: Basil Blackwell, 1992.

Tilly, Charles, ed. *The Formation of National States in Western Europe.* Princeton: Princeton University Press, 1975.

Tomaszewski, Jerzy. "The National Question in Poland in the Twentieth Century." Pp. 293–316 in Mikulas Teich and Roy Porter, eds., *The National Question in Europe in Historical Context.* Cambridge: Cambridge University Press, 1993.

Rzeczpospolita wielu narodów [Republic of Many Nations]. Warsaw: Czytelnik, 1985.

Vakar, Nicholas P. *Belorussia: The Making of a Nation.* Cambridge, Mass.: Harvard University Press, 1956.

Vasileva, Darina. "Bulgarian Turkish Emigration and Return." *International Migration Review* 26 (1992), 342–52.

Verdery, Katherine. "Nationalism and National Sentiment in Post-Socialist Romania." *Slavic Review* 52 (1993), 179–203.

"Whither 'Nation' and 'Nationalism'?" *Daedalus* 122, no. 3 (1993), 37–46.

Vitkovskaia, G. C. *Vynuzhdennaia migratsiia: problemy i perspektivy* [Forced Migration: Problems and Perspectives]. Moscow: Institut narodno-khoziaistvennogo prognozirovaniia, Rossiiskaia Akademiia Nauk, 1993.

Von Hagen, Mark. "The Great War and the Mobilization of Ethnicity in the Russian Empire." Manuscript (1995).

Vujacic, Veljko. "Communism and Nationalism in Russia and Serbia ." Ph.D. dissertation, University of California at Berkeley, 1995.

Vujacic, Veljko, and Victor Zaslavsky. "The Causes of Disintegration in the USSR and Yugoslavia." *Telos* 88 (1991), 120–40.

Wehler, Hans-Ulrich. "Polenpolitik im deutschen Kaiserreich." Pp. 184–202 in Wehler, *Krisenherde des Kaiserreichs.* 2nd edn. Göttingen: Vandenhoeck and Ruprecht, 1979.

Weiner, Myron. "The Macedonian Syndrome: An Historical Model of International Relations and Political Development." *World Politics* 23, no. 1 (1970), 665–83.

"Rejected Peoples and Unwanted Migrants in South Asia." Pp. 149–78 in Weiner, ed., *International Migration and Security.*

"Security, Stability, and International Migration." Pp. 1–35 in Weiner, ed., *International Migration and Security.*

Weiner, Myron, ed. *International Migration and Security.* Boulder, Colo.: Westview Press, 1993.

Young, Crawford. *The Politics of Cultural Pluralism.* Madison: University of Wisconsin Press, 1976.

Zaionchkovskaia, Zhanna. "Effects of Internal Migration on the Emigration from the USSR." Paper presented at conference on "Prospective Migration and Emigration From the Former Soviet Union," Santa Monica, Calif., 1991.

Zaionchkovskaia, Zhanna, ed. *Byvshii SSSR: vnutrenniaia migratsiia i emigratsiia* [The Former USSR: Internal Migration and Emigration]. Moscow: Institut problem zaniatosti, Rossiiskaia Akademiia Nauk, 1992.

Migratsionnaia situatsiia v Rossii: sotsial'no-politicheskie aspekty [The Migration Situation in Russia: Social-Political Aspects]. Moscow: Institut narodno-khoziaistvennogo prognozirovaniia, Rossiiskaia Akademiia Nauk, 1994.

Migratsionnye protsessy posle raspada SSSR [Migration Processes After the Breakup of the USSR]. Moscow: Institut narodnokhoziaistvennogo prognozirovaniia, Rossiiskaia Akademiia Nauk, 1994.

Zaslavsky, Victor. "Nationalism and Democratic Transition in Post-Communist Societies." *Daedalus* 121, no. 2 (Spring 1992), 97–121.

Zaslavsky, Victor, and Yuri Luryi. "The Passport System in the USSR and Changes in Soviet Society." *Soviet Union* 6, no. 2 (1979), 137–53.

Zolberg, Aristide. "Contemporary Transnational Migrations in Historical Perspective: Patterns and Dilemmas." Pp. 15–51 in Mary M. Kritz, ed., *U.S. Immigration and Refugee Policy.* Lexington, Mass.: D.C. Heath, 1983.

"The Formation of New States as a Refugee-Generating Process." *Annals of the American Academy of Political and Social Science* 467 (1983), 24–38.

Zolberg, Aristide, Astri Suhrke, and Sergio Aguayo. *Escape From Violence: Conflict and the Refugee Crisis in the Developing World.* New York: Oxford University Press, 1989.

Index

agrarian reform
  as nationalizing strategy, 91–2, 100–1
Albania and Albanians, 7, 56, 70, 73, 108,
  112n
Algeria, 175
Anschluss (joining of Austria to Germany),
  119–20
anti-Semitism, 85–6, 93–7, 132, 152n
Armenia
  as ethnically homogeneous successor
    state, 44, 104n
  as external national homeland, 108
  migration of Russians from, 170
Armenians
  and ethnic unmixing in Transcaucasia,
    170n
  as national minority, 7, 56
  as "Russian-speakers," 143
  claims for border revision, 38n
  dispersion of, 36, 56
  genocidal deportation of from Turkey,
    152n
assimilation
  and blurring of group boundaries, 48,
    56n
  and concept of *rossiiane*, 142n
  and concept of "Russian-speakers,"
    143
  competitive pressures for, 50n
  formal protection against, 105
  in Habsburg Empire, 27, 35
  in interwar Poland, 86, 88–9, 93–4,
    99–100, 101–2
  in nation-building literature, 80
  in nationalizing states, 86, 88–9,
    99–100, 101–2
  minority resistance to, 35, 57
  of Poles in Germany, 164
  of Polish Jews, 93–4
  of Russians in Soviet successor states,
    50n, 173
  of Turks in Bulgaria, 155

of Ukrainians outside Ukraine,
  56n
see also dissimilation; Germanization;
  Magyarization; nationalism,
  nationalizing; nationalizing state;
  Polonization; Russification
Austria, post-Habsburg, 119–20, 122,
  125, 133, 160–1, 162, 163
  see also Habsburg Empire
autonomy, 8, 52, 57, 60, 69, 75, 84, 123,
  134, 173, 174
  competing conceptions of, 39–40
  cultural, 129, 130, 130n
  extra-territorial, 40n
  territorial, 39–40, 50, 50n, 174
Azerbaijan, 38n, 56
  as nationalizing state, 108
  migration of Armenians from, 170n
  migration of Azeris to, 170n
  migration of Russians from, 170

Balkan Wars, 154, 167
Baltic nations and states, 38n, 47, 175,
  176
  migration of Russians to, 170
  see also Estonia; Latvia; Lithuania
Belarus, 139
  dual citizenship agreement with Russia,
    144n
  migration of Russians to, 170
  weakness of nationalizing nationalism in,
    47, 104n, 106n
Belarusians
  as "Russian-speakers," 143
  in interwar Poland, 7, 86, 92, 94–5,
    97–103, 107n
  in non-Slavic Soviet successor states,
    151n
Belorussia: *see* Belarus
Bismarck, Otto von, 117, 119
  reserve *vis-à-vis* transborder Germans,
    114–15, 116

193

DATE DUE

		THESIS	
		MAY 1 5 2013	
MAY 20 2002			
MAY 1 6 2005			
OCT - 7 2005			
THESIS			
MAY 1 3 2011			
MAY 1 6 2014			
THESIS			